INTERNET
ROADSIDE
ATTRACTIONS

Sites, sounds & scenes along the
**information
superhighway**

INTERNET
ROADSIDE
ATTRACTIONS

Sites, sounds & scenes along the
information superhighway

Gareth Branwyn

Sean Carton

Luke Duncan

Tom Lichty

Donald Rose

Shannon Turlington

Jan Weingarten

VENTANA
PRESS

Internet Roadside Attractions:
  Sites, Sounds & Scenes Along the Information Superhighway
Copyright © 1995 by Gareth Branwyn, Sean Carton, Luke Duncan, Tom Lichty, Donald Rose, Shannon Turlington, Jan Weingarten

Library of Congress Cataloging-in-Publication Data

Internet roadside attractions: sites, sounds & scenes along the information superhighway / Gareth Branwyn ... [et al.]. -- 1st ed.
       p. cm.
     ISBN 1-56604-193-7
     1. Internet (Computer network) -- Directories.
   TK5105.875.I57I573 1995
   025.04--dc20   94-40134
                                                    CIP

Book design: Marcia Webb
Cover design: John Nedwidek, emDesign
Technical review: Gary Moore
Index service: Dianne Bertsch, Answers Plus
Editorial staff: Angela Anderson, Walter R. Bruce III, Tracye Giles, Nathaniel Mund, Pam Richardson, Jessica Ryan
Production staff: Patrick Berry, Cheri Collins, John Cotterman, Dan Koeller, Lance Kozlowski, Dawne Sherman, Marcia Webb
Proofreader: Eric Edstam

First Edition 9 8 7 6 5 4 3 2 1
Printed in the United States of America

Ventana Press, Inc.
P.O. Box 2468
Chapel Hill, NC 27515
919/942-0220
FAX 919/942-1140

Limits of Liability and Disclaimer of Warranty

Trademarks

Trademarked names appear throughout this book. Rather than list the names and entities that own the trademarks or insert a trademark symbol with each mention of the trademarked name, the publisher states that it is using the names only for editorial purposes and to the benefit of the trademark owner with no intention of infringing upon that trademark.

About the Authors

Gareth Branwyn, aka *GB*

Gareth Branwyn is a regular contributor to *Wired* magazine, the senior editor of *bOING bOING* (a pop culture humor mag) and the former Street Tech editor of *Mondo 2000*. His book publishing credits include *Mosaic Quick Tours,* available in Mac and Windows versions (Ventana Press), *Flame Wars* (Duke University Press), *Virtual Reality Casebook* (Van Nostrand Reinhold), *The Multimedia Home Companion* (Warner Books) and *The Millennium Whole Earth Catalog* (Harper San Francisco). As a hypermedia designer Gareth is co-creator of the critically acclaimed *Beyond Cyberpunk!*, an electronic compendium of cyberculture. He has been a flag-waving Net citizen since 1987.

"It's a really exciting time to be on the Net—things are changing so rapidly, especially with the World Wide Web. The Net has created a virtual community which is exciting to belong to. I crave intellectual stimulation, and the Net allows one to snag other people; we can each put out our own net and catch others' ideas and responses to our queries."

Sean Carton, aka *SC*

 Sean, whose interest in computers dates back to his boyhood days of growing up on a farm miles from the closest neighbor, recently served as technical advisor for Ventana Press's *Mosaic Quick Tours,* available in Mac and Windows versions. An accomplished writer presently working as a graphics specialist, Sean has contributed to *bOING bOING* and *Link* magazines, and is currently working on *bOING bOING's Happy Mutant Handbook* (Putnam Berkeley, 1995).

Sean received his MA in English from the University of Maryland and has been involved with the Internet for six years. His goal is to write full-time, combining his knowledge of computers with his interest in writing.

"The exciting thing is that the Net allows the ordinary person to reach more people than ever. It brings people together and allows for more communication," says Sean. "One can do things that were previously not possible—like combining all forms of media."

Luke Duncan, aka *LAD*

Luke is the youngest of the *Internet Roadside Attractions* contributors. At the age of 20 he is already an experienced Internet online developer and online programmer for Ventana Online.

Currently a junior majoring in Narrative Studies at the University of North Carolina at Chapel Hill, Luke edits and designs graphics for and serves on the editorial board of *Cyberkind*, a Net zine.

"The Internet makes distances disappear. It lets you talk in real time to people in your field from different parts of the world. In regards to research, it opens everything up, making it much easier to communicate with people in your field."

Tom Lichty, aka *TL*

Tom is the author of the highly acclaimed *Official America Online Tour Guide* and *America Online's Internet* (both available in Mac and Windows versions). His credits also include *Desktop Publishing With Word for Windows* and *Mac, Word & Excel Desktop Companion*. All of these titles are published by Ventana Press.

The retired director of the University of Oregon Micro Computer Program in Portland, Tom raises Asian pears at his Oregon farm and navigates the Net between harvests.

Donald Rose, Ph.D., aka *DR*

Author of *Minding Your Cybermanners on the Internet* (Alpha Books), and contributor to *Cyberlife!*, Donald earned a Ph.D. in computer science from the University of California at Irvine in 1989. As a graduate student he began doing stand-up comedy and improvisation. Now, as a writer, Donald strives to combine his computer knowledge with humorous style.

A 12-year veteran of the Internet, Donald has lectured internationally on computer topics ranging from artificial intelligence to the Internet.

"Explosive growth of the Internet will fuel the use of artificial intelligence," states Donald. "It will evolve from providing just static data to real, creative, informative knowledge. People will go from being overwhelmed by the Net to overjoyed."

Shannon Turlington, aka *ST*

A full-time writer and aspiring mystery author, Shannon is the author of *Walking the World Wide Web* (published by Ventana Press) and editor of Ventana Online's "Nifty Site of the Week." She also publishes and edits *Cyberkind*, a Net zine.

"The Net is the most exciting thing I've come across," says Shannon. "I believe it will totally change the way we live within the next several years. We will do everything on the Net: shopping, banking, travel reservations, etc.

"The Net makes the world a much smaller place. Email makes all people more approachable. You can talk to anyone whereas you wouldn't just pick up the phone and call someone you don't know."

Jan Weingarten, aka *JW*

A noted computer author, Jan most recently has been a co-author of *Visual Guide to Paradox* and the *Smart-Suite Desktop Companion*, both published by Ventana Press. In addition, she contributed all the listings to the second editions of Ventana's *Internet Tour Guides*.

Jan's interests range from theater (she attended the London School of theater) to massage therapy (which she practices in between book deadlines).

"The Net is amorphous," says Jan. "Its potential is very exciting. Even though it's in its infancy, there's a lot of cool stuff out there. We'll see it explode over the next year as we see an increase in accessibility and a decrease in cost."

CONTENTS

England 74

Brit Chat

Environment 75

Biosphere & Ecology Discussion List • Earth Science Information Network • Ecological Society of America • EcoNet • EnviroGopher • EnviroLink

Erotica 79

Fanny Hill • Poetry & Prose

Food & Drink 80

Coffee • Food & Nutrition Information Center • Grapevine Wine Drinkers • Hot Hot Hot • Mothercity Espresso • Restaurant Le Cordon Bleu • Vegetarian Recipes

Frequently Asked Questions Lists 83

USENET FAQs

Fun 84

Doctor Fun • Electronic Fortune Cookies • The Exploratorium • Graffiti Wall • Lego Bricks Server • On This Day... • Penpal Network • Tarot Information • Techno/Rave Archive • The Toy Box • Urban Folklore • What's in a (Long) Name

Games 91

Abyss IV (DikuMUD) • Addventure • Advanced Dungeons & Dragons Discussion List • Apocalypse IV MUD (DikuMUD) • BatMUD, A World Apart • BU's Interactive WWW Games • Chess Archive • ChromeMUSH (TinyMUSH) • Doom • Foosball • Games Mania • Games of Death MUD (DikuMUD) • GarouMUSH (TinyMUSH) • Genocide (LPMud) • Global MUSH (MUSH) • GrimneMUD (DikuMUD) • InfinityMUD (LPMud) • Internet Hunt • Initgame • Let's Play Jeopardy • Magic Deck Master • MicroMuse • MUME "Multi Users in Middle Earth" (DikuMUD) • NannyMUD (LPMud) • Nanvaent • NuclearWar (LPMud) • Othello Across the Net • Overdrive (LPMud) • Paradox • The Revenge of the End of the Line (LPMud) • Spatial Wastes (MUSH) • The Sprawl (MOO) • Star Trek Email Game • Star Wars MUSH • Sword & Crown • ToonMUSH III (TinyMUSH) • Video Games Chat • WWW Addict's Pop-Culture Scavenger Hunt

Network Resource Tools • InterLinks Internet Access • International Internet Association • Internaut • Internet Connections List • Internet Mail Guide • Internet Mailing Lists • Internet Phone Books & Email • Internet Resource Guide • The Internet Society • Internet Talk Radio • The Internet Tools List • InterNIC • Online Texts About the Internet • Planet Earth Home Page • SUSI Search Engine • Testing Newsgroups & Mailing Lists • Unique & Interesting Net Resources • USENET 101 • What's New on comp.infosystems.announce?

Archie • The Internet Adapter™

Best of the Net • Best of the Web • CERN WWW Virtual Library • List of Commercial Services on the Web • Nexor List of Web Robots • The Virtual Tourist • The Web Overview at CERN • The WebCrawler • What's New With NCSA Mosaic • World Wide Web Chat • The World Wide Web Worm

CMU English Server • Master Gopher at UMN • SunSITE • World Wide Web Home • WU Archive • Yahoo—A Guide to the WWW

Conspirators Unite • Rumor Mill

Computer-Assisted Reporting & Research • Medialist

MARVEL Language & Linguistics • Spanish Counting Books

Information Law Alert • The Legal Domain Network • Pepper & Corazzini, L.L.P.

Introduction

It's a changing world. Everyday, I see the signs. An email address at the end of the evening news. Internet television shows, cover stories on weekly news magazines, theme calendars, books. Not trickling into existence, but WHAM! Internet as superstar, infobahn headlines, screaming cybermania.

You already know all that—you've perused in the Internet section of a bookstore or computer store, or flipped through the Internet offerings of a catalog, to find *Internet Roadside Attractions*. Your kids or co-workers are online. Your mother has read about the Internet. Even your out-of-touch-with-life neighbor has an email address. Everybody's getting wired.

However the Net, the great conglomeration of networks around the world, hasn't been a household term for very long. When I was first introduced to it way back in 1984, only a few thousand of us were connected to the Internet, which offered little more than email and a few file archives—not much to see. I left it for more interesting things, like girls (un-PC as it may be, I can't bring myself to call eighth graders women).

When I revisited the Internet five years later, deciding finally to knuckle down and become a hacker, the community of "Netters" numbered almost a hundred thousand, talking up a storm on mailing lists and newsgroups, and transferring megabytes each day from file archives all over the world.

In 1992, when I landed my first Internet job, the one-million-user mark had been reached; and the megabytes had turned into gigabytes. It was still primarily a Net ruled by the government and the universities. Even so, odds are that as recently as 1992, you probably had never heard of the Internet.

Today, more than 25 million people communicate through the Net, and more are joining by the hour. Gigabyte references have given way to terabytes, and cyberspace is alive and thriving.

And the speed of transition is revving up. Among the numerous factors affecting growth is a sudden phenomenon called "the commercialization of the Internet." By the end of 1994, media conglomerates Time Warner, Viacom/Paramount and Fox, as well as the Rolling Stones, the Home Shopping Network and the White House, were all online.

An early pioneer in the commericialization of the Internet was SunSITE. Sun Microsystems, wanting a site similar to the site Apple had hosted for years, put its Internet home under the auspices of hacker/poet Paul Jones at the University of North Carolina at Chapel Hill. But instead of having the site dedicated to Sun-related information, Sun took a different approach. Only part of the Sun information archive (SunSITE) was devoted to Sun information; the rest was to be devoted to experiments in electronic publishing.

Paul, aided by a staff of students (my first official Internet job) and former students, tapped the Internet's content potential with SunSITE. Here you will find everything from technical information about Sun systems to dinosaur exhibits to today's menus in the best restaurants in Paris. As you read *Internet Roadside Attractions* and explore the CD-ROM, you'll find SunSITE listed in the **Internet Giants** category, as well as many of its rich offerings scattered in subject categories throughout the book.

Success stories like this have ignited interest in commercializing the Net. And with the advent of the World Wide Web and the groundbreaking Web reader Mosaic, the drab, text-based Internet of yore is increasingly being replaced with the colorful sizzle and pop of the multimedia-rich hypermedia. Images now burst forth from the screen in vibrant color; sounds and music fill the Web page; and most important, distributed hypermedia allows readers to click on words or phrases and jump to related coverage in other nooks and crannies of the Net, a virtual world of information at your fingertips.

✻

Navigating With *Internet Roadside Attractions*

In a few years, more people will be wired than not, and most industries will have a presence in cyberspace. Even today, shoppers can browse "virtual storefronts," listening to music, mulling over merchandise, ordering and paying for goods online. Students can attend class online. The latest research, up-to-the-minute news and weather can be accessed over the Net.

But finding your way through this maze can be daunting. *Internet Roadside Attractions* is your cyberspace map, pointing you to some of the best sites on the Net. Reviewed here are more than 500 places our team of authors recommends. Here you will find the Vatican and the Louvre, the White House and the Smithsonian. Visit the Electric Gallery for beautiful and elegant Haitian Art. See the world down under at the Guide to Australia. After gazing at the stars at the Mt. Wilson Observatory, get down to Earth with hobbits and such visiting MUME (Multi Users in Middle Earth), one of the first examples of text-based virtual reality.

The book is arranged in alphabetical order, with generous cross-referencing to make it all the more valuable as a resource. In addition to a review (followed by the initials of the contributing author), the access information for each site is listed. We've used URLs for accessing information. (More on URLs in a minute.)

The Cybernauts Behind *Internet Roadside Attractions*

Internet Roadside Attractions is the perfect antidote to the Internet laundry lists that abound. Our authors have made sure of that, adding lots of anecdotes and insights into what makes an Internet resource worth exploring.

The team of reviewers includes such noted authors and cybernauts as Gareth Branwyn, Sean Carton, Luke Duncan, Tom Lichty, Donald Rose, Shannon Turlington and Jan Weingarten. Be sure to check out their "home pages," both on Ventana Online and in the "About the Authors" section near the front of this book. You can easily identify their contributions to the book by looking at the initials following each review. We wanted to capture not only their favorite places, but also their voices and opinions in this opinionated book.

But wait...this is not just a book. *Internet Roadside Attractions* is also a CD-ROM and boasts an online companion. Read on.

Let the CD-ROM Do Your Walking

Now, if you find typing in these long URL addresses, listed under the Access heading in each listing, a grind, we can empathize. But type no longer. On the CD-ROM accompanying *Internet Roadside Attractions* we have provided the entire contents of this book in WWW hypertext. Fire up your Internet connection, pop the CD-ROM into your drive and you are good to go.

Free Mosaic

The CD-ROM also includes both Windows and Mac versions of the complete Ventana Mosaic. Available from the "ReadMe" front interface, this excellent Web browser provides you with the tools necessary to get up on the Web and use the URLs as listed in the book, not to mention the ability to take advantage of the wonderful world of the World Wide Web and its hypermedia essence.

Tools & Coffee

First things first. My assumption is that you have an Internet connection. (If you don't, there's information in the back of the book on how to get our *Internet Membership Kit*, which will get you hooked up. Well? What are you waiting for? I promise to wait right here until you get one.)

You will find six main types of Internet resources in this book: mailing lists, USENET newsgroups, telnet sites, FTP sites, Gophers and World Wide Web (WWW) archives.

With the exception of mailing lists, the tools listed above roughly follow a client/server model. Let's explore the client/server, a popular buzzword these days.

This is the short and sweet definition given to me by the SunSITE sage, Simon Spero. He likens an Internet computer running various servers (like SunSITE) to a shelf of bottomless coffee cans (each of which is a server) divided up into many compartments, which in turn are also divided up into compartments, and so on down to the coffee. The compartments are directories or folders within the server. The coffee is the files within those directories.

Imagine yourself with a coffee cup. You want some coffee, so you go to a coffee can and scoop up the kind of java you want, from the compartments you want, from the can you want. The cup is your client. Now remember, the coffee cans are bottomless, so there is always enough joe for the next person with a cup, and often coffee cans have more than one cup in them at a time. If you like the coffee you can keep it, and if you don't you can throw it away and go back for different coffee in a different compartment, perhaps in a different can, perhaps on a different shelf. That is the nature of client/ server interactions.

This model oversimplifies a little. Many clients serve special purposes and only provide access to a specific server. An FTP client only works with FTP servers, and Gopher clients only work with Gopher servers. Thankfully this problem has been addressed by the developers of World Wide Web (WWW) clients, the first attempts at Internet multiclients. I like to think of it as a universal coffee cup. That's why the addresses in *Internet Roadside Attractions* support the Web.

URL as a Second Language

URLs (Uniform Resource Locators) are a standard addressing convention, designed for use with World Wide Web browsers, through which you can access not only the Web sites but virtually any resource on the Internet. Let's see what this strange thing called a URL looks like:

protocol://computer.hostname:port/directory/subdirectory/.../file

The protocol is the kind of server (actually, the kind of language the server speaks). The computer.hostname element is the Internet hostname of the computer where the server resides. The port is the numerical connection point where the server can be found, if it is different from the default. Directories and subdirectories are the paths down to the file, which is what will ultimately be returned to the client.

Even if you're using a tool or client other than WWW, you can get there from here. URLs can be easily rewritten to work with Telnet, Gopher, FTP and newsgroups. (Mailing lists and chat channels are a little different; see the **Chat** and **Mailing Lists** sections below.)

World Wide Web

This is the protocol URLs were designed for. WWW files are transmitted via HTTP, or HyperText Transport Protocol. I won't break down this example, since it would be entered as is into a WWW client, which takes URLs as standard input. (This example is the SunSITE Vatican archive, reviewed in the **History, World** section of this book.)

http://sunsite.unc.edu/expo/vatican.exhibit/Vatican.exhibit.html

If you're using a WWW client or Web browser (such as Ventana Mosaic), all you have to do is select Open URL from the File menu (in most clients) and type in the address provided in the Access line at the end of each review.

Telnet

Telnet is a little strange in that it is not strictly client/server. When you visit a telnet resource, you are actually connecting to a remote computer. The "coffee" returned is not a file or a directory listing, but rather a connection to the remote computer. Your WWW client will launch a telnet tool when it encounters a telnet URL.

A telnet tool usually requires a hostname and sometimes a port. In this example, from the **ToonMUSH III** listing in the **Games** section of this book, the hostname is **brahe.phys.unm.edu** and the port is **9999**:

telnet://brahe.phys.unm.edu:9999/

News

USENET newsgroups and Gopher are at opposite ends of the spectrum. Newsgroups have the simplest URL implementation and Gopher has the most complex. A specialized newsreader needs you simply to specify the newsgroup you want to access.

In this example, from the **USENET 101** review, the newsgroup is **news.announce.newusers**:

news:news.announce.newusers

Gopher

At the far end of the spectrum, the Gopher URL can look weird. This example is the FAQ (Frequently Asked Questions) Central archive:

**gopher://gopher.cs.ttu.edu/11/Reference%20Shelf/
FAQs%20%28Frequently%20Asked%20Questions%29**

Trust me, this is not as confusing as it looks. First, let's translate the escape codes. Any time you see a % in a Gopher URL, it precedes an escape code. In this example, %20 is a space, %28 is an open parenthesis and %29 is a close parenthesis (these are about the only escape codes you'll run into). Now you have a URL that reads:

**gopher://gopher.cs.ttu.edu/11/Reference Shelf/FAQs (Frequently
Asked Questions)**

The 11 is simply a code that says the last item in the URL—FAQs (Frequently Asked Questions)—is a Gopher directory. Other codes you may see include 00 for a text file or I9 for an image.

When a specialized Gopher client prompts you to connect to a Gopher server, you just enter the hostname (**gopher.cs.ttu.edu**). When the top-level menu is returned, simply follow the path downward. In this example, you would select **Reference Shelf** from the top-level menu and **FAQs (Frequently Asked Questions)** from the **Reference Shelf** menu.

Don't worry, it gets easier from here on out.

FTP

FTP, or File Transfer Protocol, is very straightforward and follows exactly the generic URL I gave at the beginning of this section. The following example is a list of Internet tools:

ftp://ftp.rpi.edu/pub/communications/internet-tools.html

A specialized FTP client would first ask for the hostname (**ftp.rpi.edu**). You then have the option of entering the path, **/pub/ communications**, or following the directories down one by one until you get to the one containing the file itself (**internet-tools.html**).

Mailing Lists

Mailing lists work a little differently than the other tools. The first Access address in each mailing list review tells you how to subscribe to the list. It's written as an email address, like this one from the children's literature mailing list:

to subscribe, send email to **listserv@bingumb.cc.binghamton.edu**

In your email, be sure to include the line **subscribe kidlit-l,** followed by your name. After you've subscribed, send mail that you want distributed to the list to the second address given in the Access information for each listing, as in the following:

Send messages to **kidlit-l@bingumb.cc.binghamton.edu**

Chat

Chat can be accessed in one of two distinct ways: (1) through a chat client, or IRC (Internet Relay Chat); (2) through simple telnet. (See the **Chat** section of this book for details on this exciting new Internet tool.)

Internet Roadside Attractions Online

Now for the best part of the book: included on *Internet Roadside Attraction*'s CD-ROM is a link labeled "Visit Ventana Online." There you have the option of registering your new book and thus receiving an account with Ventana Online. Simply add your code key (on the card behind your CD). Then your account name and password will let you access the continuously updated *Internet Roadside Attractions Online Companion*!

If you have experienced difficulties with slow WWW accesses, special Ventana hybrid media technology lets you access all images on the online companion from your CD, allowing you to access information many times faster than with regular Internet documents!

No more messy URLs. Just point and click to shoot the moon. Check out the "Installing the CD-ROM" and "Accessing the Online Companion" pages at the back of the book for more details.

Visiting Ventana Online

The *Internet Roadside Attractions Online Companion* is part of the Ventana Visitor's Center, a rich resource that offers you the latest information on the Internet. Whether it's software, online content or the best computer books available, Ventana Online offers it.

The Nifty Site of the Week is a regular visiting point for many experienced Net surfers. Selected and annotated by *Internet Roadside Attractions* author Shannon Turlington, the Nifty Site is, quite literally, always something new.

The Online Companions Archive is where you'll find the *Internet Roadside Attractions Online Companion*, as well as online companions for many other Ventana Press books. Use Photoshop? The *Photoshop f/x Online Companion* has the most complete collection of filters and extensions in cyberspace, annotated with instructions, comments and before-and-after shots. That's just the tip of the cyberial glacier.

The Ventana Visitor's Center Software Archive has every tool available for both the novice and master Netsurfer. Culled from every online companion (including the one for this book), this archive contains every freely available piece of software mentioned in a Ventana cyberbook.

There is nothing better than a rest stop on a long journey, and the Ventana Visitor's Center was designed to be that rest stop for the Internet. Stop in for coffee—I'll see you there!

You're Off

This is your guide to a rich and adventurous cybertour. Good health, God speed and good luck. There's a frontier out there. And with Gareth, Sean, Luke, Tom, Donald, Shannon and Jan as your guides, you're in good hands. (Be sure to check out their "home pages" before you start your journey.)

If you get a chance, drop me a line and let me know what treasures you find out there.

See you among the wires,

Dykki Settle
Vice President, Ventana Online
settle@vmedia.com
Winter 1995

A

African-Americans

The African-American Mosaic

A rich resource guide for the study of black history and culture, this online exhibit covers 500 years of black experience in the Western Hemisphere. As a sampler of the Library of Congress's African-American collection you'll find graphics and text of relevant sources of black history, including maps, treatises, memoirs and historical photographs. You can click on the inline images for a larger, more detailed view of the documents. Each section is several WWW pages long. All in all a huge, information-packed archive. —*ST*

Access: **http://lcweb.loc.gov/exhibits/African.American/intro.html**

Aliens

Aliens Have Invaded Cyberspace!

Bill Barker was a gallery artist living in Reno, Nevada, when in 1992, someone gave him a reprint of a bizarre article on alien invasion and abduction. He became fascinated with the subject and people's seemingly sincere tales of flying saucers and aliens among us. With tongue firmly planted in cheek, Barker began doing a series of stark black-and-white drawings, using an alien motif. He saw this as an interesting way to speak about "alienation" in all of its forms and the fears that people have about being controlled by unseen forces. The response to Barker's work, done behind the mask of a mysterious entity called the Schwa Corporation, has been phenomenal. Barker has developed a line of "alien defense products" based on his Schwa characters and themes, and these items are hot. He's developing a whole line of cheap alien objets d'art and has even been approached by a toy and a clothing company who are tickled by his strange sense of humor and his almond-headed aliens with the big, not-so-friendly eyes. —*GB*

Access: **http://www.scs.unr.edu/homepage/rory/schwa/schwa.html**

Angst

Beyond Emoticons

If you promise not to worry about it, subscribe to **alt.angst,** an appropriate home for all the anxiety-ridden people on the planet. It's soul food for the paranoid appetite, as long as they don't take it away... —*TL*

Access: **news:alt.angst**

Animation

See also Cartoons.

Warner Brothers Central

Want to find out Bugs Bunny's middle name or vital statistics on other Warner Brothers' cartoon stars? Looking for your favorite Warner Brothers cartoon on video tape or laser disc? This is the place to ask. You can also inquire about Warner Bros. merchandise. —*LAD*

Access: **news:alt.animation.warner-bros**

Art Clips for the ASCII

Access: **news:alt.ascii-art.animation**

See Art: Art Clips for the ASCII for a review.

University of California at Irvine Bookstore

Access: **http://bookweb.cwis.uci.edu:8042/**

See Books: University of California at Irvine Bookstore for a review.

Anthropology

General Anthropology Discussion List

Here you can discuss anthropology with like-minded individuals, including students and professors. It's usually hard to find good discussions about anthropology, but the discussions will come to you when you subscribe to this mailing list. —*LAD*

Access: to subscribe, send email to **listserv@tamvm1.tamu.edu**

Send messages to **anthro-l@tamvm1.tamu.edu**

Archaeology

Archaeology List

This discussion list focuses on problems with archaeology excavation and research. It features announcements of relevant conferences, calls for papers, bibliographies and publications. It also serves as a repository for public domain software related to archaeological studies. —*LAD*

Access: to subscribe, send email to **listserv@tamvm1.tamu.edu**

Send messages to **arch-l@tamvm1.tamu.edu**

ArchNet

ArchNet is a huge database that provides access to archaeological resources available on the Internet, categorized by geographical region and subject. An attractive button bar enables you to move quickly through the information. Visit archaeological regions all over the world. Or access information by subject, including geo-archaeology, historical archaeology, ethnoarchaeology and archaeological software. The main highlight is the site tours section, which links to hypertext site and survey reports. Through this link, you can take an archaeological survey in the Egyptian desert or visit a Roman fort in Scotland. —*ST*

Access: **http://spirit.lib.uconn.edu/ArchNet/ArchNet.html**

This graphical button bar makes it easy to locate archaeological information at ArchNet.

Dead Sea Scrolls Exhibit

Access: **http://sunsite.unc.edu/expo/deadsea.scrolls.exhibit/ intro.html**

See **History, World: Dead Sea Scrolls Exhibit** *for a review.*

ARCHITECTURE

Architectural Resources

Here you can browse architectural images and AutoCAD 3D images. Also, read an essay on lunar architecture and look at a few pictures of what people envision buildings would look like on the moon. —*LAD*

Access: **gopher://libra.arch.umich.edu/**

What architecture might look like on the moon.

Art Serve

Access: **http://rubens.anu.edu.au/**

*See **Art: Art Serve** for a review.*

ART

ANIMA: Arts Network for Integrated Media Applications

Billed as "the creative cultural information source," ANIMA is divided into sections covering events, electronic art magazines, online art projects and the tools and technologies used in contemporary art. A "Guide to Online Galleries" reviews online art projects and spaces and provides hotlinks to them. —*GB*

Access: **http://wimsey.com/anima/ANIMAhome.html**

 **Arts Network for Integrated Media**

ANIMA's logo.

Art Clips for the ASCII

Looking for a nice piece of art to email to a friend? Then check out **alt.ascii-art**. You can ask about pictures you're looking for, ranging from flowers and castles to Beavis and Butt-head. You can also find animated ASCII art from **alt.ascii-art.animation**. The offerings here may not be as sophisticated as an MPEG file, but they don't take up much space either. —*LAD*

Access: **news:alt.ascii-art** *AND* **news:alt.ascii-art.animation**

An ASCII image of a bat from alt.ascii-art.

Art Links on the World Wide Web

Art galleries on the Web are scattered far and wide, but once found, they reveal an amazing amount of new and innovative art, music, video, photography and 3D renderings. This page contains links to most of the major and minor galleries on the Web. —*GB*

Access: **http://amanda.physics.wisc.edu/outside.html**

Art Serve

Art history and architecture students will love this immense database of art and architecture images that can speed up research time. Art connoisseurs will also enjoy the variety of exhibitions located at this site. A prints database of 2,800 images covers art history from the 15th to the 19th century. Accompanying that is a collection of 2,500 images of classical architecture. While the databases are the star attraction at this site, don't miss the exhibits, which include the architecture of Islam and contemporary Hong Kong architecture. —*ST*

Access: **http://rubens.anu.edu.au/**

The Electric Gallery

As you'll see at this online gallery, Haitian art is rich with color and texture, depicting themes ranging from politics to voodoo. The gallery features paintings that hang permanently in museums as well as original art for sale. From the lobby, go on a walking tour of the exhibits, learn the history of Haitian art or view selected paintings by artist or title. On the walking tour, you'll pass through rooms where you can view thumbnails of paintings and purchase those you like as you see them by connecting directly to an online order form. —*ST*

Access: **http://www.egallery.com/egallery/**

A

FineArt Forum Online

FineArt Forum Online is a monthly electronic newsletter that covers art and technology issues, produced by the Art, Science and Technology Network, a virtual organization. In the newsletter, archived online at FTP, Gopher and World Wide Web sites, read announcements of events and news items happening in the world of electronic art. You'll also find an Online Directory, where you can connect to other Internet resources for art and technology. Enter the directory for the Inter-Society for the Electronic Arts for even more information about this new art medium. —*ST*

Access: **gopher://gopher.msstate.edu:70/11/Online_services/ fineart_online** *OR* **http://www.msstate.edu/Fineart_Online/ home.html**

Fine-Art Networking

This discussion group distributes information on using computers in the fine arts. Topics range from using computers to create art to using computers to analyze art. You can also discuss computer animation and computer-aided fabrication of art. —*LAD*

Access: to subscribe, send email to **listserv@rutvm1.rutgers.edu**

Send messages to **fine-art@rutvm1.rutgers.edu**

Kaleidospace

Kaleidospace is devoted to the promotion, distribution and placement of independent artists, musicians, performers, CD-ROM authors, writers, animators and filmmakers. Artists provide samples of their work, which Kaleidospace integrates into a multimedia document. Artists pay flat rentals to showcase their work; Internet users may order from the artists online, as well as by phone, fax, email and snail mail. Kaleidospace provides placement for artists wishing to showcase their work to agents, directors, gallery owners, publishers, record labels and other industry professionals. Kaleidospace also offers Gopher and FTP services at **Gopher.kspace.com** and **ftp.kspace.com**, respectively. —*GB*

Access: **http://kspace.com/**

Krannert Art Museum

Walk through exhibits of sculpture, paintings, modern art, antiquities, African art and pre-Columbian pieces at this virtual museum. In each exhibit, you can view thumbnail images of selected art pieces. Click on the graphic to get a much larger inline image and a description of the piece. Proceed through the exhibits on a preset guided tour or jump directly to the area that most interests you. After wandering through the museum, stop at the Palette Cafe and Bookstore for a light lunch or pastry. —*ST*

Access: **http://www.ncsa.uiuc.edu/General/UIUC/ KrannertArtMuseum/KrannertArtHome.html**

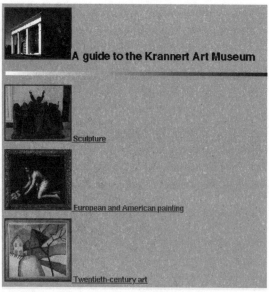

A guide to the Krannert Art Museum

Sculpture

European and American painting

Twentieth-century art

Follow this electronic guide to view online art exhibits at the Krannert Art Museum. (Copyright 1994 University of Illinois at Urbana-Champaign.)

The OTIS Project

OTIS is a place for "image-makers and image-lovers to exchange ideas, collaborate and, in a loose sense of the word, meet." It is also a repository of images and information available for public perusal and participation. Exhibits of OTIS work have been held in cities around the globe. —*GB*

Access: **http://sunsite.unc.edu/otis/otis.html**

```
Welcome to...


      tttttttt mmmm   mmmm  1111      twotwotwotwo
     t  tt  t  mmmm mmmm    11           two  two
        tt     mm mmm mm    11           two  two
        tt     mm  m  mm    11    ####    two  two
        tt     mm  m  mm    11    ####    two  two
        tt     mm     mm    11           two  two
        tt     mm     mm    11           two  two
      tttt     mmmm   mmmm  1111      twotwotwotwo

            Mudlib Development Site

Tmi-2 is running the TMI-2 1.1.1 mudlib on MudOS 0.9.19.4.3

Current users: Lem, Jeearr, Kupe, Grendel, Eldrich, Wyrmslayer, Kamini,
Terry, Gothic, Eyes, and Firedoom.

By what name do you wish to be known?
```

The OTIS home page.

Strange Interactions: Art Work by John E. Jacobsen

Experience a one-person art show of drawings, paintings and prints using the Internet as a publicly accessible gallery with a potential audience of over 25 million. Jacobsen created the exhibition himself as a way of expanding art out of the locally accessible sphere of conventional galleries and into the globally accessible one of the Internet. View Jacobsen's works through GIFs and read descriptions of each work written by the artist. This one-person show is a pleasure to tour and a great application of the Internet. —*ST*

Access: **gopher://amanda.physics.wisc.edu:70/11/show** *OR*
http://amanda.physics.wisc.edu/show.html

Le WebLouvre

That's right, the world-famous French art museum is online. Among the exhibits hosted have been a French medieval art demonstration, a collection of well-known paintings from famous artists and a tour around Paris, the Eiffel Tower and the Champs-Elysees. —*GB*

Access: **http://mistral.enst.fr/~pioch/louvre/**

 Dalí, Salvador: Dated Works (1904-1989)

[Surrealism]

- Apparition of Face and Fruit Dish on a Beach (1938)
- The Ghost of Vermeer of Delft, which can be used as a Table (1934)
- The Metamorphosis of Narcissus (1938)
- Spain (1938)

Salvador Dali on Le WebLouvre.

World Wide Web Art Navigator

A collection of brief descriptions of hotlinked sites to get you started on your quest for art in the labyrinth of the Web. —*GB*

Access: **http://www.uiah.fi/isea/navigator.html**

Alternative X

Access: **http://marketplace.com/0/alt.x/althome.html**

See Internet, Publishing: Alternative X for a review.

Cyberpoet's Guide to Virtual Culture

Access: **http://128.230.38.86/cgvc/cgvc1.html**

See CyberCulture: Cyberpoet's Guide to Virtual Culture for a review.

Electronic Cafe

Access: **http://www.cyberspace.org/u/ecafe/www/index.html**

See *Cyberculture: Electronic Cafe* for a review.

Gallery of Interactive Online Geometry

Access: **http://www.geom.umn.edu/apps/gallery.html**

See *Mathematics: Gallery of Interactive Online Geometry* for a review.

The Jerusalem Mosaic

Access: **http://shum.cc.huji.ac.il/jeru/jerusalem.html**

See *World Cultures: The Jerusalem Mosaic* for a review.

Labyrinth Electronic Publishing Project

Access: **http://www.honors.indiana.edu/docs/lab/laby.html**

See *Magazines & Publications: Labyrinth Electronic Publishing Project* for a review.

Smithsonian Images

Access: **ftp://photo1.si.edu/images/**

See *Photography: Smithsonian Images* for a review.

Underworld Industries' Web's Edge

Access: **http://kzsu.stanford.edu/uwi.html**

See *Music: Underworld Industries' Web's Edge* for a review.

Astronomy

Mt. Wilson Observatory

Visit a real space observatory through the WWW. First go on a multimedia walking tour to get a feel for the grounds and find out the
history of the observatory. Then read about the telescopes and other
astronomical equipment at the observatory. Professional services at
the site include scientific papers and robotics research. A page for
amateur astronomers has lots of fun things, including a constellation
quiz where you prove your knowledge of the night sky. One attraction is the Special Jupiter Page, where you can view Jupiter photos
taken with the observatory's 100-inch telescope before and after the
Levy-Shoemaker comet's impact. —*ST*

Access: **http://www.mtwilson.edu/**

Welcome to the Planets

Gathered at this one site is a collection of the best images from
NASA's planetary exploration programs for an overall introduction
to our solar system. Click on a planet's picture in the graphical
menu to access the planet's distance from the sun, mass, surface
temperature and a range of other useful facts. This data is followed
by images of the planet taken by NASA space probes and telescopes, complete with descriptions of how each photo was taken
and what it shows. A section on small bodies features close-ups of
asteroids and comets. Tour the solar system through this fascinating
image gallery. —*ST*

Access: **http://stardust.jpl.nasa.gov/planets/**

B

A graphical menu takes you on a tour of the solar system at Welcome to the Planets.

BBSes

(Bulletin Board Systems)

ISCA BBS

On ISCA BBS, a bulletin board at the University of Iowa, users can read messages from various forums ranging from Computers to The Lighter Side. Users can also send mail to other users or messages to those who are online at the same time. The site also features extensive help files, and the "who" list shows people who are available to help. —*LAD*

Access: **telnet://bbs.isca.uiowa.edu:23/**

LaUNChpad to the Internet

At the University of North Carolina at Chapel Hill, you'll find LaUNChpad, a student-run limited Internet service provider. Once you log in, you can create an account so that you can send and receive mail from other 'padders. If you mail in a privilege request form, you can send mail to anyone on the Internet. LaUNChpad also provides access to a full USENET newsfeed, Gopher and Lynx, plus online help from the student SysOps. —*LAD*

Access: **telnet://launch@launchpad.unc.edu/**

An image from the LaUNChpad WWW pages representing what LaUNChpad does: allow you to see the world from a different perspective.

BIOLOGY

IUBio Archive for Biology

The IUBio Archive showcases molecular biology research and drosophila research data. You can search molecular data, download software compatible to most operating systems and catch up on the latest biology news. The archive also includes outside links to other sites housing documents of interest to anyone interested in biology. —*LAD*

Access: **gopher://fly.bio.indiana.edu/**

B

Virtual Frog Dissection Kit

Squeamish about cutting up real frogs in biology courses? Didn't like the idea of taking a frog's life for science? Real-life dissection may become obsolete with virtual-dissection kits like this one, in which you can take apart an entire frog on your computer screen. A tutorial walks you through the process, then you can go to it—turn the frog over or remove the skin and organs. An image-mapped version of the kit displays each organ's name and function when you click on it. When you're done, you can put the whole frog back together again. Try that with the real thing. —*ST*

Access: **http://george.lbl.gov/ITG.hm.pg.docs/dissect/info.html**

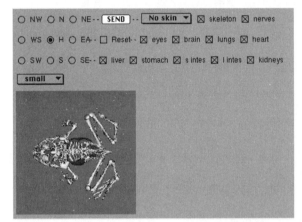

Dissect a virtual frog like this one using this online interactive kit. (Courtesy of Lawrence Berkeley Laboratory through work sponsored by the U.S. Department of Energy, Energy Research Division, Office of Scientific Computing.)

Smithsonian Natural History Archive

Access: **gopher://nmnhgoph.si.edu/**

*See **Natural History: Smithsonian Natural History Archive** for a review.*

BIZARRE

EVIL! Mud (TeenyMUD)

You know that you're in for a wild ride when you type something wrong and the MUD responds "What the ____ was that? (Maybe you should type 'help'... nah, forget it. You're hopeless.)" Yikes! EVIL! Mud (yes, all caps; they're very particular about that) lives up to its name in just the sheer orneriness of its interface, not to mention the people who populate it. Expect mayhem, expect nastiness; hell, you better expect just about anything when you dare to tread here. Not to say that it's not fun living on the dark side once in a while.... —SC

Access: **telnet://intac.com:23/**

Mayhem awaits on EVIL! Mud.

Vampyres Only

Join other creatures of the night on the "Vorld Vide Veb" at this site packed with vampire stuff. Follow the "Interview With a Vampyre" link for FAQs on vampires, their origins, causes of vampirism, making your own fangs and 20 other topics. The "Walpurgis Nacht" link leads to electronically available fiction about vampires. "Fangdom" links to lists of vampire books and movies, some of which are reviewed, as well as song lists, role-playing books, nonfiction books, Dracula editions, etc. The Pont du Lac gallery has inline portraits of vampires gathered from all over the Internet. —*ST*

Access: **http://www.wimsey.com/~bmiddlet/vampyre/ vampyre.html**

Meet vampires like these at the Vampyres Only WWW page.

BOATING

The Nautical Bookshelf

Made for "Sea Dogs" and "Landlubbers," the Nautical Bookshelf includes information about nautical books and how to get them along with an online guide to the books. The Nautical Bookshelf features boating tips, a FAQ about nautical books and also tells you how to get a nautical book for free! —*LAD*

Access: **gopher://gopher.nautical.com/**

Images of six different sailboats.

Books

See also Libraries; Literature.

Electronic Books

If you've ever wondered what books you can read on the Internet, here you can browse the books based on author, call number or title. You can also search for certain books. You can find links to the works of Lewis Carroll and Herman Melville. Or you can read such classics as the *Scarlet Letter* and the *Oedipus Trilogy.* —*LAD*

Access: **gopher://gopher.tc.umn.edu:70/11/Libraries/ Electronic%20Books**

Future Fantasy Bookstore

On the Internet, your local bookstore for science fiction, fantasy and mysteries is always open. An interactive catalog browser lets you search the full catalog of books by genre, author, title or date of publication. You're sure to find your favorite science fiction, fantasy and mystery authors in this large inventory. Select the books you want to order from a hyperlinked list and place orders online. The store also carries t-shirts, games, statuary, magazines, audio tapes and software, so set aside time for browsing. —*ST*

Access: **http://www.commerce.digital.com/palo-alto/ FutureFantasy/home.html**

Future Fantasy is the Internet's local science fiction and fantasy bookstore.

B

Jayhawk

This is an archive for *Jayhawk*, a sci-fi novel by Mary K. Kuhner, originally posted to the Net in 144 installments. Here each part is available separately and each includes a story background. —*GB*

Access: **http://www.klab.caltech.edu/~flowers/jayhawk/**

Umney's Last Case by Stephen King

Even the master of mass-market fiction can be found on the WWW. This 21-page novella from King's anthology *Nightmares and Dreamscapes* was published electronically before it ever saw print, the first commercially published hypertext short story. The bilingual WWW edition has both English and German versions. You'll even find a few surprise links in the text to sound effects that enhance the story. Don't bypass this model of future trade publishing on the Internet and Stephen King's first appearance on the WWW. —*ST*

Access: **http://www.eu.net/king/**

University of California at Irvine Bookstore

This online bookstore has it all: books, music, even UCI souvenirs. First you'll find a huge inventory of academic and general books, including a technical-books section and a large selection of fiction and poetry. Next, go to the music catalog for over 30,000 classical and jazz CDs. The store also has a unique collection of Japanese animation materials. The whole inventory can be searched for something specific and products ordered through email. If you just like to browse, take a look at the exhibitions section, featuring multimedia displays such as a travel guide to Hawaii or a West Coast jazz photography exhibit. —*ST*

Access: **http://bookweb.cwis.uci.edu:8042/**

Douglas Adams

Access: **news:alt.fan.douglas-adams**

*See **Humor: Douglas Adams** for a review.*

Alice's Adventures in Wonderland

Access: **gopher://spinaltap.micro.umn.edu/11/Ebooks/By%20Title/Alice**

See Literature, Titles: **Alice's Adventures in Wonderland** *for a review.*

The Doomsday Brunette by John M. Zakour

Access: **http://zeb.nysaes.cornell.edu/CGI/ddb/demo.cgi**

See Science Fiction: **The Doomsday Brunette** *by John M. Zadour for a review.*

Electronic Books Archive

Access: **gopher://spinaltap.micro.umn.edu:70/11/Ebooks**

See Literature, Collections: Electronic Books Archive for a review.

Electronic Texts From CCAT

Access: **gopher://ccat.sas.upenn.edu:3333**

See Literature, Collections: Electronic Texts From CCAT for a review.

Fanny Hill

Access: **ftp://ftp.netcom.com/pub/noring/books**

See Erotica: **Fanny Hill** *for a review.*

Moon Travel Handbooks

Access: **gopher://gopher.moon.com:7000/11/**

See Travel: Moon Travel Handbooks for a review.

The Nautical Bookshelf

Access: **gopher://gopher.nautical.com/**

*See **Boating: The Nautical Bookshelf** for a review.*

Unraveling the URL

Most of the Internet resources reviewed in this book are identified by URLs (Uniform Resource Locators), a standardized addressing system designed to be used with Web browsing software (such as Ventana Mosaic, included on the CD-ROM at the back of this book). URL addresses can refer to World Wide Web sites, which are accessed using the HyperText Transport Protocol (HTTP), as well as sites using other Internet protocols, including FTP, Gopher, telnet and newsgroups.

URL addresses consist of four parts: **protocol://hostname.domain:port/path**.

- The **protocol** indicates the type of site on which the resource is located.
- The **hostname.domain** is the Internet address of the site.
- The **port** is the numerical connection point where the server can be found. (The port is usually not necessary to include, since most protocols default to a specific port.)
- The **path** is the specific location of the resource. This might be a directory name, a file name, or both. (Some URLs include no path at all.)

The URL for the Ventana Online Visitor's Center home page looks like this:

http://www.vmedia.com:80/home.html

This tells us that the Visitor's Center home page is the file **home.html**, located at the World Wide Web site **www.vmedia.com**, port **80**.

Following are typical URLs for FTP, Gopher and telnet sites (note that you must have a telnet client properly installed and configured in order to initiate telnet sessions with Mosaic):

ftp://ftp.vmedia.com:21/pub/

gopher://gopher.vmedia.com:70/

telnet://kells.vmedia.com:23/

Newsgroup URLs look a little bit different: **news:newsgroup**. For example,

news:comp.infosystems.www

If you're not using Ventana Mosaic or another Web browser, simply translate the elements of a URL address into whatever format is appropriate for your client.

Online Book Initiative

Access: **gopher://gopher.std.com:70/11/obi**

See Libraries: Online Book Initiative for a review.

Project Gutenberg

Access: **gopher://gopher.msen.com:70/11/stuff/gutenberg**

See Literature, Collections: Project Gutenberg for a review.

Rare Books Discussion

Access: to subscribe, send email to **listserv@rutvm1.rutgers.edu**

Send messages to **exlibris@rutvm1.rutgers.edu**

See Literature: Rare Books Discussion for a review.

Science Fiction Newsgroups

Access: **news:rec.arts.sf.misc**

See Science Fiction: Science Fiction Newsgroups for a review.

Science Fiction Resource Guide

Access: **ftp://gandalf.rutgers.edu/pub/sfl/sf-resource.guide.html**

See Science Fiction: Science Fiction Resource Guide for a review.

Ventana Online

Access: **http://www.vmedia.com/**

See Computers, Resources & Publications: Ventana Online for a review.

BOTANY

Flora of North America

If you're interested in botany or just wonder about the plant life in North America, the Flora of North America (FNA) project will be of interest to you. You can browse introductory material or search more specific material about pteridophytes and gymnosperms. You can also download illustrations from FNA publications. —*LAD*

Access: **gopher://mobot.mobot.org:70/11/fna**

Azaleas from the Missouri Botanical Gardens.

Business & Finance

Department of Commerce Database

Here you can find information from the National Trade Data Bank (NTDB), the office of the Secretary of Commerce, and the national budget. If you own or work for a small company interested in exporting, you can find information from the NTDB that was previously only available to Fortune 500 companies. —*LAD*

Access: **gopher://gopher.stat-usa.gov/**

Entrepreneurs on the Web

Visit an online meeting place where entrepreneurs can access useful information and offer their goods and services to other entrepreneurs. Gathered here are business information resources from all over the Internet, including a frequently asked questions list on advertising on the Internet and information about World Wide Web advertising services. Many goods and services are available from other entrepreneurs on the Web as well, including computers, software, business handbooks, and consulting, marketing and financial services. —*ST*

Access: **http://sashimi.wwa.com/~notime/eotw/EOTW.html**

FinWeb

This meta-resource for financial resources collected from all over the Internet should be your first stop in seeking online financial information. From here, connect to stock market databases, investment services and interactive quote servers. A working-papers archive covers financial and economics topics. Hook up to publications like Dowvision—full-text articles from the *Wall Street Journal*, *New York Times* and Dow Jones News Service—or the *Financial Executive Journal* from NASDAQ. You can also link to other financial World Wide Web servers such as the World Bank, or make connections to law, insurance and government information on the Internet. —*ST*

Access: **http://riskweb.bus.utexas.edu/finweb.html**

Grant & Funding Information Resources

If you need to know about grants, here's the place to go. This resource from the Library of Congress includes GrantsNet, an electronic network being piloted by the Department of Health and Human Services. GrantsNet provides you with access to a wide range of grant information, from funding opportunities to finding the right contact person for a specific grant program. You can locate and learn all about Net resources on grants with A Grant Getter's Guide to the Internet, investigate grant procedures and protocols for NIH and National Science Foundation grants, and find out what's happening with collaborative research and intellectual exchanges in Eastern Europe and the former Soviet Union via the International Research & Exchanges Board. —*Chris Colomb*

Access: **gopher://marvel.loc.gov/11/global/ref/gran**

Internet Business Center

This resource is a must-see for any professional interested in using the Internet for business purposes, whether it's marketing, sales or public relations. This is also the first place to look for breaking Internet business news and new commercial sites. A Hot Sites feature displays first-rate examples of Internet business applications. A Cool Posts link features articles culled from newsgroups, mailing lists and WWW sites related to doing business on the Internet. Net Nuggets provides nuggets of information about Internet infrastructure elements to aid in your understanding of the Internet. Finally, a list of entertainment links called "After Hours" allows you to relax after a hard day's work. —*ST*

Access: **http://www.tig.com/IBC/**

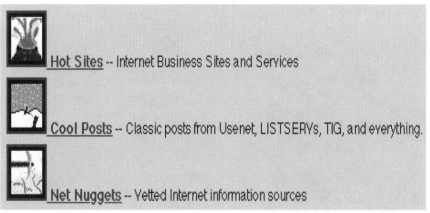

Get all your Internet business information at the Internet Business Center.

Internet Business Directory

Here you'll find listings of over 200 home pages for companies on the Internet. The searchable catalog of companies includes telecommunications services, networking services, software companies, computer vendors and more, all with lengthy descriptions. Graphical catalogs for some businesses have company overviews and listings of services and products. Use an email application form to list your own business in the directory. The directory also hosts the Internet Better Business Bureau, where you can use an online complaint form to report abuses of the Internet by commercial interests. —*ST*

Access: **http://ibd.ar.com/**

Quote Com

Get the latest stock quotes over the Internet through this financial market service. Get up to five free quotes per day, or expand into subscription services, which include an end-of-the-day portfolio update, foreign stock and commodity data, and custom quote software. Custom-design a personal stock portfolio that receives updates, daily news items and email alarms of important activities regarding the companies in the portfolio. Take a free test run of Quote Com's services today to determine if they should become your investment information source on the Internet. —*ST*

Access: **http://www.quote.com/**

A variety of investment services is available at Quote Com.

List of Commercial Services of the Web

Access: **http://www.directory.net/**

See **Internet, World Wide Web: List of Commercial Services on the Web** *for a review.*

CANADA

Canada Open Government Pilot

Take a class in Canadian government at this informative site. Here you can visit the Canadian Senate, Parliament and Supreme Court. Important government documents are available for public viewing, including NAFTA and GATT. You'll also find links to government departments, such as the National Library, health-care groups and the Department of National Defense. A Development Kit that other governments can use to build their online information systems includes software and instructions that can be downloaded from the site. Every country can use this model of an online government-info system as an example for their own information sites. —*ST*

Access: **http://debra.dgbt.doc.ca/opengov/index.html**

The Official Touring Guide of New Brunswick

Hop in your virtual automobile and travel along various scenic drives through New Brunswick, Canada, stopping at towns to sightsee. Or opt for the Discovery Byway along lesser traveled back roads off the main routes. For fun, visit "The World's Highest and Wildest Tides" or take a whale-watching expedition. Several pamphlets are provided to make your trip to New Brunswick a better one. For example, a handbook lists things to do for free in New Brunswick; another lists children's attractions. There are also guides to shopping along the drives and a list of Tourist Information Centers. —*ST*

Access: **http://www.cuslm.ca/tourist/welcome.html**

Canadian Radio

Access: **http://debra.dgbt.doc.ca/cbc/cbc.html**

See *Radio: Canadian Radio* for a review.

Travels With Samantha

Access: **http://www-swiss.ai.mit.edu/samantha/travels-with-samantha.html**

See *Travel: Travels With Samantha* for a review.

CAREER

The Academic Position Network

The Academic Position Network (APN) is an online position announcement service for higher education introduced in 1992. Announcements include faculty, administration and staff positions as well as graduate assistant and fellowship positions. Announcements are transmitted to the APN office by email or fax, and then placed on Gopher for access worldwide. Academic institutions are charged a one-time fee to place an online position announcement. The announcement remains on the network until removal instructions are received from the placing institution. All entries represent positions where searches are currently in process, and there is no charge to browse or search the APN files by authorized Internet educational users. —*Chris Colomb*

Access: **gopher://wcni.cis.umn.edu:11111**

CareerMosaic

This meta-resource is an invaluable guide to potential employers, information about careers and events in human resources. A clickable map leads you to all the information inside. Learn about hot companies and new products and technologies, information that can help you land a job with an up-and-coming company. Also find out about employers' benefits, sites and lifestyles around the world to help you make career decisions. College students will find a listing of special opportunities as co-ops or interns. A job-resources library features articles about managing and advancing your career. —ST

Access: **http://www.careermosaic.com/**

CareerMosaic makes it easy to find the perfect job.
(Trademark of Bernard Hodes Advertising.)

The Online Career Center

The Online Career Center is a terrific aid for finding employment. OCC is owned, managed and controlled by employers through a nonprofit association. It is a single source for employers placing employment advertising and reaches over 20 million users of national online networks, including users of Prodigy, CompuServe, America Online, Delphi, BIX and GEnie. Corporate members include such heavyweights as AT&T, Du Pont and Eastman Kodak.

The Online Career Center features a job-listing database with keyword search, a resume database, and a database of company information and profiles for the over 100 member companies. There are no charges for employers to access your resume, and entering your resume is free if done online. —*Chris Colomb*

Access: **gopher://garnet.msen.com:9062/**

```
       Internet Gopher Information Client v2.0.15

                      * Search Jobs

-->█ 1.  Browse Jobs:      Jobs and Profiles By Company/
    2.  Browse Jobs:      Jobs By State/
    3.  Browse Jobs:      Jobs By City/
    4.  Keyword Search:   Contract Jobs <?>
    5.  Keyword Search:   Search All Jobs <?>
    6.  Northeast:        CT/ME/MA/NH/NY/RI/VT <?>
    7.  East:             DE/MD/NJ/PA/VA/WV/DC <?>
    8.  Midwest:          IL/IN/KS/KY/MI/OH/WI <?>
    9.  South:            AL/FL/GA/MS/NC/SC/TN <?>
   10.  North Central:    IA/MN/NE/ND/SD <?>
   11.  South Central:    AR/LA/MO/OK/TX <?>
   12.  West:             AZ/CA/CO/HI/NV/NM/UT <?>
   13.  Northwest:        AK/ID/MT/OR/WA/WY <?>
   14.  Canada:           All Provinces <?>
   15.  International:    International Jobs/



Press █ for Help, █ to Quit, █ to go up a menu      Page: 1/1
```

Some of your options at the Online Career Center Gopher.

CARTOONS

See also Animation.

Doctor Fun

Access: **http://sunsite.unc.edu/Dave/drfun.html**

*See **Fun: Doctor Fun** for a review.*

Warner Brothers Central

Access: **news:alt.animation.warner.bros**

*See **Animation: Warner Brothers Central** for a review.*

CHAT

See also MUDs, MOOs & MUSHes.

Chat About Chat

The place to go to chat about chat; one of the USENET newsgroups. If you really love IRC, think of **alt.irc** as an asynchronous (non-real-time) channel with IRC itself as the topic, a place to further foster the spirit of online community that starts with the IRC channels. Of course, things can progress in the opposite direction too; people may meet on IRC, get an idea for a new channel or want to talk more in real-time mode, and hence go to IRC to continue conversing. If you are *really* addicted to IRC, think of trying the **alt.irc.recovery** newsgroup instead. —*DR*

Access: **news:alt.irc**

Chat Detox

Another IRC-related newsgroup on USENET, this one for those recovering from IRC addiction. Don't snicker; it really does happen. Many IRC users admit the fact that overuse leads to feelings of isolation and/or results in spending less time with loved ones and friends in the real world. This newsgroup serves a function not unlike an online AA meeting. Substitute the term IRCoholics for Alcoholics and you get the idea; addicts as well as those who've recovered give support, testimonials, advice, engage in debates, etc. And if someone wants to learn how to avoid becoming an IRC addict in the first place, **alt.irc.recovery** can be useful for such a person as well. —*DR*

Access: **news:alt.irc.recovery**

Chatting in the Hot Tub

Get virtually wet! This is one of the longest-running and most popular of IRC channels; it's almost always teeming with people. Other channels come and go, but there always seems to be a #hottub or #hottub2 or something similar around on IRC. Author and Internet expert Howard Rheingold has described #hottub as "an ongoing flirtation space...mostly heterosexual." You'll probably call it "fun." Meant to simulate a hot tub, you never know what the topic of conversation will be (which, of course, is pretty much what it's like when talking to others in a *real* hot tub). In fact, its popularity may be due to this very fact—that there are no built-in restrictions implied by the channel name, as there often are with other channels. Whatever the reason, jump on in; towels are optional. —*DR*

Access: Run IRC client, specifying desired IRC server, *OR* telnet to a telnettable server; do command **/join #hottub**

Connecting to the IRC

IRC is the acronym for Internet Relay Chat, the client/server technology that enables Netters to communicate in real time. The best way to connect to the IRC is to have an IRC client installed on your computer system. If you are on a UNIX system, you would normally start an IRC client by typing **irc** at the command prompt. If that doesn't work, try talking to your system administrator. Since the IRC can impact on resources, organizations vary in their rules about IRC use.

If you don't have an IRC client, or can't access one, you can try telnetting to a host (server) that provides IRC services. These sites may limit access to a certain number of users and to non-peak hours. (See client and server lists in the **Publicly Accessible IRC Servers** and the **Telnettable Server Hosts That Provide IRC** sidebars at the end of this **Chat** section.) The IRC FAQ, available many places online, describes where to obtain clients for various machines (UNIX, Windows, Mac, etc.) and also provides a list of servers that enable Netters to use IRC. —*DR*

Pull a Stool Up to the #ircbar

The main feature of #ircbar is the Barman. His job is to serve the customers with drinks, provide them with information on how to make over 60 cocktails, and information on the operators. To find out more about this, type the following into irc: **/msg barman4 help**

The Barman runs the bar, and that's what the people come in for—to get served by the Barman. Of course, without real liquor you may not get real drunk—unless you count getting drunk on conversation, as many IRCers do. (In fact, there's a USENET newsgroup for recovering IRCoholics; see **Chat Detox** in the **Chat** section.) The #ircbar channel (you can also try #IRCBar or #IRCbar) has been going since 1993, and has gradually become more and more popular. People have requested to become operators. The channel and Barman have brought a lot of people together to form good friendships. And who knows; maybe we'll meet too! Hope I R C you on IRCbar. —*DR*

Access: Run IRC client, specifying desired IRC server, *OR* telnet to a telnettable server; do command **/join #ircbar**

Navigating the Chaotic Soup of IRC

Channels can come and go on IRC, but there still tend to be hundreds available for chatting every day, sometimes even thousands. The reviews of channels listed in this book will give you some of the best or most intriguing ones to try—a set to start with rather than randomly "jumping in" to the often-chaotic soup of IRC. —*DR*

30-Something Chat

Many IRCers recommend this channel for good times. Mainly geared for those over 30 (and yet you can even trust them at times :-). Generally under 40 also applies, since there are usually other channels (e.g., #40plus) for higher age markers. But don't be "non-plussed" if you're not 30-plus; even members of Generation neXt are welcome (or whatever other Generation-? Age-of-? group you want to be part of, even if that group is just a party of one). —*DR*

Access: Run IRC client, specifying desired IRC server, *OR* telnet to a telnettable server; do command **/join #30plus**

The Undernet

Many people, even IRC users, still do not know about the Undernet—but, to quote AT&T, you will. What is it? A second IRC network, essentially; a kind of "mirror IRC." Why is it good to know about? First, because the "good ol' IRC" is becoming overloaded with users; second, many channels are getting overpoliticized. Fortunately, regulars on the Undernet are trying hard to make this new chat network into a place where good manners and higher chat quality is the norm.

So check it out. If you and some others want to create a new channel and keep it fairly free of mass intrusion, the Undernet might be a better place to create it; you can always go back to your fave IRC channels whenever you want. In general, not only might you find some discussions better on Undernet, with a higher signal-to-noise ratio, but you can get that first-on-my-block-to-see-the-next-cool-thing feeling. Even if it may only last a short time (i.e., until everybody buys this book!). —*DR*

Access: Run IRC client, specifying desired Undernet server, *OR* telnet to a telnettable Undernet server; do same commands (**/join #<channelname>**) you'd do for IRC channels. (You might need to change the port number for your chosen Undernet server.)

Brit Chat

Access for #England IRC channel: Run IRC client, specifying desired IRC server, *OR* telnet to a telnettable server; do command **/join #England**

Access for #England WWW home page: **http://www.fer.uni-lj.si/~iztok/england.html**

See **England: Brit Chat** *for a review.*

Doom

Access: Run IRC client, specifying desired IRC server, *OR* telnet to a telnettable server; do command **/join #doom**

*See **Games: Doom** for a review.*

EnviroGopher

Access: **gopher://envirolink.org/**

*See **Environment: EnviroGopher** for a review.*

Global Chat

There are a number of very popular channels devoted to various nationalities. In addition to **Brit Chat** (reviewed in the **England** section) and **Russian Chat** (listed in the **Russia** section), some of the most active are **#viet**, **#korea**, **#hk** (Hong Kong, I presume), **#taiwan**, **#aussie** or **#australia**, **#sweden**, **#germany**, **#francais** and **#francaise**, and **#europe** (for that unified feeling). Naturally, I cannot list them all, and some may not use English as the primary language. But if you get out a (recent!) globe, it'll be the next best thing to a real world tour. —*DR*

Film Talk

Access: Run IRC client, specifying desired IRC server, *OR* telnet to a telnettable server; do command **/join #movies**

*See **Movies: Film Talk** for a review.*

Gulf War IRC Logs

Access: **ftp://sunsite.unc.edu/pub/academic/communications/logs/Gulf-War/**

*See **History, World: Gulf War IRC Logs** for a review.*

Hack Chat

Access: Run IRC client, specifying desired IRC server, *OR* telnet to a telnettable server; do command **/join #hack**

See Computers, Resources & Publications: Hack Chat for a review.

Initgame

Access: Run IRC client, specifying desired IRC server, *OR* telnet to a telnettable server; do command **/join #Initgame**

See Games: Initgame for a review.

Internet Services List

Access: **telnet://csd4.csd.uwm.edu/**

See Internet, Resources: Internet Services List for a review.

Jeopardy

Access: Run IRC client, specifying desired IRC server, *OR* telnet to a telnettable server; do command **/join #jeopardy**

See Games: Jeopardy for a review.

Macintosh Chat

Access for #macintosh IRC channel: Run IRC client, specifying desired IRC server, *OR* telnet to a telnettable server; do command **/join #macintosh**

Access for #macintosh WWW home page: **http://disserv.stu.umn.edu/~thingles/PoundMac/**

See Macintosh: Macintosh Chat for a review.

C

MediaMOO

Access: **telnet://purple-crayon.media.mit.edu:8888/**

See **MUDs, MOOs & MUSHes: MediaMOO** *for a review.*

Netsex

Access: Run IRC client, specifying desired IRC server, *OR* telnet to a telnettable server; do command **/join #netsex**

See **Sex: Netsex** *for a review.*

Poetry in Motion

Access: Run IRC client, specifying desired IRC server, *OR* telnet to a telnettable server; do command **/join #poems**

See **Poetry: Poetry in Motion** *for a review.*

Report Chat Channel

Access: Run IRC client, specifying desired IRC server, *OR* telnet to a telnettable server; do command **/join #report**

See **News: Report Chat Channel** *for a review.*

Here Today, Gone Tomorrow

Note that some of the channels reviewed in this book may be gone when you try to join them; such is the ephemeral nature of IRC. If a channel *is* still around, this indicates its ongoing popularity. On the other hand, you can actually create your own channel (by joining one that does not currently exist). Hence, you, the reader, might be the one to create a great new future roadside attraction! So get to it! (And if you *do* get a great new channel going, maybe we'll include it in the next edition of *Internet Roadside Attractions*. You never know!) —DR

Russian Chat

Access: Run IRC client, specifying desired IRC server, *OR* telnet to a telnettable server; do command **/join #russian**

*See **Russia: Russian Chat** for a review.*

Russian Coup IRC Log

Access: **ftp://sunsite.unc.edu/pub/academic/communications/ logs/report-ussr-gorbatchev**

*See **History, World: Russian Coup IRC Log** for a review.*

Truth or Dare

Access: Run IRC client, specifying desired IRC server, *OR* telnet to a telnettable server; do command **/join #netsex**

*See **Sex: Truth or Dare** for a review.*

Vidgames

Access: Run IRC client, specifying desired IRC server, *OR* telnet to a telnettable server; do command **/join #vidgames**

*See **Games: Vidgames** for a review.*

World Wide Web Chat

Access: Run IRC client, specifying desired IRC server, *OR* telnet to a telnettable server; do command **/join #www**

*See **Internet, World Wide Web: World Wide Web Chat** for a review.*

Publicly Accessible IRC Servers

If you have an IRC client, point it to one of the servers below or others you know of. Note that IRC server ports are assumed to be 6667 unless otherwise indicated and most clients will assume 6667 if you do not specify a port. —*DR*

U.S. Sites

For more, read IRC FAQ, reviewed in the **Internet, Resources: FAQ (Frequently Asked Questions) Central** section in this book, or *Internet World* magazine, Nov/Dec 94, p. 60.

irc.colorado.edu (Colorado; try port 6665 or 6666 if 6667 gives trouble)

irc.math.ufl.edu (Florida)

irc.uiuc.edu (Illinois)

cs-pub.bu.edu (Boston)

European Sites

olymp.wu-wien.ac.at 6666 (Austria)

irc.funet.fi (Finland)

Australia

ircserver.cltr.uq.oz.au

Telnettable Server Hosts That Provide IRC

If you do not have an IRC client, try telnetting to one of these servers (until you get time to FTP a client from one of the many IRC-related repositories you'll find online!). —*DR*

U.S. Sites

telnet sci.dixie.edu 6677

telnet sci.dixie.edu 7766

telnet exuokmax.ecn.uoknor.edu 6668

telnet wildcat.ecn.uoknor.edu 6677

telnet wildcat.ecn.uoknor.edu 7766

telnet skywarrior.ecn.uoknor.edu 6677

telnet skyraider.ecn.uoknor.edu 6677

telnet intruder.ecn.uoknor.edu 6677

European Sites

telnet irc.tuzvo.sk 6668

telnet obelix.wu-wien.ac.at 6996

telnet obelix.wu-wien.ac.at 6677

telnet obelix.wu-wien.ac.at 7766

telnet obelix.wu-wien.ac.at 6969

telnet caen.fr.eu.undernet.ord 6677

telnet telnet1.eu.undernet.org 6677

telnet telnet2.eu.undernet.org 6677

CHILDREN

See also Education, Students.

Kids On Campus Internet Tour

Every year, the Cornell Theory Center has a Kids On Campus day where kids and computers come together. The theme for the 1994 day was "Navigating the Information Superhighway," and the folks at Cornell created this huge image map of street signs to guide the kids through the various Net resources available to them. Plunk the little ones down in front of this and let 'em go to town! —*GB*

Access: **http://www.tc.cornell.edu:80/Kids.on.Campus/KOC94**

Some signs found on the Kids On Campus site.

Spanish Counting Books

Mr. Buckman and his students created a very cute book to teach kids how to count in Spanish. The pages were drawn by his kindergarten students using KidPics. There are audio links that let you hear the students reading the numbers out loud. You can even download an entire self-running slide show of the project. —*GB*

Access: **http://davinci.vancouver.wsu.edu/buckman/ SpanishBook.html**

Children, Youth & Family Consortium Clearinghouse

Access: **gopher://tinman.mes.umn.edu:80**

See Social Issues: Children, Youth & Family Consortium Clearinghouse for a review.

Children & Youth Literature List

Access: to subscribe, send email to **listserv@bingvmb.cc.binghamton.edu**

Send messages to **kidlit-l@bingvmb.cc.binghamton.edu**

See Literature, Collections: Children & Youth Literature List for a review.

CICNet Select K–12 Internet Resources

Access: **gopher://gopher.cic.net:3005**

See Education, Students: CICNet Select K–12 Internet Resources for a review.

SchoolHouse Gopher Server

Access: **http://crusher.bev.net:70/1/Schoolhouse/kids**

See Education, Students: SchoolHouse Gopher Server for a review.

CLASSICS

The Classics

Interested in ancient cultures? You can find discussions about the classical periods of the ancient civilizations. Most of the threads discuss literature or academic writings of the classical periods of Rome, Greece and Egypt. —*LAD*

Access: **news:sci.classics**

Le radici della memoria, *an ancient piece of artwork.*

Latin Texts

This article of classical texts includes works in the Latin language and commentaries on these works. Inside, you'll find files from the MALIN Project and from Project Libellus. The MALIN Project texts are not in the public domain but are freely distributable over the Internet. They include documents in the original Latin suitable for historical study. Project Libellus holds a much bigger archive of public-domain texts, including Latin-language works from Cicero,

Caesar, Nepos and Livy as well as commentaries from Holmes. Latin scholars are sure to find this library of classical texts a valuable resource. —*ST*

Access: **gopher://wiretap.spies.com:70/11/Library/Classic/Latin**

Unraveling the URL

Most of the Internet resources reviewed in this book are identified by URLs (Uniform Resource Locators), a standardized addressing system designed to be used with Web browsing software (such as Ventana Mosaic, included on the CD-ROM at the back of this book). URL addresses can refer to World Wide Web sites, which are accessed using the HyperText Transport Protocol (HTTP), as well as sites using other Internet protocols, including FTP, Gopher, telnet and newsgroups.

URL addresses consist of four parts: **protocol://hostname.domain:port/path**.

- The **protocol** indicates the type of site on which the resource is located.
- The **hostname.domain** is the Internet address of the site.
- The **port** is the numerical connection point where the server can be found. (The port is usually not necessary to include, since most protocols default to a specific port.)
- The **path** is the specific location of the resource. This might be a directory name, a file name, or both. (Some URLs include no path at all.)

The URL for the Ventana Online Visitor's Center home page looks like this:

http://www.vmedia.com:80/home.html

This tells us that the Visitor's Center home page is the file **home.html**, located at the World Wide Web site **www.vmedia.com**, port **80**.

Following are typical URLs for FTP, Gopher and telnet sites (note that you must have a telnet client properly installed and configured in order to initiate telnet sessions with Mosaic):

ftp://ftp.vmedia.com:21/pub/

gopher://gopher.vmedia.com:70/

telnet://kells.vmedia.com:23/

Newsgroup URLs look a little bit different: **news:newsgroup**. For example,

news:comp.infosystems.www

If you're not using Ventana Mosaic or another Web browser, simply translate the elements of a URL address into whatever format is appropriate for your client.

Thesaurus Linguae Graecae

The Thesaurus Linguae Graecae (TLG) is an electronic database of ancient Greek literature from the period between Homer and A.D. 600, plus relevant historical, lexicographic and scholastic texts. The database is usually disseminated on CD-ROM; find out how to order it at this Gopher site. You can also view the table of contents for the CD-ROM, get licensing agreements, read over pricing policies and access an order form. Extras include a quick-reference file of addenda and corrigenda and the latest issue of the TLG newsletter that you can read free. —*ST*

Access: **gopher://tlg.cwis.uci.edu:7011**

Comics

Comics Collectors

Comics collectors shouldn't pass up the opportunity these newsgroups offer. You can join discussions of comics trivia and rumors. There's even a group devoted to X-books. You can also find people selling comics you might not find elsewhere. —*LAD*

Access: **news:rec.arts.comics.*(misc, marketplace, xbooks, creative)**

Computers

See also Macintosh; Microsoft Windows.

Computers, Graphics

Art Links on the World Wide Web

Access: **http://amanda.physics.wisc.edu/outside.html**

See **Art: Art Links on the World Wide Web** *for a review.*

Fine-Art Networking

Access: to subscribe, send email to **listserv@rutvm1.rutgers.edu**

Send messages to **fine-art@rutvm1.rutgers.edu**

See Art: Fine-Art Networking for a review.

Index to Multimedia Sources

Access: **http://cui-www.unige.ch/OSG/MultimediaInfo**

See Multimedia: Index to Multimedia Sources for a review.

Rob's Multimedia Lab

Access: **http://www.acm.uiuc.edu/rml/**

See Multimedia: Rob's Multimedia Lab for a review.

━━━━━ Computers.Hardware ━━━━━

Internet Shopping Network

Access: **http://www.internet.net/**

See Shopping: Internet Shopping Network for a review.

Macintosh Newsgroup

Access: **news:comp.sys.mac.*(apps, comm, games, hardware, misc, programmer, system)**

See Macintosh: Macintosh Newsgroup for a review.

PC Newsgroup

Access: **news:comp.sys.ibm.pc.*(hardware, programmer, soundcard, games, misc)**

See Computers, Resources & Publications: PC Newsgroup for a review.

======= Computers, Programming =======

C Programming

The answer to just about any C question you can imagine can be found on this newsgroup. You have access to C gurus around the world. In addition, you can learn lots of tips by reviewing the answers to other peoples' questions. —*LAD*

Access: **news:comp.lang.c**

======= Computers, Resources & Publications =======

Babel Computer Terms

A glossary of computer-oriented abbreviations and acronyms. It's a shame that there are no definitions included; some of these abbreviations are quite obscure. Just knowing that POPF stands for Pop Flags isn't enough. What on earth are Pop Flags? Still, a source of worthwhile clues to the many obscure references found in computer and telecom documents and discussions. —*GB*

Access: **ftp://ftp.temple.edu/pub/info/help-net**

Computer Folklore

The newsgroup alt.folklore.computers is a busy group about computer nostalgia. They've discussed almost everything at one time or another, so be sure to read this group for a while before you contribute. —*TL*

Access: **news:alt.folklore.computers**

Computer Resource Bonanza

The mother lode of all Mac, DOS and Windows computer resources is the **garbo.uwasa.fi** FTP site at the University of Vaasa, in Finland. The site is resplendent with games, fonts, utilities, graphics, icons, multimedia files—enough stuff to make even Garbo blush with abundance. —*TL*

Access: **ftp://garbo.uwasa.fi/**

Computer Risks & Other Hazards

The comp.risks newsgroup offers several long digests per month about risks to the public from computers and computer users. As the Internet matures, the intellectual analysis offered by this newsgroup is not only pertinent, but praiseworthy. The newsgroup is fully moderated; on the average, its digests are released weekly. —*TL*

Access: **news:comp.risks**

Computer Underground Digest

Computer Underground Digest (CuD) is a moderated weekly electronic journal/newsletter dedicated to the sharing of information and to the presentation and debate of diverse views. The quality of this publication is praiseworthy: the topics are contemporary, the prose is sensible, and the price is free. —*TL*

Access: to subscribe, send email to **listserv@uiucvmd.bitnet**

Current Cites

Current Cites is a bibliography of current journal articles relating to computers, networks, information issues and technology. Telnet to **melvyl.ucop.edu** and at the prompt, enter the command **show current cites.** —*TL*

Access: **telnet://melvyl.ucop.edu/**

Dr. Dobb's Journal

Dr. Dobb's Journal—the quintessential PC magazine—is available online in text format, fully suited to your word processor. —*TL*

Access: **ftp://ftp.mv.com/pub/ddj/**

Hack Chat

Hackers here talk about each other or their accomplishments, for the most part. Of course, if you've always wanted to *pretend* to be a hacker or talk like one, here's your chance. (But don't tell anyone I recommended it. Hackers or their related kin can be a very cliquish bunch.) —*DR*

Access: Run IRC client, specifying desired IRC server, *OR* telnet to a telnettable server; do command **/join #hack**

PowerPC News

The latest news on the PowerPC, along with some of the most up-to-date and interesting information about the Internet and personal computing and technology in general. You can get it mailed directly to your email account, or you can wait a couple of days and read it here as a Web text. —*GB*

Access: **http://power.globalnews.com/**

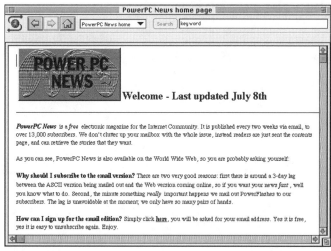

PowerPC News home page.

Subscribing to Mailing Lists & Electronic Publications

To subscribe to a discussion list, send the following message from your email account:

subscribe <list name> <Your Name>

<list name> is the name of the group. Send this message to the "to subscribe" address listed in the Access information. Include the message in the message section of the email, not in the subject line, because most listservers ignore the subject line. —*LAD*

PC Newsgroup

If you have a PC, you'll want to read one of these newsgroups. If you've ever been frustrated at your computer (and you can't get through to customer service), you'll want the resources of the PC gurus of the Internet community. If you've never been frustrated, tell me your secret. —*LAD*

Access: **news:comp.sys.ibm.pc.*(hardware, programmer, soundcard, games, misc)**

TidBITS

Adam C. Engst's *TidBITS* is one of the best documents to whiz through cyberspace. Published weekly, it covers a broad wavefront of computer hardware, software and industry news and reviews (mostly from a Mac perspective). The Web site features an index of back issues and the current issue in HTML form. One neat feature is that references within an issue to past articles in *TidBITS* are hot-linked. —*GB*

Access: **http://www.dartmouth.edu/Pages/TidBITS/ TidBITS.html**

Ventana Online

To find books and software on computer programming, desktop publishing and the Internet, among many more computer-related subjects, try this easy-to-use, graphical catalog. Navigate the pages of detailed information using a graphical button bar and pull-down menu. A graphical map of the Ventana "world" lets you enter a number of buildings on-site. Choose the Library to see the shelves of books and software for sale. As a Ventana customer, you'll also want to explore the Ventana Visitor's Center, where you find online companions to Ventana books (including this one), free software archives and the "nifty site of the week." —*ST*

Access: **http://www.vmedia.com/**

Choose books like these off the shelf at Ventana's virtual bookstore.

Computer Networks & Internet Guides

Access: **gopher://riceinfo.rice.edu:70/1/Subject/Networks**

*See **Internet, Resources: Computer Networks & Internet Guides** for a review.*

Computer Professionals for Social Responsibility

Access: **gopher://locust.cic.net:70/11/CPSR**

*See **Technology: Computer Professionals for Social Responsibility** for a review.*

Digital Future

Access: **gopher://marketplace.com/11/fyi**

See *Magazines & Publications:* **Digital Future** *for a review.*

EFFector Online

Access: **gopher://gopher.eff.org/00/about.eff**

See *Cyberculture: EFFector Online for a review.*

Electronic Frontier Foundation

Access: **gopher://gopher.eff.org/00/about.eff**

See *Cyberculture: Electronic Frontier Foundation for a review.*

FAQ (Frequently Asked Questions) Central

Access: **gopher://gopher.cs.ttu.edu/11/Reference%20Shelf FAQs%20%28Frequently%20Asked%20Questions%29**

See *Internet, Resources: FAQ (Frequently Asked Questions) Central for a review.*

Internaut

Access: **http://www.zilker.net/users/internaut/index.html**

See *Internet, Resources: Internaut for a review.*

PCWeek Best News Sources & Online Mags

Access: **ftp://www.ziff.com/~pcweek/best-news.html**

See *Magazines & Publications:* **PCWeek** *Best News Sources & Online Mags for a review.*

University of Indiana Windows Resource

Access: **ftp://ftp.cica.indiana.edu/pub/pc/win3/**

See Microsoft Windows: University of Indiana Windows Resource for a review.

▬▬▬ Computers.Security ▬▬▬

Viruses!

If you download from the Internet or a BBS, you need to be vigilant about computer viruses. On comp.virus, you get information about viruses and tips on cleaning them up with minimal damage to your data. *—LAD*

Access: **news:comp.virus**

Fight Viruses

A quick tip: don't forget to scan any files you download from public places for viruses. You can FTP McAfee Associates' scan program from **ftp://oak.oakland.edu/pub/msdos/virus/scanv###.zip** to get the latest version. *—LAD*

Clipper Chip Archive at the English-Server

Access: **gopher://english-server.hss.cmu.edu:70/** choose directories **Cyber/Clipper**

See Cryptography: Clipper Chip Archive at the English-Server for a review.

Computer Professionals for Social Responsibility

Access: **gopher://locust.cic.net:70/11/CPSR**

See Technology: Computer Professionals for Social Responsibility for a review.

Bruce Sterling

Access: **gopher://english-server.hss.cmu.edu:70/** choose
directories **Cyber/Bruce Sterling**

*See **Cyberculture: Bruce Sterling** for a review.*

■■■■■■ Computers, Software ■■■■■■

See also Macintosh; Microsoft Windows.

Internet Shopping Network

Access: **http://www.internet.net/**

*See **Shopping: Internet Shopping Network** for a review.*

Mac Everything

Access: **ftp://sumex-aim.stanford.edu/**

*See **Macintosh: Mac Everything** for a review.*

Robert Lentz's Macintosh Resources

Access: **http://www.astro.nwu.edu/lentz/mac/home-mac.html**

*See **Macintosh: Robert Lentz's Macintosh Resources** for a review.*

University of Indiana Windows Resource

Access: **ftp://ftp.cica.indiana.edu/pub/pc/win3/**

*See **Microsoft Windows: University of Indiana Windows Resource**
for a review.*

Consumer Services

Consumer News & Reviews

As Big Brother encroaches further into our lives, what's a poor consumer to do? The best thing is to make sure you know your rights. Lots of good stuff here on credit, travel and other consumer-related issues. Be sure to check out "What to do when they ask for your Social Security Number." Do you have any options when asked for your Social Security number? This article gets into the history of Social Security numbers, the Privacy Act of 1974, and how to deal with governmental and other entities who want your number. —*JW*

Access: **gopher://gopher.uiuc.edu1/News/consumers**

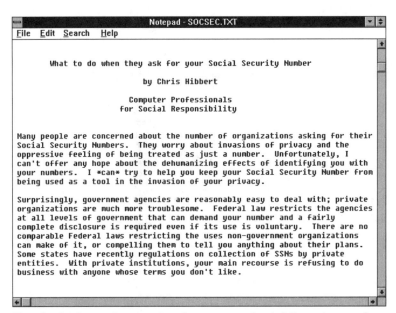

You don't always have to hand over your Social Security number—read all about it.

CRYPTOGRAPHY

Clipper Chip Archive at the English-Server

Are you wondering if Big Brother is listening? This archive of Clipper Chip information will give you the lowdown. The Clipper Chip, an encryption technique proposed by the National Security Administration, would let the government wiretap any files moving along the Information Superhighway and has stirred up a major debate on the Internet. In this archive, read about the background of the Clipper Chip, articles for and against the device, and warnings about the FBI Phone Act. —*ST*

Access: **gopher://english-server.hss.cmu.edu:70/** choose directories **Cyber/Clipper**

CYBERCULTURE

CyberNet

The Webmasters at CyberNet believe that the Internet has gotten far too boring, that it's lost its pioneering edge. They are dedicated to preserving "the unconventional nature of the Internet." They include a lengthy list of Web sites pushing the edges of art, science, culture and taste. —*GB*

Access: **http://venus.mcs.com/~flowers/html/gcybernet.html**

Funky. Shake your booty!

Hazardous. May cause brain damage.

Kitsch. Oh, how very lovely.

Noise. Boom, boom, boom, twang!

Populaire Culture. Putting the pop back in culture.

CyberNet's HotLink icons.

Cyberpoet's Guide to Virtual Culture

Those who are interested in learning more about "cyberculture," the nexus of pop culture, high technology and fringe science, should check out Cyberpoet's Guide to Virtual Culture. This is a popular watering hole for cybernauts. Includes essays on various aspects of cyberculture, a cyberspace lexicon and dictionary, and a huge hot-linked database of art, pop culture, cyberculture, music, electronic magazines and more. —*GB*

Access: **http://128.230.38.86/cgvc/cgvc1.html**

EFFector Online

EFFector Online is the online publication of the Electronic Frontier Foundation (see review below). EFFector Online serves as a watch-dog over cyberspace, including privacy, freedom and First Amendment rights. You might also investigate the Foundation's "Zine Stand," which can be accessed via FTP at **etext.archive.umich.edu** in the **/pub/zines-by-subject** directory. —*TL*

Access: **gopher://gopher.eff.org/00/about.eff**

Electronic Cafe

The Electronic Cafe (or "ecafe" to its regulars) is a place to explore music, art, literature and virtual community. It's a place for people to meet, learn, share ideas and come together in ways that only the Net can make possible. —*GB*

Access: **http://www.cyberspace.org/u/ecafe/www/index.html**

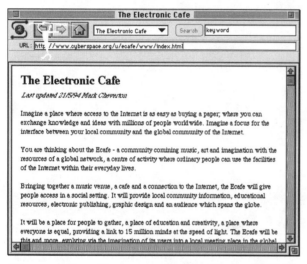

You can get anything you want at the Electronic Cafe.

Electronic Frontier Foundation

The Electronic Frontier Foundation (EFF) was founded in July 1990 to ensure that the principles embodied in the U.S. Constitution and the Bill of Rights are protected as new communications technologies emerge. EFF has been at work since then, through education, legal council and public debate, helping to shape the nation's communications policies and infrastructure. Their ultimate goal is nothing less than the creation of an electronic democracy. The EFF Gopher site contains many of their papers, articles, newsletters, action alerts and organizational materials. Other publications related to computer culture and legal issues are also stored here, as is the EFF's Guide to the Internet. —*GB*

Access: **gopher://gopher.eff.org/00/about.eff**

Internet Coffee Machine

It's late in the day, you've been Web walking for hours and boy are your hands tired. You want a little pick-me-up, but you don't want the nagging jitters of caffeine. How about a virtual cup o' joe? One at a safe distance—say, the United Kingdom? The Trojan Room Coffee Pot lives at the University of Cambridge in England. A special camera is trained on the pot, taking a picture of it every second. That picture is then digitized and made available to the Cambridge Web server. By typing the URL below, you can access the currently available image to see how much coffee is in the pot. —*GB*

Access: **http://www.cl.cam.ac.uk/coffee/coffee.html**

Internet Hot Tub

If you think the Internet coffee and Coke machines are silly, how about the Internet Hot Tub! That's right—someone in Ann Arbor, Michigan, has their outdoor hot tub connected to a Sun Workstation. By sending email to the tub, you can find out how it's doing. —*GB*

Access: send email to **hottub@hamjudo.mi.org**

Miller Genuine Draft Tap Room

You might expect this Web site to be nothing more that a shameless plug for Miller beer, but it's much more. It's a fresh and fun online lifestyle magazine. It bills itself as a "virtual tap room," but that's misleading since there's little in the way of interactive chatting. There's a feedback page where you can tell the Webmasters what you'd like to see in future issues, and they seem to take it to heart. Currently, the Tap Room has articles on art, fashion, sports, city life, social issues and entertainment. Coverage centers on New York, Atlanta, Chicago, Austin, LA, San Francisco, Seattle, Miami and cool happenings on the Net. This site is a great example of Net-based advertising that gives the user a lot in exchange for product exposure/identification. —*GB*

Access: **http://www.mgdtaproom.com/**

neXus Home Page

neXus contains information and links that lean heavily toward the more "cyberpunk" edges of the Net. You'll find links to rave culture and music, hacking and the computer underground, industrial music and the well-known electronic compendium of cyberculture, the FutureCulture FAQ. —*GB*

Access: **http://www.cis.ksu.edu/~solder/nexus.html**

Bruce Sterling

The father of cyberpunk has his own archive on the Internet. Here you can read the entire text of Sterling's famous book, *The Hacker Crackdown*, a nonfiction manifesto on hacking, the government crackdown on computer crimes, and electronic free expression. You'll also find many shorter articles and speeches by Sterling on subjects related to cybertechnology, such as artificial life, computer gaming and cyberspace. A complete bibliography lists all of Sterling's works. —*ST*

Access: **gopher://english-server.hss.cmu.edu:70/** choose directories **Cyber/Bruce Sterling**

Alternative X

Access: **http://marketplace.com/0/alt.x/althome.html**

See **Internet, Publishing: Alternative X** *for a review.*

bOING bOING

Access: **http://www.zeitgeist.net/public/Boing-boing/bbw3/ boing.boing.html**

See **Zines: bOING bOING** *for a review.*

CYCLING

The Global Cycling Network

The Global Cycling Network, or VeloNet, is a storehouse of electronic information for cycling enthusiasts. It includes information about bicycle organizations around the world and how to contact them, announcements submitted by other cyclists, and information about meeting other cyclists. It also features a search of all the information on the Gopher. —*LAD*

Access: **gopher://cycling.org/**

A cyclist looking over the Horsetooth Reservoir in Colorado.

Unraveling the URL

Most of the Internet resources reviewed in this book are identified by URLs (Uniform Resource Locators), a standardized addressing system designed to be used with Web browsing software (such as Ventana Mosaic, included on the CD-ROM at the back of this book). URL addresses can refer to World Wide Web sites, which are accessed using the HyperText Transport Protocol (HTTP), as well as sites using other Internet protocols, including FTP, Gopher, telnet and newsgroups.

URL addresses consist of four parts: **protocol://hostname.domain:port/path**.

- The **protocol** indicates the type of site on which the resource is located.
- The **hostname.domain** is the Internet address of the site.
- The **port** is the numerical connection point where the server can be found. (The port is usually not necessary to include, since most protocols default to a specific port.)
- The **path** is the specific location of the resource. This might be a directory name, a file name, or both. (Some URLs include no path at all.)

The URL for the Ventana Online Visitor's Center home page looks like this:

http://www.vmedia.com:80/home.html

This tells us that the Visitor's Center home page is the file **home.html**, located at the World Wide Web site **www.vmedia.com**, port **80**.

Following are typical URLs for FTP, Gopher and telnet sites (note that you must have a telnet client properly installed and configured in order to initiate telnet sessions with Mosaic):

ftp://ftp.vmedia.com:21/pub/

gopher://gopher.vmedia.com:70/

telnet://kells.vmedia.com:23/

Newsgroup URLs look a little bit different: **news:newsgroup**. For example,

news:comp.infosystems.www

If you're not using Ventana Mosaic or another Web browser, simply translate the elements of a URL address into whatever format is appropriate for your client.

DICTIONARIES

See also Reference.

Dictionary Library

While it might seem odd that a site in Germany is the main link point to a bunch of English dictionaries, this service is undeniably useful. Here you can gain access to a number of literary, grammatical and lexigraphical reference books. Includes *American English, Webster's, Roget's Thesaurus, The Oxford Dictionary of Familiar Quotations* and an online computer dictionary. Plus many more. —*GB*

Access: **http://math-www.uni-paderborn.de/HTML/ Dictionaries.html**

Hacker's Dictionary

Confusing your ROM and RAM, your bits and bytes? Wondering what the expression "film at eleven" really means? Look no further than the Hacker's Dictionary, aptly characterized in its preface as "a comprehensive compendium of hacker slang illuminating many aspects of hackish tradition, folklore and humor." Not just a dictionary of techspeak, the Hacker's Dictionary provides insight and illumination into the culture and philosophy of all things hackish. Be sure and stop by—the introduction alone is worth the visit. And after all, you don't want to be thought of as a "suit," do you? —*Chris Colomb*

Access: **gopher://gopher.cs.ttu.edu/11/Reference%20Shelf/ Hacker%27s%20Dictionary**

Babel Computer Terms

Access: **ftp://ftp.temple.edu/pub/info/help-net**

See Computers, Resources & Publications: Babel Computer Terms for a review.

The Virtual Reference Desk

Access: **gopher://mobot.mobot.org:70/11/fna**

See *Reference: The Virtual Reference Desk* for a review.

DRAMA

Historical Costuming

Access: **gopher://riceinfo.rice.edu:70/11/.subject/Textiles/ Hist.cost**

See *History, World: Historical Costuming* for a review.

The Oedipus Trilogy

Access: **gopher://spinaltap.micro.umn.edu/11/Ebooks/ By%20Title/oedipus**

See *Literature, Titles: The Oedipus Trilogy* for a review.

Shakespeare's Complete Plays

Access: **gopher://english-server.hss.cmu.edu:70** choose the directories **Drama/Shakespeare**

See *Literature, Collections: Shakespeare's Complete Plays* for a review.

Drugs

Forum for Discussion of Concerns of Drinking & Driving

This discussion list was created to discuss concerns regarding drinking and driving and its implications in our society. —*LAD*

Access: to subscribe, send email to
listserv@admin.humberc.on.ca

Send messages to **add-l@admin.humberc.on.ca**

Education

Education. Institutions

Ralph Bunche School

Visit a Harlem elementary school that has joined the WWW community. Browse the two student newspapers and read articles written by the students. Or connect to the school's Gopher, where you can access student work, science projects and the background of the school. A big attraction here is the illustrated Spanish alphabet, created by the students. A menu of Spanish vocabulary words for every letter in the alphabet connects to original artwork by the students illustrating each vocabulary word. At this site, elementary-school students have the chance to show off their special projects while learning through the Internet. —*ST*

Access: **http://mac94.ralphbunche.rbs.edu/**

By Chris Glover & Felipe Paulino Email: Chrisg@ralphbunche.rbs.edu
Felipep@ralphbunche.rbs.edu

*Learn Spanish at the Ralph Bunche School. (Art by Chris
Glover and Felipe Paulino, P.S. 125, 1993–1994.)*

Diversity University (MOO)

This may be a taste of the future of education. Diversity University,
run by the Embry Riddle Aeronautical University in Daytona Beach,
Florida, is not a game. It's a serious experiment into the future of
collaborative learning and telecommunication. Here, a virtual campus provides a place where teachers and classes can meet, teach,
learn and interact, regardless of the physical location of those involved. Grab your virtual backpack and get to class! —SC

Access: **telnet://erau.db.erau.edu:8888/**

Diversity University

*Diversity University: the future
of learning.*

Globewide Network Academy

Visit the world's first completely online university. The campus is
entirely virtual, with classes and office hours taking place in participating MOOs. At the WWW site, learn all about the history of the
university. Then take a look at some of the special projects going on,

such as an experiment to generate hypertext textbooks on various subjects for teaching over the Internet. Visit the GNA Library for course-specific resources; there's even a campus bookstore. By sending in an interactive form through email, you can join the Globewide Network Academy mailing list, volunteer to teach a course or sign up to be a student. —*ST*

Access: **http://uu-gna.mit.edu:8001/uu-gna/**

Honolulu Community College

Honolulu Community College is the site of many WWW "firsts," and is a model of a WWW campus-wide information system (CWIS). The first interactive map on the WWW was created here and takes you all over campus. You can also connect to course catalogs, faculty and student publications, an academic calendar and student organizations. Exhibits include interesting sculpture on campus, including the Berlin Wall Freedom monument, and an interactive geographic map of WWW sites throughout the world. Don't miss Dinosaurs in Hawaii, a multimedia dinosaur museum, or the archive of videos of campus life. —*ST*

Access: **http://www.hcc.hawaii.edu/**

Harbor Skyline (2.5 megs)

The camera slowly pans from the fifth floor of Building 2, showing the downtown waterfront skyline, starting with the Dole pineapple cannery in the distance, moving to Building 5, and showing the campus sculpture *Stage Set - Mise en Sc&eacutene</I>* down below. In the first few frames, you can just make out the large Dole pineapple water tank, now gone.

Honolulu Community College was the first WWW site to use multimedia as in this movie archive.

CERFnet Research

The California Education and Research Federation Network, CERF-net, a regional network operating throughout California, was established in 1989 to advance science and education by "assisting the interchange of information among research and educational institutions through high-speed data communications techniques." That's the official description of the resource. For those of us who aren't affiliated with one of California's 300 research and education centers, however, CERFnet offers an FTP service (**ftp.cerf.net**) that's especially rich in content, including an extensive repository of Internet information in the **internet/readings** and **internet/resources** directories. The **pub/infomagic-cd** directory reveals a gold mine of Internet data, including the "Hitchhiker's Guide to the Internet." —*TL*

Access: **ftp://ftp.cerf.net/**

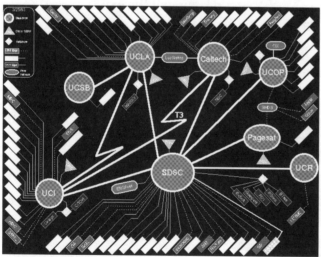

The CERFnet topology map.

CICNet Select K–12 Internet Resources

At this useful Gopher server, educators, administrators and students find pointers to K–12 resources available on the Internet. More than just a list of resources, these listings have complete descriptions, including Internet addresses, contact information, login and logout procedures, notes about particularly useful files and often a sample session. From the server, connect to K–12 resources on Gopher, World Wide Web, telnet and FTP sites, or get a list of useful mailing lists. You'll also find library catalogs, classroom activities and projects, education-related publications, news flashes and training aids, all in one handy spot. —ST

Access: **gopher://gopher.cic.net:3005**

Eisenhower National Clearinghouse for Mathematics & Science Education

The Eisenhower National Clearinghouse's stated mission is "encouraging the adoption and use of K–12 curriculum materials and programs...which improve teaching and learning in mathematics and science by providing better access to resources." To this end, the Clearinghouse maintains a "comprehensive, multimedia collection" of materials and programs for educators. You'll also find links to other math and science related Net sites, as well as info about federal programs, educational research, and related newsletters and journals. —JW

Access: **gopher://enc.org:70**

Public Broadcasting System

Dust off that old thinking cap. Learn about personal finance and money management. Or the world of abnormal psychology. Or being an effective teacher. Or any of the many topics available via telecourse through PBS's Adult Learning Services. If you're a teacher or involved in any organization that uses educational resources, be sure to take a look at PBS MATHLINE, PBS ONLINE, PBS VIDEO and K–12 Learning Services. —JW

Access: **gopher://gopher.pbs.org:70**

Bulfinch's Mythology

Access: **gopher://gopher.vt.edu:10010/11/53**

See *Mythology: Bulfinch's Mythology* for a review.

Colorado Alliance of Research Libraries

Access: **telnet://pac.carl.org/**

See *Libraries: Colorado Alliance of Research Libraries* for a review.

Dartmouth Dante Project

Access: **gopher://gopher.lib.virginia.edu:70/11/alpha/dante**

See *Literature, Authors: Dartmouth Dante Project* for a review.

The Exploratorium

Access: **http://www.exploratorium.edu/**

See *Science: The Exploratorium* for a review.

Or access: **gopher://gopher.exploratorium.edu**

See *Fun: The Exploratorium* for a review.

Historical Documents & Speeches

Access: **gopher://dewey.lib.ncsu.edu:70/1/library/stacks/historical-documents-US**

See *History, World: Historical Documents & Speeches* for a review.

The JASON Project

Access: **http://seawifs.gsfc.nasa.gov/JASON.html**

See *Science: The Jason Project* for a review.

Knowledge One

Access: **http://KnowOne-WWW.Sonoma.edu/**

See **Reference: Knowledge One** for a review.

Latin Texts

Access: **gopher://wiretap.spies.com:70/11/Library/Classic/Latin**

See **Classics: Latin Texts** for a review.

Safari 1994: Barkley Sound Expedition

Access: **http://oberon.educ.sfu.ca/splash.htm**

See **Oceanography: Safari 1994: Barkley Sound Expedition** for
a review.

Thesaurus Linguae Graecae

Access: **gopher://tlg.cwis.uci.edu:7011**

See **Classics: Thesaurus Linguae Graecae** for a review.

▬▬▬ Education.Students ▬▬▬

See also Children.

SchoolHouse Gopher Server

Not pretty by WWW standards, but this Gopher site is a great resource for kids and teachers. A lot of links here. —GB

Access: **http://crusher.bev.net:70/1/Schoolhouse/kids**

Project GeoSim

Access: **gopher://geosim.cs.vt.edu/**

See *Geography: Project GeoSim* for a review.

Spanish Counting Books

Access: **http://davinci.vancouver.wsu.edu/buckman/ SpanishBook.html**

See *Children: Spanish Counting Books* for a review.

▪▪▪▪▪ Education, Teachers ▪▪▪▪▪

The Academic Position Network

Access: **gopher://wcni.cis.umn.edu:11111**

See *Career: The Academic Position Network* for a review.

CICNet Select K–12 Internet Resources

Access: **gopher://gopher.cic.net:3005**

See *Education, Resources: CICNet Select K–12 Internet Resources* for a review.

The Labyrinth

Access: **http://www.georgetown.edu/labyrinth/ labyrinth-home.html**

See *Medieval Studies: The Labyrinth* for a review.

SchoolHouse Gopher Server

Access: **http://crusher.bev.net:70/1/Schoolhouse/kids**

See *Education, Students: SchoolHouse Gopher Server* for a review.

EMERGENCIES

Emergency & Disaster Information Services

Fire, floods and pestilence. You hope they never happen to you, but arming yourself with information is the best way to make sure you're ready for whatever comes. Learn how to prepare for natural and other disasters, what to do if a disaster hits and who to call for what. Check out the figure below—Under USDA Disaster Relief Information, there's even a whole section on emotional stress after disasters. And last but not least, a link to other safety information resources on the Net. All in all, an essential and comprehensive disaster resource. —*JW*

Access: **gopher://marvel.loc.gov/11/global/ref/disaster**

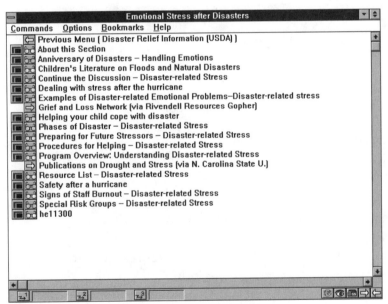

```
Emotional Stress after Disasters
Commands   Options   Bookmarks   Help
     Previous Menu ( Disaster Relief Information (USDA) )
     About this Section
     Anniversary of Disasters – Handling Emotions
     Children's Literature on Floods and Natural Disasters
     Continue the Discussion – Disaster-related Stress
     Dealing with stress after the hurricane
     Examples of Disaster-related Emotional Problems–Disaster-related stress
     Grief and Loss Network (via Rivendell Resources Gopher)
     Helping your child cope with disaster
     Phases of Disaster – Disaster-related Stress
     Preparing for Future Stressors – Disaster-related Stress
     Procedures for Helping – Disaster-related Stress
     Program Overview: Understanding Disaster-related Stress
     Publications on Drought and Stress (via N. Carolina State U.)
     Resource List – Disaster-related Stress
     Safety after a hurricane
     Signs of Staff Burnout – Disaster-related Stress
     Special Risk Groups – Disaster-related Stress
     he11300
```

Where to turn for emotional support after a disaster.

ENCYCLOPEDIAS

See also Reference.

Britannica Online

The *Encyclopedia Britannica*'s online test site. Still in the beta test phase, but there are articles you can browse. Lets you search on keywords. Supports both form searches (Mosaic 2.x) and list searches (Mosaic 1.x). This will be a paid subscription service when it is up and running. —*GB*

Access: **http://www.eb.com/**

ENGLAND

Brit Chat

#England is a regular channel on IRC, and the people who visit there tend to be very friendly. In fact, the channel description states its subtitle as "The Friendly Channel™"; if they bothered to trademark such a name, they must be serious about being amiable! This channel has never just been for people from England; people all over the world meet here and become regular visitors to this virtual English Channel (pun intended ;-). And, like a growing number of IRC channels, #England now has a WWW page where channel enthusiasts can, among other things, find a list of common visitors to #England on IRC, as well as a growing collection of picture files (GIFs) of channel users. In effect, such WWW pages expand the community feeling that IRC channels often foster, and #England's does the job very well. (In fact, some call it the best IRC-channel-related Web page yet constructed; try it for yourself and see.) —*DR*

Access for #England IRC channel: Run IRC client, specifying desired IRC server, *OR* telnet to a telnettable server; do command **/join #England**

Access for #England WWW home page: **http://www.fer.uni-lj.si/~iztok/england.html**

London Information Guide

Access: **http://www.cs.ucl.ac.uk/misc/uk/london.html**

See Travel: London Information Guide for a review.

Environment

Biosphere & Ecology Discussion List

This discussion list focuses on topics relating to the biosphere, pollution, CO-2 effect, ecology, habitats and the climate. Anything that influences the biosphere is acceptable for discussion and debate. *—LAD*

Access: to subscribe, send email to **listserv@ubvm.cc.buffalo.edu**

Send messages to **biosph-1@ubvm.ccbuffalo.edu**

Earth Science Information Network

The Consortium for International Earth Science Information Network (CIESIN, pronounced "season") was created to address environmental data management issues raised by the U.S. Congress and the Administration.

CIESIN provides Gopher access to the NASA Earth Observation System Data and Information System, including the "Environmental Internet Catalog." Other topics include health, history, humanities, law, moleclear biology, nutrition, oceanography, politics, weather and meteorology. *—TL*

Access: **gopher://gopher.ciesin.org/**

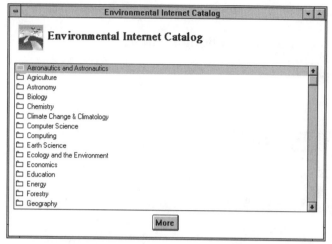

Seen through a window from America Online's Gopher client, CIESIN's Environmental Internet Catalog offers a wealth of information on governmental issues.

Ecological Society of America

This list draws ecologists who wish to exchange information and find out about job and funding opportunities, as well as catch up on Society information. It also serves as a forum for discussion of current topics in ecology, and as a resource for people looking for information about research projects. —*LAD*

Access: to subscribe, send email to **listserv@umdd.bitnet**

Send messages to **ecolog-l@umdd.bitnet**

EcoNet

EcoNet is a member of the Association for Progressive Communications (APC), a worldwide organization of like-minded computer networks. APC aims to provide a global communications network dedicated to the free and balanced flow of information. Operating within APC, you'll find the Institute for Global Communications (IGC), which hosts EcoNet, PeaceNet, ConflictNet and LaborNet. IGC offers a Gopher site in San Francisco that's especially rich in environmental resources. —*TL*

Access: **http://www.igc.apc.org/igc/en.html**

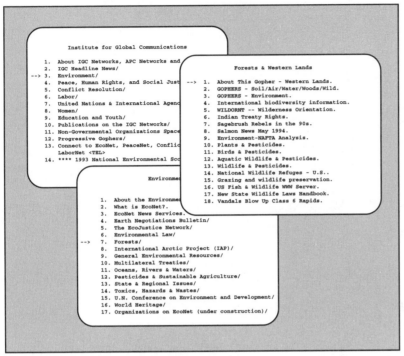

```
            Institute for Global Communications

     1.  About IGC Networks, APC Networks and
     2.  IGC Headline News/
-->  3.  Environment/
     4.  Peace, Human Rights, and Social Just
     5.  Conflict Resolution/
     6.  Labor/
     7.  United Nations & International Agenc
     8.  Women/
     9.  Education and Youth/
    10.  Publications on the IGC Networks/
    11.  Non-Governmental Organizations Space
    12.  Progressive Gophers/
    13.  Connect to EcoNet, PeaceNet, Conflic
         LaborNet <TEL>
    14.  **** 1993 National Environmental Sco
```

```
                       Forests & Western Lands

-->  1.  About This Gopher - Western Lands.
     2.  GOPHERS - Soil/Air/Water/Woods/Wild.
     3.  GOPHERS - Environment.
     4.  International biodiversity information.
     5.  WILDORNT -- Wilderness Orientation.
     6.  Indian Treaty Rights.
     7.  Sagebrush Rebels in the 90s.
     8.  Salmon News May 1994.
     9.  Environment-NAFTA Analysis.
    10.  Plants & Pesticides.
    11.  Birds & Pesticides.
    12.  Aquatic Wildlife & Pesticides.
    13.  Wildlife & Pesticides.
    14.  National Wildlife Refuges - U.S..
    15.  Grazing and wildlife preservation.
    16.  US Fish & Wildlife WWW Server.
    17.  New State Wildlife Laws Handbook.
    18.  Vandals Blow Up Class 6 Rapids.
```

```
                       Environme

     1.  About the Environme
     2.  What is EcoNet?.
     3.  EcoNet News Services.
     4.  Earth Negotiations Bulletin/
     5.  The EcoJustice Network/
     6.  Environmental Law/
-->  7.  Forests/
     8.  International Arctic Project (IAP)/
     9.  General Environmental Resources/
    10.  Multilateral Treaties/
    11.  Oceans, Rivers & Waters/
    12.  Pesticides & Sustainable Agriculture/
    13.  State & Regional Issues/
    14.  Toxics, Hazards & Wastes/
    15.  U.N. Conference on Environment and Development/
    16.  World Heritage/
    17.  Organizations on EcoNet (under construction)/
```

Starting at the top of the IGC Gopher, Econet's abundance is revealed in menu after menu.

EnviroGopher

EnviroGopher, a project of the EnviroLink network, is an archive of environmental information. It also has links to other sources about the environment. A link to EnviroChat lets you talk to others about environmental issues. —*LAD*

Access: **gopher://envirolink.org/**

Icon of the EnviroLink Network, which sponsors the EnviroGopher.

Unraveling the URL

Most of the Internet resources reviewed in this book are identified by URLs (Uniform Resource Locators), a standardized addressing system designed to be used with Web browsing software (such as Ventana Mosaic, included on the CD-ROM at the back of this book). URL addresses can refer to World Wide Web sites, which are accessed using the HyperText Transport Protocol (HTTP), as well as sites using other Internet protocols, including FTP, Gopher, telnet and newsgroups.

URL addresses consist of four parts: **protocol://hostname.domain:port/path**.

- The **protocol** indicates the type of site on which the resource is located.
- The **hostname.domain** is the Internet address of the site.
- The **port** is the numerical connection point where the server can be found. (The port is usually not necessary to include, since most protocols default to a specific port.)
- The **path** is the specific location of the resource. This might be a directory name, a file name, or both. (Some URLs include no path at all.)

The URL for the Ventana Online Visitor's Center home page looks like this:

http://www.vmedia.com:80/home.html

This tells us that the Visitor's Center home page is the file **home.html**, located at the World Wide Web site **www.vmedia.com**, port **80**.

Following are typical URLs for FTP, Gopher and telnet sites (note that you must have a telnet client properly installed and configured in order to initiate telnet sessions with Mosaic):

ftp://ftp.vmedia.com:21/pub/

gopher://gopher.vmedia.com:70/

telnet://kells.vmedia.com:23/

Newsgroup URLs look a little bit different: **news:newsgroup**. For example,

news:comp.infosystems.www

If you're not using Ventana Mosaic or another Web browser, simply translate the elements of a URL address into whatever format is appropriate for your client.

EnviroLink

The EnviroLink Network, the largest online environmental information service on the planet, reaches well over 450,000 people in 95 countries. It offers mailing lists (for sending U.S. Mail, not the Internet variety), the world's largest online environmental archive, a World Wide Web/Mosaic interface and anonymous FTP at

envirolink.org. Among all these things, the Network's "Enviro-Gopher" offers a legislative scorecard that tracks the environmental performance of the nation's legislators.

Access: **http://envirolink.org/about.html**

```
Highest Scoring Individuals and Delegations
-------------------------------------------
Highest Scoring Delegations:
Senate: New Jersey 97%, Massachusetts 94%,
Connecticut 85%, Vermont 85%, Wisconsin 85%
House: Vermont 95%, Rhode Island 90%, Maine
85%, Massachusetts 83%, Connecticut 80%,
Hawaii 80%.

Highest Scoring Individuals:
Senate: Lieberman (Connecticut) 100%, Kerry
(Massachussetts) 100%, Lautenberg (New
Jersey) 100%, Metzenbaum (Ohio) 100%,
Leahy (Vermont) 100%
House: Woolsey (California) 100%, Lantos
(California) 100%, Eshoo (California) 100%,
Becerra (California) 100%, Andrews, T.
(Maine) 100%, Vento (Minnesota) 100%,
Nadler (New York) 100%, Shepherd (Utah) 100%
```

The EnviroLink Network's legislative scorecard is always current and is the best way to keep track of your elected representatives' environmental performance.

U.S. Department of Energy

Access: **http://www.doe.gov/**

*See **Government, U.S.: U.S. Department of Energy** for a review.*

EROTICA

Fanny Hill

John Cleland's 1749 erotic masterpiece *Fanny Hill* returns to the literary frontier in the form of a hypertext offering by John Noring. Appearing in the Windows Help format, the file is fully searchable; bookmarks facilitate your return to favorite sections, and jump lines abound. —*TL*

Access: **ftp://ftp.netcom.com/pub/noring/books**

Poetry & Prose

The newsgroup rec.arts.erotica is a moderated forum of prose and poetry, complete with a 1-to-10 ratings system. The moderator keeps the content on a creditable level and keeps noise to a minimum. Submissions range from 17-syllable haiku to 17-installment series. —*TL*

Access: **news:rec.arts.erotica**

Food & Drink

Coffee

When you want to talk up one of the world's favorite legal drug, hang out here to find out about all things caffeine-related. You can swap coffee recipes and find out the best coffee mail order places. Or you can just read the diatribes instant coffee inspires. —*LAD*

Access: **news:alt.coffee**

A picture of a coffee pot from the Internet Coffee Machine.

Food & Nutrition Information Center

The Food and Nutrition Information Center (FNIC) provides information and educational materials on food and nutrition. You can find out about conferences, publications, software and the National Agriculture Library. The FNIC also houses the USDA/FDA food-borne illness education information center. —*LAD*

Access: **gopher://cyfer.esusda.gov:70/11/fnic**

Grapevine Wine Drinkers

Grapevine is an archive for wine lovers. You can find an archive of the **rec.food.drink** newsgroup and reviews of wines from Australia, Italy and the USA. You can send in reviews to be included in the archive. —*LAD*

Access: **gopher://gopher.opal.com:70/11/grapevine**

An image of vintage wine.

Hot Hot Hot

Make a stop in the Internet's "coolest hot-sauce shop." Here you'll find over 100 products, all guaranteed to spice up your life. Check out the catalog selections by heat level, geographic origin, ingredients or name. Icons by every product show at a glance how hot it is. Click on the order button right next to any product to add it to your shopping list; when you're done browsing, send off your whole order through an interactive form. You'll have a "hot" time browsing through this colorful catalog. —*ST*

Access: **http://www.presence.com:1235/H3/**

Choose sauces by level of "heat" in the Hot Hot Hot catalog. (Copyright 1994 Hot Hot Hot and Presence.)

Mothercity Espresso

This guide will lead you to the best coffeehouses in the North American crown city of espresso—Seattle, Washington. The listings describe the coffee, atmosphere and location of each recommended coffeehouse. You'll even see the place for yourself through inline photographs. The little things that make each coffeehouse unique are described, like the kind of beans they use, the way they froth their milk or the weird artistic types who hang out there. —*ST*

Access: **http://www.seas.upenn.edu/~cpage/mothercity.html**

Visit Seattle coffeehouses like the Caffé D'arte at Mothercity Espresso. (Copyright 1994 Virticulturalist IT.)

Restaurant Le Cordon Bleu

By the time you have scrolled through this exhibit of French culinary arts you'll be ravenous. The site features a collection of recipes taught at Le Cordon Bleu by master chefs, representing classical French cuisine. After reading a history of the cooking school, choose from a week's worth of full menus, with an appetizer, entree and dessert. Each menu is linked to recipes for every dish featured. You'll definitely want to try them all after viewing the full-color photographs of selected dishes that accompany them. —*ST*

Access: **http://sunsite.unc.edu/expo/restaurant/restaurant.html**

Vegetarian Recipes

Internet vegetarians can find recipes on dishes from falafel to applesauce cake. Even if you're not a vegetarian, this site also has a vast store of fat-free recipes. —*LAD*

Access: **ftp://ftp.geod.emr.ca/pub/Vegetarian/Recipes**

The move toward a vegetarian world.

Frequently Asked Questions Lists

USENET FAQs

Get the FAQs, the whole FAQs and nothing but the FAQs. As you may or may not recall, FAQ stands for "frequently asked question," and this Gopher has the FAQs for just about every USENET news-group in the known universe. Be a savvy netizen and get the inside skinny before you barge in on a newsgroup. A peek at the FAQ can often prevent an embarrassing cyber faux pas. —*JW*

Access: **gopher://mudhoney.micro.umn.edu:70/00/Gopher**

FAQ (Frequently Asked Questions) Central

Access: **gopher://gopher.cs.ttu.edu/11/Reference%20Shelf/ FAQs%20%28Frequently%20Asked%20Questions%29**

*See **Internet, Resources: FAQ (Frequently Asked Questions) Central** for a review.*

FAQ Up First

Before posting to any newsgroup, read the FAQ for the newsgroup beforehand. Not doing so can get you flamed very quickly. My favorite place to find FAQs is at **http://www.cis.ohio-state.edu/ hypertext/faq/usenet/FAQ-List.html**. —*LAD*

Doctor Fun

Doctor Fun is a single-panel cartoon by David Farley distributed every weekday over the Internet. Doctor Fun has been in produc-tion since September 1993. The cartoons are rendered in vivid colors and uploaded to the Net as 24-bit JPEG images. Farley's work has appeared in *Spy, Punch* and *Campus Life,* and he has done work for King Features and Recycled Paper Products. —*GB*

Access: **http://sunsite.unc.edu/Dave/drfun.html**

Make your day with a cartoon from Doctor Fun.

Electronic Fortune Cookies

Among the many thought/quote/meditation-for-the-day ("fortune-cookie") services, one is an email "bounce-back" service that responds only when you ask it to. To receive a fortune cookie on demand, send email to the address listed below with the words "send quote" in the message field. You'll receive return mail within a few hours. —*TL*

Access: to subscribe, send email to **listserv@oes.orst.edu**

Send messages to **almanac@oes.orst.edu**

The Exploratorium

Man, does this one bring back memories. When the Exploratorium was in its infancy, I lived about two blocks from the Palace of Fine Arts in San Francisco (that's where it's located). It was this huge, cavernous room. Concrete walls, kinda dark, very funky. And you could play all these cool games that actually taught you something.

The Exploratorium calls itself "a museum of science, technology, and human perception." Methinks they are too modest. Now, through the magic of modern technology, you can share my Exploratorium experience. (Also check out Shannon Turlington's review of the Exploratorium Web site in the **Science** section.) —*JW*

Access: **gopher://gopher.exploratorium.edu**

Graffiti Wall

Do you feel the urge to vandalize the walls of the World Wide Web? Or do you just need to express yourself? The Graffiti Wall is the place for you. Here you'll find a whole Web page of stuff people wrote down just because they felt like it. Virtual graffiti can include graphics, links to other WWW sites or just random thoughts. To add your own graffiti WWW-style, use the handy interactive form. You can also insert HTML enhancements, such as links to your favorite WWW places or a picture of yourself. —*ST*

Access: **http://www.honors.indiana.edu/~cdent/the.graffiti.html**

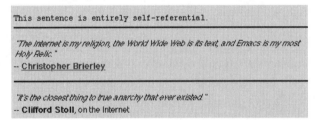

A sample of virtual graffiti left behind on the WWW Graffiti Wall.

Lego Bricks Server

Here Lego fans can catch a sneak preview of the newest product line or get information on specific Lego sets, including parts lists. Lego designers show off their work through pictures of home-built construction projects. For more advanced builders, get rules for Lego games, such as Lego War, or instructions on how to build complicated projects, like robots. You can even learn how to power your Lego models with electricity or solar energy. A menu of projects such as animated movies and flight simulators will provide enough ideas to fill up your spare time playing with Legos. —*ST*

Access: **http://legowww.itek.norut.no/**

On This Day...

You might also try the "On-this-day" mailing list. Subscribers receive a daily listing of interesting birthdays, events, religious holidays and astronomical events. —*TL*

Access: to subscribe, send email to **geiser@pictel.com**

Penpal Network

If you hate opening an empty email mailbox, check out **soc.penpals.** You can post information about yourself or reply to others' posts. Plus, you can befriend Internauts from around the world. You may even end up with a free guided tour of any city on the map. —*LAD*

Access: **news:soc.penpals**

Tarot Information

Get your fortune read by the WWW using this tarot-card server. The interactive program provides a simple 3-card reading to answer all your pressing questions about your future. Or opt for the full 16-card Celtic reading. Think about your problem, let your vibes travel over the Internet, and then hit the hyperlink to get a personal reading chosen randomly from a virtual tarot deck. The computer lays out the cards and then interprets them for you. —*ST*

Access: **http://cas.ucla.edu/repository/useful/tarot.html**

Let the WWW tell your fortune at the tarot server.

Techno/Rave Archive

For information about raves and locations near you, this is the place to go. You can find out when a rave is scheduled near you or read treatises on the merits of raving. You can even check other countries for raves in case you'll be traveling and don't want to miss out on raving. —*LAD*

Access: **gopher://gopher.hyperreal.com:70/11/raves**

Rave (rāv)

v. 1. To speak wildly, irrationally or incoherently; 2. To roar; rage; 3. To speak with wild enthusiasm. n. 1. The state or act of raving. 2. Informal. An extravagantly enthusiastic opinion or review. 3. Slang. A dance usually lasting throughout the night where loud techno music is played. —*LAD*

The Toy Box

In this virtual toy box, you'll find unique playthings probably not available elsewhere on the Internet. Listen to the song of the day, a digital clip of new and unusual music submitted by users. Access the Written Word page for humorous essays, such as Fabio's Top Ten Pick-up Lines and the Tonya Harding Fan Club Page. Float into space with a selection of images from the Mars Probe. Visit the Internet Candy Dish to receive a handful of Valentine candy hearts with inspiring messages, or wander through the Field of Clovers, where you'll find lots of three-leaf clovers but only one four-leaf. —*ST*

Access: **http://orange-room.cc.nd.edu/ToyBox/ToyBox.html**

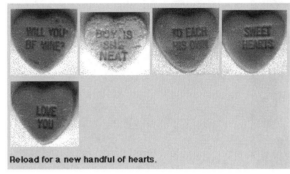

Reload for a new handful of hearts.

Get a handful of Valentine hearts from the Internet Candy Dish.

Urban Folklore

Tread lightly in the **alt.folklore.urban** newsgroup: newbies are baited regularly. The traps are benign, however, and the humor is gentle. This newsgroup's volume, however, is prodigious. As cud goes, **alt.folklore.urban** is a substantial wad, but it's worth the chew. —*TL*

Access: **news:alt.folklore.urban**

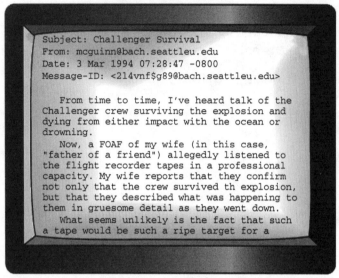

```
Subject: Challenger Survival
From: mcguinn@bach.seattleu.edu
Date: 3 Mar 1994 07:28:47 -0800
Message-ID: <214vnf$g89@bach.seattleu.edu>

     From time to time, I've heard talk of the
Challenger crew surviving the explosion and
dying from either impact with the ocean or
drowning.
     Now, a FOAF of my wife (in this case,
"father of a friend") allegedly listened to
the flight recorder tapes in a professional
capacity. My wife reports that they confirm
not only that the crew survived th explosion,
but that they described what was happening to
them in gruesome detail as they went down.
     What seems unlikely is the fact that such
a tape would be such a ripe target for a
```

*Bait for sure: respond to this message with something like
"Wow! Do you think that's true? The video was so realistic!"
and watch what happens.*

What's in a (Long) Name

For the fun of it, see if your newsreader will subscribe to
alt.this.group.has.the.longest.name.of.any. alt.group.there.is.just.
to.mess.up.your.newsreader. It works with some readers well
enough for folks to post. —*TL*

Access: **news:alt.this.group.has.the.longest.name.of.any.alt.
group.there.is.just.to.mess.up.your.newsreader**

Rumor Mill

Access: **news:talk.rumors**

See **Intrigue: Rumor Mill** *for a review.*

Vermont Teddy Bear Company

Access: **http://www.service.digital.com/tdb/vtdbear.html**

See **Shopping: Vermont Teddy Bear Company** *for a review.*

Games

Abyss IV (DikuMUD)

Abyss IV would be your fairly standard run-around-and-kill-monsters MUD if it weren't for the tone of absolute bloodlust that runs through this place. Not for the weak of heart or those who get unnaturally attached to their characters. Like real life, you can be certain you'll die here. Loads of fun. —SC

Access: **telnet://129.89.68.89:4000/**

A spooky screen welcomes you to Abyss IV.

Addventure

Addventure is a choose-your-own-adventure game with a twist—you can add your own creations to the game. Once you enter the game, proceed through various rooms, all of which were created by previous players. Because of its collaborative nature, the game moves into a variety of unknown plot twists. If you reach a point where no one has ever been before, you get to make up rooms for other players to use. This game has been going on since June 1994, and promises to be more unpredictable than conventional choose-your-own-adventure games. —ST

Access: **http://helios.acm.rpi.edu/addventure/**

Advanced Dungeons & Dragons Discussion List

This list offers a forum for discussing the Advanced Dungeons and Dragons and Dungeons and Dragons Role-Playing Game. Discussions range from campaigns and modules to new spells, monsters and rules. Interpretation and clarification of rules are also discussed. —*LAD*

Access: to subscribe, send email to **listserv@gitvm1.bitnet**

Send messages to **adnd-l@gitvm1.bitnet**

Apocalypse IV MUD (DikuMUD)

Descend into the seven circles of hell. Scale impassable peaks. Battle through hopeless and impossible quests. Sound like your usual Monday morning? Nope! It's Apocalypse IV MUD, an ever-expanding world populated with dastardly thieves, arrogant mages, muscle-bound warriors and supposedly pious clerics—all duking it out in a never-ending quest of world domination. Apocalypse IV lets players submit their own areas, so you can be assured you'll never get bored. On top of all that, it now seems to have a permanent home at West Virginia University, so it should be up for years of hack and slash adventure. —*SC*

Access: **telnet://157.182.168.20:4000/**

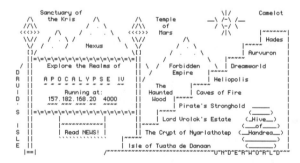

Just a sampling of the areas on Apocalypse IV.

BatMUD, A World Apart

One of the best MUDs I've seen, BatMUD boasts myriad guilds including the ability to create your own, thousands of rooms (you can download a world map from their FTP server), dozens of races, 100 levels and a wish system to further customize your character with boons and banes. There is also a newbie warehouse, for players under level 30, and a few high-level characters that offer help. This isn't a MUD for first-time MUDders though, so you might want to try another one first then come back to BatMUD when you know a little more about the basic operations of MUDs. —*LAD*

Access: **telnet://bat.cs.hut.fi:23/**

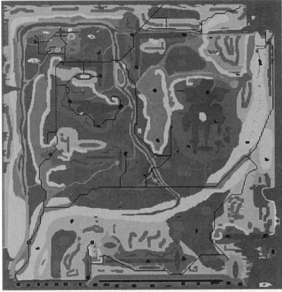

*A map of the overworld of BatMUD to help in finding new areas to explore. A new version of the map can be found at **http://bat.cs.hut.fi/batmap.html**.*

BU's Interactive WWW Games

The first interactive multiplayer games page on the Web. Play against a computer in a game of tic-tac-toe or pegs, try to solve the 9-puzzle—the sliding tiles game—or risk your virtual life playing

Hunt The Wumpus in real time against other denizens of the Net. Things are a bit primitive at this point, but it's a harbinger of things to come. —*GB*

Access: **http://www.bu.edu/Games/games.html**

Chess Archive

This archive includes information about connecting to the Internet Chess Server, where you can play other Internauts or the ICS computer. Help files for ICS are available for downloading. You can also download computer chess games for most operating systems. —*LAD*

Access: **ftp://ics.onenet.net/pub/chess**

A computer representation of pawns on a chess board from the Chess Archive.

ChromeMUSH (TinyMUSH)

OK razorgirls and console cowboys! You think you have what it takes to survive in the gone-to-hell world of the 21st century? Can you rely only on your wits and implants to make a name for yourself in the seamy underworld that is ChromeMUSH? It doesn't get any more cyberpunk than this—leave the meat behind and jack in to this lightfast intense role-playing world. One caution—the machine that maintains this MUD seems to be more fickle than your typical AI. Best connections are on weekends. —*SC*

Access: **telnet://colossus.acusd.edu:4444/**

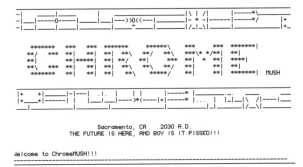

```
Sacramento, CA    2030 A.D.
THE FUTURE IS HERE, AND BOY IS IT PISSED!!!

Welcome to ChromeMUSH!!!
```

Grab your cyberdeck and jack in to ChromeMUSH.

Doom

This channel is a cousin of #vidgames (see review later in this section) but goes into more detail about a specific game—you guessed it, Doom. On #doom you can meet other players of this wildly popular (some say addictive) game. And some IRCers like to find other IHHD players too; IHHD refers to the special "Internet Head-to-Head Daemon" software some people use, which can link PCs and let folks play Doom against other humans over the Net. (Note: some "Doomers" may want to try finding a **#modemdoom** channel if #doom is not active for some reason.)

Related channels include **#falcon3.0** and **#bolo**, where aspects of these other games are discussed by their respective fanatics (I mean, players). And now that DOOM II is being released, don't be surprised if a **#doomII** channel begins taking up IRC bandwidth sometime in the near future. —*DR*

Access: Run IRC client, specifying desired IRC server, *OR* telnet to a telnettable server; do command **/join #doom**

Final Frontiers II

Final Frontiers II is a MOO based on the world of *Star Trek: The Next Generation* and *Star Trek: Deep Space Nine*. You can join forces with the Federation, Klingons, Rihannsu (Romulan), Ferengi, Dominion, or try it on your own. Final Frontiers II has simulated space to practice your piloting abilities for the real thing. You can rise in rank in whichever organization you choose and even build additions to the Final Frontiers Universe. —*LAD*

Access: **telnet://ugly.microserve.net:2499/**

Logo of the United Federation of Planets, one of the key groups on Final Frontiers II.

Foosball

Here you can get the official rules for foosball as well as advice for improving your game. Instructional guides can be downloaded that also offer tips on special trick shots. Watch a British cartoon about foosball and find a listing of public playing locations. —*LAD*

Access: **ftp://conrad.harvard.edu/pub/foosball/**

A British cartoon about foosball.

Games Mania

This site has something for everyone interested in board or Internet games. It also includes information about role-playing games, computer games, arcade games and Magic: The Gathering. You can also find links to other games-oriented sites across the Net. —*LAD*

Access: **gopher://gwis.circ.gwu.edu:70/11/ Student%20Organizations/Sports%5cHobby%5cRecreational/ GWU%20Gamers%20Society**

Unraveling the URL

Most of the Internet resources reviewed in this book are identified by URLs (Uniform Resource Locators), a standardized addressing system designed to be used with Web browsing software (such as Ventana Mosaic, included on the CD-ROM at the back of this book). URL addresses can refer to World Wide Web sites, which are accessed using the HyperText Transport Protocol (HTTP), as well as sites using other Internet protocols, including FTP, Gopher, telnet and newsgroups.

URL addresses consist of four parts: **protocol://hostname.domain:port/path**.

- The **protocol** indicates the type of site on which the resource is located.
- The **hostname.domain** is the Internet address of the site.
- The **port** is the numerical connection point where the server can be found. (The port is usually not necessary to include, since most protocols default to a specific port.)
- The **path** is the specific location of the resource. This might be a directory name, a file name, or both. (Some URLs include no path at all.)

The URL for the Ventana Online Visitor's Center home page looks like this:

http://www.vmedia.com:80/home.html

This tells us that the Visitor's Center home page is the file **home.html**, located at the World Wide Web site **www.vmedia.com**, port **80**.

Following are typical URLs for FTP, Gopher and telnet sites (note that you must have a telnet client properly installed and configured in order to initiate telnet sessions with Mosaic):

ftp://ftp.vmedia.com:21/pub/
gopher://gopher.vmedia.com:70/
telnet://kells.vmedia.com:23/

Newsgroup URLs look a little bit different: **news:newsgroup**. For example,

news:comp.infosystems.www

If you're not using Ventana Mosaic or another Web browser, simply translate the elements of a URL address into whatever format is appropriate for your client.

Games of Death MUD (DikuMUD)

Caught in a time-warp gone bad, you're suddenly thrust out of your comfortable reality and dumped right into the middle of the ruin that is GOD MUD. The world as you know it is gone. Here, radioactive monsters rule the landscape and all but the few who are strong enough fear for their lives with every turn. GOD MUD is based on the good ol' Diku formula with lots of monsters and a standard layout. But there's a lot here to make this MUD stand out from the crowd. Take on GOD, if you think you have the guts. —*SC*

Access: **telnet://cyberspace.com:4000/**

GarouMUSH (TinyMUSH)

Put down that Anne Rice novel and go play the real thing! Garou-MUSH is one of many MUSHes based on White Wolf's "Story-teller" games. Set in the fictitious city of St. Claire, Washington, Garou's universe has always included the supernatural beings that we suspected were lurking in the closet. Werewolves, vampires and their ilk coexist with the mortal world, but carry out their lives as part of a shadowy underworld that few mortals ever see. Garou-MUSH is heavily dependent on role-playing rather than gaming; and players must go through a rigorous creation procedure where they create detailed backgrounds, descriptions and motivations for their characters. Intense and highly absorbing. —*SC*

Access: **telnet://kyriath.cygnuys.com:7000/**

Subscribing to Mailing Lists & Electronic Publications

To subscribe to a discussion list, send the following message from your email account:

subscribe <list name> <Your Name>

<list name> is the name of the group. Send this message to the "to subscribe" address listed in the Access information. Include the message in the message section of the email, not in the subject line, because most listservers ignore the subject line. —*LAD*

Genocide (LPMud)

Genocide is where you go if you want to kill, pure and simple. There is no adventure here, no quests and precious little chit chat. Genocide is one long series of ongoing wars, fought and won for status and points. In this natural extension of the player-killing MUD genre, you arrive as a ghost. In this form, you can wander around and check out the MUD. But when a war starts, watch out! You must scramble to gather the goods and then move even faster to annihilate your fellow players. When it's over, the dead are swept away, the victorious rewarded, and the whole thing starts all over again. Fun! —*SC*

Access: **telnet://pip.shu.edu:2222/**

Global MUSH (MUSH)

You really can be all things to all people, and Global MUSH is here to prove it. Not content to be your usual "hang around and chat" MUSH or the just-as-usual wizards and warriors type place, Global MUSH lives up to its global theme by providing areas for fantasy, sci-fi, adventure and city themes as well as college and beach areas! Who needs real life? Friendly to the core, Global MUSH is the great Whitman's Sampler of text-based virtual realities—you never know what you're gonna get. —*SC*

Access: **telnet://lancelot.cif.rochester.edu:4201/**

GrimneMUD (DikuMUD)

Ready to hack and slash? Billing itself as "the worst of the hack and slash MUDs," GrimneMUD does all it can to live up to its name. No namby-pamby stuff here—just pure adventure, lots of treasure, and evil monsters galore. If you give no quarter nor ask for any back, GrimneMUD is the place to hang out. On the other hand, its also a great place for newbies because the equipment is plentiful, the supplies cheap, and you get to dive right in without a lot of preliminary chitchat and begging for coins from the local wizards and such. If you're some wuss who wants to stand back and watch the action, forget it. Go hang out on some Toon MUSH, you big baby, and stay away from Grimne. —SC

Access: **telnet://gytje.pvv.unit.no:4000/**

Just one of the fun people you can expect to meet on the GrimneMUD.

InfinityMUD (LPMud)

You won't get bored here. Sure, Infinity is a pretty classic MUD, but it's also populated with some of the friendliest people this side of the Rainbow Festival. Newbies are usually welcomed here with showers of gifts and lots of smiles and hugs. Plus, as soon as you can extricate yourself from all the touchy-feely, there's a huge world out there to explore. Find yourself a quest and head out! Adventure awaits. —SC

Access: **telnet://infinity.ccs.neu.edu:3000/**

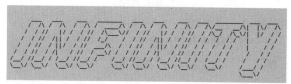

Good times and friendly people await you at InfinityMUD.

Internet Hunt

This contest leads you on a scavenger hunt all over the Internet to find the answers to trivia questions that can only be answered using Internet resources. The Hunt questions, released on the first of every month, cover the spectrum of information available on the Internet. At the Hunt's Gopher server, you'll find the latest set of questions as well as a history of the Hunt, the official rules, lists of individual and team winners, and prize lists. You can also access an archive of past Hunt questions and results. Prove yourself to be an Internet wizard by taking part in the Internet Hunt. —*ST*

Access: **gopher://gopher.cic.net:70/11/hunt**

```
--------------------------------------------------------
Question 1  (3 points)
(Question designed by Carole Leita, John Makulowich, Kimberley Robles)

I'm going to be visiting Berkeley, CA next month and am in a
wheelchair. I'd like a list of wheelchair-accessible bookstores
(including addresses, phone #'s, specialities, etc.)

--------------------------------------------------------
Question 2  (5 points)
(Question designed by Alan Shapiro and Karen Schneider)

What airline flys between Chicago, Alanta, Newark, and Florida
for one-way prices ranging from $69 to $149?  The toll-free
number would also be helpful.

--------------------------------------------------------
```

Questions like these will stump you at the Internet Hunt.

Initgame

An IRC (chat) channel meant for relaxation and fun, Initgame offers an endless game of Initials. (Try #initgame if you cannot find #Initgame.) One user at a time is the host of this ongoing game, usually changing his or her nickname to a string of letters that stand for specific bits of information. For example, JL_MAAR: the J and L represent the person's first and last name; the M is for male (F=female); the first A is for American (N=not); the second A is for Alive (D=dead); and R is for Real (F=fictional). Players ask simple Yes or No queries of the host, such as listing a set of potential jobs or general job areas (abbreviated to a few letters) that the famous person in question may (or may not) have engaged in. For instance, in my example, "TV flm" would get a "Yes" (since TV was the right job area), and "Tlk" would get a "Yes," because my JL stands for talk-show host Jay Leno. (Do the command **/recap** to get a summary of all information gathered so far in the game. The first user to guess right becomes the new host, and the game continues.) —*DR*

Access: Run IRC client, specifying desired IRC server, *OR* telnet to a telnettable server; do command **/join #Initgame**

Let's Play Jeopardy

The chat channel #jeopardy is a virtual experiment of sorts, an attempt to add a bit of creative entropy and a dash of chaos to an established classic game show. The essence: This channel is an ongoing game of Jeopardy, where contestants answer questions (oops!—I meant enter questions to match given answers), just like on the TV show. An IRC user can jump in and out at any time, playing as many rounds as one likes. The game never ends.

Other elements unique to this IRC incarnation: There are no virtual buzzers; instead, the fastest typist to enter the correct answer (I mean question) wins. Also, there's an automated online "robot" (referred to as Alexbot) that runs things, and requires players to precede each sentence with the name "Alex" so that the 'bot can recognize players' entries. In addition, the number of players is not limited to 3, as in the TV version; on IRC, the number varies, usually averaging about 30 at any given time.

Is this the future of game shows? Is Alexbot more human than Alex Trebek? Try #jeopardy and see. (One tip: you may want to create a macro to automatically type "Alex" for you, to speed your typing!) —*DR*

Access: Run IRC client, specifying desired IRC server, *OR* telnet to a telnettable server; do command **/join #jeopardy**

Magic Deck Master

Looking for tips on building that unbeatable Magic deck for the popular Magic: The Gathering card game? Well, no deck is truly unbeatable, but you can still get your questions answered plus some handy tips on card combinations. You can also get info about buying singles from the marketplace newsgroup. —*LAD*

Access: **news:rec.games.deckmaster** *AND*
news:rec.games.deckmaster.marketplace

MicroMuse

MicroMuse, a multi-user simulation developed at the Massachusetts Institute of Technology, features explorations, adventures and puzzles with redeeming social, cultural and educational content. This service is becoming overrun and MIT is threatening to disconnect it from the Net. As it now stands, a message appears saying that the MicroMuse is no longer available to the public, but if you then issue the command **connect guest** you may get in. —*TL*

Access: **telnet://michael.ai.mit.edu** and log in as **guest**.

The Metaverse

The novel *Snow Crash*, by Neal Stephanson, describes the MUSE of the 21st Century as a "Street": a grand boulevard that circles a black sphere measuring 65,536 kilometers in circumference. Vendors rent real estate along its right of way, which players are invited to enter. Each player adopts an "avatar" (a synthetic embodiment) of his or her choosing. Players wear audio/video helmets, and the simulation is presented at 72 frames per second with a resolution of 2000 by 2000 pixels (times two: a different image is presented for each eye). It's all very elaborate and surprisingly believable. If you're a MUD/MUSE fan, this book is a must. —*TL*

MUME "Multi Users in Middle Earth" (DikuMUD)

Evil Orcs and good Hobbits, mysterious Men and steadfast Dwarves—they're all here in MUME, a faithful re-creation of J.R.R. Tolkien's world of Middle Earth. Not only an adventuring MUD, but an intensely detailed role-playing world, MUME has the details down, even to the point of having different languages and dialects for the different races. Even if you don't have any experience with Tolkien's work, MUME provides a rich world to live in and an exciting place to play. Be warned, though—great powers await you on the other side! —SC

Access: **telnet://lbdsun4.epfl.ch:4242/**

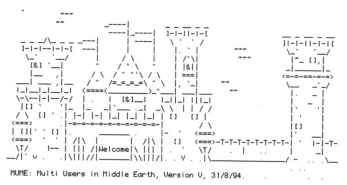

MUME: Multi Users in Middle Earth, Version V, 31/8/94.

Middle Earth can be yours when you enter MUME.

NannyMUD (LPMud)

Why the "nanny" in NannyMUD? Maybe because that's who you'll be crying for after a bit of time on this classic adventure MUD. Based in Sweden at the MUDs-a-plenty Lysator site, NannyMUD is a busy place—loaded with players, quests and good ol' fashioned killing. Not for the faint-hearted or weak-willed. Make sure your life is in order before you drop by here. —SC

Access: **telnet://mud.lysator.liu.se:2000/**

Mats, the tireless god of NannyMUD.

Nanvaent

Nanvaent at first seems to be much like other combat MUDs. You have the standard fighter and wizard guilds, skills, stats and 100 levels. But if you log in, you'll soon find out that your life on Nanvaent might not be as prolonged as on other MUDs. You can only die a certain number of times before you can't come back from the dead. It makes you more careful with your character, and less willing to sacrifice it for a special equipment or other rewards. —*LAD*

Access: **telnet://corrour.cc.strath.ac.uk:3000/**

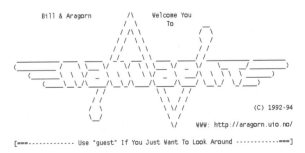

The login screen for Nanvaent.

NuclearWar (LPMud)

Ever feel like kicking some mutant butt? Harbor a secret wish to join an outlaw gang but can't seem to give up that aversion to blood and dirt? Here, several hundred years in the future, gangs and megacorps rule the earth after the Big One was dropped. So you better stop being such a dern pansy and figure out how you're gonna survive, you wimp! Luckily, you can actually live a bit longer than you probably deserve here, and in the process get some serious cyberpunk adventuring done. Buck up, tighten your belt, and jack in to NuclearWar. —*SC*

Access: **telnet://nuclearwar.astrakan.hgs.se:4080/**

Danne Soli, one of the administrators of NuclearWar, coding new MUD terrors.

Othello Across the Net

Now you can play Othello whenever you want without having to worry about finding an opponent! Just log on to the Internet Othello Server (IOS) and look for a game. IOS is a text-based server that keeps a database of wins and losses for registered users. The online help files explain the theory of the game for those unfamiliar with the game and how to use the IOS interface. —*LAD*

Access: **telnet://faust.uni-paderborn.de:5000/**

```
<ios> BOARD of GAME   5. (darkleaf vs. Darkleaf)
                         increment:    0
   BLACK   (*)            A B C D E F G H      WHITE   (O)
   [  0] darkleaf        1 - - - - - - - - 1   [  0] Darkleaf
   time : 00:13:54 (120) 2 - - - - - - - - 2   time : 00:15:00 (120)
   discs :  2            3 - - - - - - - - 3   discs :  2
   moves :  4            4 - - - O * - - - 4   moves :  4
   d3 c4 f5 e6           5 - - - * O - - - 5   E3 F4 C5 D6
                         6 - - - - - - - - 6
                         7 - - - - - - - - 7
                         8 - - - - - - - - 8
OPPONENT'S TURN           A B C D E F G H      [00]: PA  00:00:00   +0.00
```

A screen capture of the beginning of a game of Othello.

Overdrive (LPMud)

A wild and savage land awaits you when you enter Overdrive. It's a huge and cruel world here, with little help lying around and few sympathies from its inhabitants. You must rely on your wits if you want to survive the day. A friendly help system will get you started on your adventures in Overdrive, but you gotta have a silver tongue to live long. Richly detailed and fabulously complex, Overdrive will keep you coming back for more. —*SC*

Access: **telnet://castor.acs.oakland.edu:5195/**

A savage land awaits when you enter the world of Overdrive.

Paradox

Paradox is a friendly MUD that isn't too difficult for newbies to get started in. Paradox has many interesting guilds ranging from "Dread Lord" bounty hunters to "Cainite" vampires and areas like the Shadow Wastes and the GWAR death pit for heavy metal fans. There is an optional player-killing system for those players who find the monsters not enough of a challenge. You can opt to become a wizard when you reach level 20 or a Mortal Lord and continue playing and making your character more powerful. —*LAD*

Access: **telnet://adl.uncc.edu:10478/**

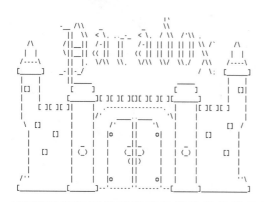

```
><][><][><][><][><][><][><][><][><][><][><][><][><][><][><][><][><][><][><]
Paradox it is: Mon Nov 21 19:46:05 1994
what name are you known, adventurer?
```

One of the many login screens for Paradox.

The Revenge of the End of the Line (LPMud)

ROEOTL (as it's known to its aficionados) may be an unwieldy acronym, but it's one heck of an eclectic place. Not content to wrap itself in the warm, fuzzy comforts of a classic hack 'n' slash adventure mode, ROEOTL flings its themes far and wide with a cool mix of fantasy, sci-fi and adventure all in one tight package. Watch your back, though, because player-killing is not only allowed—it's encouraged! He who smiles so sweetly at you when you log on may hack you to pieces as soon as you start out. Trust no one. —*SC*

Access: **telnet://mud.stanford.edu:2010/**

Spatial Wastes (MUSH)

A strange confluence of intergalactic turmoil, multidimensional travel, alien contact and generally odd occurrences, which begin on August 12, 1995. It seems that what began as a strange disappearance of the space shuttle *Discovery* has ended in the transformation of our universe and the appearance of new universes, all with their own races and needs and problems. When you descend into Spatial Wastes, be ready. This is only the beginning. —*SC*

Access: **telnet://chestnut.enmu.edu:2001/**

The Sprawl (MOO)

Taking its cue from *Neuromancer* and giving a nod to *Snow Crash*, The Sprawl is a cyberpunk/futuristic-themed MOO that emphasizes building. Players are given unlimited freedom to move and build, and this freedom has resulted in, well, a Sprawl that seems to extend endlessly into cyberspace. But wait! There's more! Using the WOO Transaction Protocol developed at Picosof, you can interact with the Sprawl through the World Wide Web as well as the more traditional telnet method. In fact, players on the Sprawl can even add Web links to their spaces, making the Sprawl the world's first multimedia MOO. Definitely worth a space on your hotlist. —*SC*

Access: **telnet://chiba.picosof.com:7777/** *AND*
http://chiba.picosof.com:7777/

The Sprawl: Cyberpunk Mecca on the Web.

Star Trek Email Game

If you're a Star Trek fan, now you can journey the final frontier. Sign on to a ship and rise in rank in Starfleet through this email roleplaying game. Many games are run simultaneously and you can read what happens in them or join in when you feel ready. —*LAD*

Access: to subscribe, send email to **listserv@gitvm1.gatech.edu**

Send messages to **stargame@gitvm1.gatech.edu**

Star Wars MUSH

A short time ago, in a computer not so far away, some dedicated Star Wars fans created an incredible virtual version of the Star Wars universe. No detail is left out here—there are over 21 races, dozens of available positions, death, intrigue, cut-throat business—and it's all waiting for you to jump right in. This is a huge and busy place, a parallel universe for all you who wish that George Lucas would get off his butt and make a sequel. Wait no more, and may the Force be with you. —*SC*

Access: **telnet://100.3.240.54:4402/**

```
    To create a new character: CREATE <name> <password>
   To connect to the guest character: CONNECT guest
    To connect to an old character: CONNECT <name> <password>
Use WHO to see which characters logged on, and QUIT to leave the MUSH.
```

Hope the Force is with you when you enter the world of Star Wars MUSH.

Sword & Crown

Shop from a large selection of role-playing games, fantasy games and other fantasy materials at this online storefront for Sword & Crown Mail Order. You'll find books, role-playing-game modules, miniatures, cards and everything else you need to play your favorite fantasy games. Browse through the catalog in your choice of a text-only or graphics-rich format. Or get instant access to the latest information about new products and releases. You have to complete a membership application to order, but once you do, you can satisfy all your gaming needs through one handy online source. —*ST*

Access: **http://www.mcs.com/~sword/html/top.html**

ToonMUSH III (TinyMUSH)

You waskly wabbit! Hop on down to Toon Town and live out your wildest Toon fantasies! Here, anything can happen and often does as normally staid people throw off the mundanity that is their normal lives and cavort around as wild and wacky Toons. Don't worry about being lost, though—most characters are recognizable from familiar boob-tube 'toons, while some are classic movie characters and some don't fit in anywhere at all. Why watch 'em when you can be 'em? Pocket those samolians and dive in. —SC

Access: **telnet://brahe.phys.unm.edu:9999/**

ToonMUSH III: your passport to Toon Town!

Video Games Chat

Join this channel for a discussion of a wide range of topics related to videogames—past, present and future. For example, some may use #vidgames to brag about their high scores (genius envy :-) and others might rebut in kind. Or IRCers might ponder puzzles they or others have found in games (especially newer ones), or discuss other problems players want answers for. Still others might bring up hidden gems and surprises to be found in certain games (especially older ones). Even the possible rise of virtual reality as the new game paradigm has been discussed here. —DR

Access: Run IRC client, specifying desired IRC server, *OR* telnet to a telnettable server; do command **/join #vidgames**

WWW Addict's Pop-Culture Scavenger Hunt

Test both your World Wide Web (WWW) and pop-culture knowledge with this fun game. Three levels each consist of a series of clues that lead you all around the pop-culture sites on the Web. You'll find easy, medium and hard questions that test your WWW know-how. If you answer all the questions correctly and find the password, you land on the winner's list. The questions cover such topics as music, entertainment and the WWW, and all the answers can be found somewhere on the Web. —ST

Access: **http://www.galcit.caltech.edu/~ta/hunt/wwwhunt.html**

Easy Level (5 Questions)

1. How many songs were in Pepsi's radio countdown show that was once hosted by Adam Curry?
2. What was the listed price of Metallica's *Garage Days Re-revisited EP* in cents?
3. How many categories in the Best of the Web '94 Awards?
4. How many cards do you get in your WWW Tarot reading?
5. How many issues of *Wired* magazine were produced in 1993?

Questions like these can lead you on a scavenger hunt all over the World Wide Web.

Lego Bricks Server

Access: **http://legowww.itek.norut.no/**

See Fun: Lego Bricks Server for a review.

Truth or Dare

Access: Run IRC client, specifying desired IRC server, *OR* telnet to a telnettable server; do command **/join #truthdare**

See Sex: Truth or Dare for a review.

University of Indiana Windows Resource

Access: **ftp://ftp.cica.indiana.edu/pub/pc/win3/**

*See **Microsoft Windows: University of Indiana Windows Resource** for a review.*

GEOGRAPHY

G

Project GeoSim

Project GeoSim is a joint research project of the Departments of Computer Science and Geography at Virginia Tech. They have created education modules for introductory geography classes including tutorial programs and simulation programs. —*LAD*

Access: **gopher://geosim.cs.vt.edu/**

Xerox PARC Map Viewer

Create your own map of any geographical location at this site. Through the interface, you can request maps of specific latitudes and longitudes; the program returns an HTML document including an inline image of the map. You control the map rendering by panning across the map, zooming in to a particular point or changing the level of detail the map provides. A color display with an accompanying legend draws in rivers, borders, roads, lakes, ferries, railroads, pipelines, parks and Indian reservations. Visit here to play with one of the best examples of interactive multimedia on the WWW. —*ST*

Access: **http://pubweb.parc.xerox.com/map/**

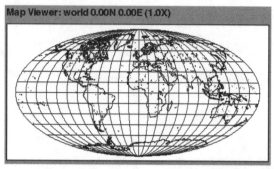

Map Viewer: world 0.00N 0.00E (1.0X)

Create maps like this one of the world at the Xerox PARC Map Viewer.

Guide to Australia

Access: **http://life.anu.edu.au/education/australia.html**

*See **World Cultures: Guide to Australia** for a review.*

GEOLOGY

Geologic Information Servers

Mine this site (pun intended) for its geological riches. It's a mega-Gopher that consists of links to just about everything earthy and scientific. Use it as a jumping off point for the Colorado School of Mines, the Earth and Marine Science Gopher at UC Santa Cruz, Carnegie-Mellon's EnviroGopher, Berkeley's Museum of Paleontology, and a whole bunch of USGS stuff (including seismology and tectonophysics info and the Pacific Marine Geology data catalog). —JW

Access: **gopher://info.er.usgs.gov:70/11/Geologic Information/**

University of California Museum of Paleontology

Access: **http://ucmp1.berkeley.edu/welcome.html**

*See **Paleontology: University of California Museum of Paleontology** for a review.*

GOVERNMENT

■■■■■ Government, U.S. ■■■■■

FCC Gopher

This is the FCC's archive of articles, releases and documents related to communications. —*GB*

Access: **gopher://gopher.fcc.gov/**

Information From the White House

Want to know what the president was doing on June 10, 1994? I sure did, so I checked out the President's Daily Schedule and came up with what you see in the figure below. If you're a political geek (or "info babe" or "dude," as politico/talk-show host Mary Matalin is wont to say), you'll loooove this place! Get the latest on press briefings, the inside scoop on health-care happenings and find out who's being appointed to what. There's also a searchable database—I did a search on AIDS and came up with over 100 references—articles, speeches and other stuff. And make sure you read the FAQ—you'll learn how to send email to the president and Congress, sign up for daily electronic publications, and search and retrieve White House documents. —*JW*

Access: **gopher://gopher.tamu.edu/11/.dir/president.dir**

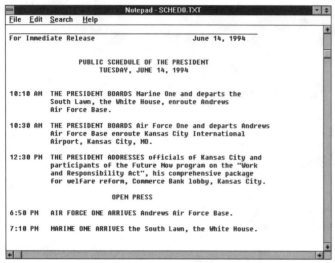

Follow the president's every move.

National Information Infrastructure

This collection of papers describes the government vision for the evolving National Information Infrastructure (NII). Here you can read for yourself how the NII will affect major aspects of society. For instance, find out how the NII will improve delivery and control costs in health care or sustain democratic and equal access to information in electronic libraries. Learn how the NII can increase the speed and efficiency of business-to-business communication to promote economic growth. There are also sections on how the NII will impact manufacturing, the environment and education. The NII could dramatically affect us all; become informed at this site. —*ST*

Access: **gopher://iitfcat.nist.gov:95**

U.S. Census Bureau Home Page

Here is proof that the Census Bureau can make public census information attractive and easy to use. Find out the projected resident population of the United States for the current day and time. Or order Census information on CD-ROM, video and maps directly through the Internet. Demographics on subjects ranging from education to retirement to buying the first home are ready to download. You can also retrieve free statistics software. If you need a break from all these numbers, visit the art gallery to view a variety of Census posters with Native-American themes. —*ST*

Access: **http://www.census.gov/**

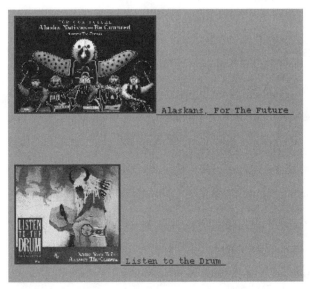

Posters from the Census Bureau's art gallery.

U.S. Department of Energy

The U.S. Department of Energy began offering its Technical Information Service (TIS) site in 1993. Among other things, TIS offers databases for the Occupational Safety and Health Administration, including standards and proposed rulemaking. —*TL*

Access: **http://www.doe.gov/**

U.S. Government Hypertexts

The official archive of the Clinton/Gore documents, this is the place to go for government information. All the White House documents are stored here, including press releases, the budget and the health-care plan. Documents like the National Performance Review are fully hyperlinked and cross-referenced, with access to supporting papers. You can also search the audio clips of the Saturday Radio

Addresses by President Clinton. For a fun detour, take the Pictorial Inaugural Tour, a photographic tour through President Clinton's inauguration. —*ST*

Access: **http://sunsite.unc.edu/govdocs.html**

U.S. State Department Travel Advisories

I'm planning to vacation in Algeria. Since my Girl Scout days, I've always believed in being prepared, so I went right to the Travel Advisories Gopher and got the advisory for Algeria. Uh, I'm glad I haven't booked a flight yet. The August 5, 1994, update tells me there was a car bomb attack against the French residential compound on August 3. As of that date, Americans in Algeria were being advised to leave. Okay, this was in August—it's December now, but still...I think I'll do a little more checking before I finalize my plans. Yeah, that's the ticket. (See also Luke Duncan's review in the **Travel** section.) —*JW*

Access: **gopher://gopher.stolaf.edu/Internet Resources/US-State-Department-Travel-Advisories**

The White House

On the Internet, the front door to the White House is literally always open. Use this Interactive Citizen's Handbook to learn all about the executive branch of government. Take a virtual tour of the White House and meet the First Family. Browse through a library of White House publications, including press releases (up to today's), policy briefings, speeches, executive orders and Congressional testimony. Listen to welcome messages from the president and vice president, and "speak out" by sending them email directly from the site. —*ST*

Access: **http://www.whitehouse.gov/**

Consumer News & Reviews

Access: **gopher://gopher.uiuc.edu/11/News/consumers**

*See **Consumer Services: Consumer News & Reviews** for a review.*

Department of Commerce Database

Access: **gopher://gopher.stat-usa.gov/**

*See **Business & Finance: Department of Commerce Database** for a review.*

Unraveling the URL

Most of the Internet resources reviewed in this book are identified by URLs (Uniform Resource Locators), a standardized addressing system designed to be used with Web browsing software (such as Ventana Mosaic, included on the CD-ROM at the back of this book). URL addresses can refer to World Wide Web sites, which are accessed using the HyperText Transport Protocol (HTTP), as well as sites using other Internet protocols, including FTP, Gopher, telnet and newsgroups.

URL addresses consist of four parts: **protocol://hostname.domain:port/path**.

- The **protocol** indicates the type of site on which the resource is located.
- The **hostname.domain** is the Internet address of the site.
- The **port** is the numerical connection point where the server can be found. (The port is usually not necessary to include, since most protocols default to a specific port.)
- The **path** is the specific location of the resource. This might be a directory name, a file name, or both. (Some URLs include no path at all.)

The URL for the Ventana Online Visitor's Center home page looks like this:

http://www.vmedia.com:80/home.html

This tells us that the Visitor's Center home page is the file **home.html**, located at the World Wide Web site **www.vmedia.com**, port **80**.

Following are typical URLs for FTP, Gopher and telnet sites (note that you must have a telnet client properly installed and configured in order to initiate telnet sessions with Mosaic):

ftp://ftp.vmedia.com:21/pub/

gopher://gopher.vmedia.com:70/

telnet://kells.vmedia.com:23/

Newsgroup URLs look a little bit different: **news:newsgroup**. For example,

news:comp.infosystems.www

If you're not using Ventana Mosaic or another Web browser, simply translate the elements of a URL address into whatever format is appropriate for your client.

G

National Archives

Access: **gopher://gopher.nara.gov/**

See *History, U.S.: National Archives* for a review.

■■■■■ Government. International ■■■■■

United Nations Documents

This site contains many documents pertaining to the United Nations and its organizations. You can browse current information and announcements regarding the UN, find environmental information and even read the UN Charter, General Assembly Documents or Security Council Resolutions. —*LAD*

Access: **gopher://nywork1.undp.org/**

The world with the ideals of the UN.

Canada Open Government Pilot

Access: **http://debra.dgbt.doc.ca/opengov/index.html**

See *Canada: Canada Open Government Pilot* for a review.

HISTORY

■■■■■■ History.World ■■■■■■

Dead Sea Scrolls Exhibit

Learn the fascinating story of the Dead Sea Scrolls through this exhibit, which describes the historical context of the Qumran community from where the scrolls may have originated and also relates the story of their discovery 2,000 years later. As you walk through the exhibit, you'll see 12 scroll fragments and 29 other objects relating to the scrolls, mostly artifacts from the Qumran site. View the scroll fragments as inline images accompanied by English translations. A text commentary relates the story of the scrolls and their discovery, backed up with secondary materials from the Library of Congress. —*ST*

Access: **http://sunsite.unc.edu/expo/deadsea.scrolls.exhibit/ intro.html**

1492 Exhibit

Rediscover the New World through an online exhibit that surveys the Mediterranean world at this dynamic turning point in its development, and goes on to explore the first sustained contact between Native-American peoples and European explorers. The exhibit covers pre-European America, the Mediterranean world, Columbus and Europe claiming America. You'll see historical drawings, manuscripts, books, maps and other items. Exhibit pieces include such diverse items as a Mexican calendar, Venetian sailing directions, Columbus's coat of arms and the first map of California. An extensive text commentary throughout gives a thorough history lesson on this important and controversial period in American history. —*ST*

Access: **http://sunsite.unc.edu/expo/1492.exhibit/Intro.html**

Gulf War IRC Logs

The 1991 Gulf War was arguably the first event to truly show off IRC's special abilities, or at least the first even to generate a lot of attention for IRC. The Gulf War IRC log site (at the location described below) is where you can read, among other things: "official" Desert Storm logs from the "report" channel; the granddaddy log of January 17, from the ironically named "peace" channel; a transcript of IRC discussions about the bombing of Israel.

These logs are not just interesting for historians of real life; they are also useful for historians of the Internet and IRC itself. Perfect for illustrating how people use IRC—even come to depend on it—for up-to-the-nanosecond news. (See also the review of **Report Chat Channel** in the **News** section.) And the logs are just plain fascinating, like being able to read scores of interwoven diaries all being written simultaneously during incredibly stressful times. —*DR*

Access: **ftp://sunsite.unc.edu/pub/academic/communications/ logs/Gulf-War/**

Historical Costuming

Do you need to reenact a Civil War battle or find out what people used to wear on the American frontier? Perhaps you just want your Halloween costume to be really accurate. This Gopher directory of the historical costuming FAQ, maintained by Shelley Johnson, will provide all the information you need. Here you'll find lists of historical costuming resources, such as places to buy authentic costumes, costuming books and magazines, and sources for fabrics, patterns and supplies. You even find tips for making authentic historical costumes from modern supplies. —*ST*

Access: **gopher://riceinfo.rice.edu:70/11/.subject/Textiles/ Hist.cost**

Historical Documents & Speeches

Divided into Pre-Constitution, Constitution and Post-Constitution documents. Pre-Constitution includes the Magna Carta, the Mayflower Compact, the First Thanksgiving Proclamation, the Declaration of Independence, Articles of Confederation and the Annapolis Convention. Constitution contains the entire Constitution, including the Bill of Rights and Amendments. The figure shows the Post-Constitution documents available. —*JW*

Access: **gopher://dewey.lib.ncsu.edu:70/1/library/stacks/ historical-documents-US**

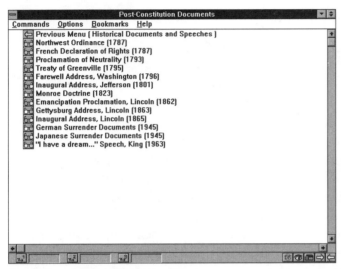

Post-Constitution documents.

History of the Renaissance

This discussion list focuses on the history of the Renaissance. Announcements, calls for papers, and newsletters are distributed to the group. Ideas and short papers can be sent to the group to receive criticism and spark debate. —*LAD*

Access: to subscribe, send email to **listserv@ulkyvm.louisville.edu**

Send messages to **renais-l@ulkyvm.louisville.edu**

Mediterranean History

This forum offers discussion and exchange of information by students and scholars of the history of the ancient Mediterranean. Newsletters, announcements for meetings and calls for papers are distributed, as well as short pieces, queries and other relevent items of interest. —*LAD*

Access: to subscribe, send email to **listserv@ulkyvm.louisville.edu**

Send messages to **ancien-l@ulkyvm.louisville.edu**

Russian Coup IRC Log

As fascinating as the Gulf War logs (see **Gulf War IRC Logs** earlier in this section), the IRC report documenting the 1991 Russian coup (or the tumultuous trek of Gorbachev, if you prefer) is the other document many point to as an early showcase of the power and benefits of IRC. The IRC log site related to the coup events (at the location described below) lets you relive, in often scary detail, the fear and ultimate determination of the Russian people. (See also **Report Chat Channel** in the **News** section.) You can track the shift in discussion tone over time: from confusion and fear to resolve and transformation to relief as the crisis fades (and the beginning of the end of communism becomes evident). Note the misspelled name of the Soviet leader at the end of the URL access information below; this *is* the spelling you must use for access, but keep in mind that Gorby was only one part of the story, with Yeltsin and the Russian people being the other main elements. Enough talking; start reading! (See **Russia: Russia Chat Channel** for additional information about the Coup and current issues.) —*DR*

Access: **ftp://sunsite.unc.edu/pub/academic/communications/ logs/report-ussr-gorbatchev**

Vatican Exhibit

At this exhibit, study 200 of the Vatican Library's most precious manuscripts, books and maps. From the main hall of the exhibit, you can enter several rooms organized by subject, including archaeology, humanism, math, music and medicine. Each room has an extensive text introduction to ground you in the history of the topic. Then you can view images of actual manuscripts from the Vatican Library, such as pages from texts by Plato and Aristotle. As you proceed through the exhibit, it tells the story of the emergence of Rome as a superpower during the Renaissance. —*ST*

Access: **http://sunsite.unc.edu/expo/vatican.exhibit/ Vatican.exhibit.html**

Electronic Texts From CCAT

Access: **gopher://ccat.sas.upenn.edu:3333**

*See **Literature, Collections: Electronic Texts From CCAT** for a review.*

History of Islam

Access: to subscribe, send email to **listserv@ulkyvm.louisville.edu**

Send messages to **islam-l@ulkyvm.lousville.edu**

*See **Religion: History of Islam** for a review.*

History of Medicine

Access: **http://www.nlm.nih.gov/hmd.dir/hmd.html**

*See **Medicine: History of Medicine** for a review.*

The Jerusalem Mosaic

Access: **http://shum.cc.huji.ac.il/jeru/jerusalem.html**

*See **World Cultures: The Jerusalem Mosaic** for a review.*

Latin Texts

Access: **gopher://wiretap.spies.com:70/11/Library/Classic/Latin**

*See **Classics: Latin Texts** for a review.*

Online Book Initiative

Access: **gopher://gopher.std.com:70/11/obi**

*See **Libraries: Online Book Initiative** for a review.*

H

Project Gutenberg

Access: **gopher://gopher.msen.com:70/11/stuff/gutenberg**

*See **Literature, Collections: Project Gutenberg** for a review.*

■■■■■ History.U.S. ■■■■■

American Memory

History buffs will love this site for its multimedia collections of American culture and history materials. One of the main attractions is a collection of 59 sound recordings of speeches from World War I. Another highlight is the Carl Van Vechten exhibit, featuring photographs of literary figures, artists and celebrities. Using an interactive form, you can search the database of 1,395 photographs. Other exhibits you'll find here are selected Civil War photographs and color photographs from the Farm Security Administration Office. Take a fascinating trip into American history at this Library of Congress archive. —*ST*

Access: **http://rs6.loc.gov/amhome.html**

Carl Van Vechten Photographs, 1932-1964
..*Portraits of literary figures, artists, and celebrities.*

Relive American history through online multimedia exhibits at American Memory.

Civil War History

This list offers a forum for discussing issues related to the history of the U.S. Civil War. Participants exchange information and express views and theories. —*LAD*

Access: to subscribe, send email to **listserv@uicvm.uic.edu**

Send messages to **h-civwar@uicvm.uic.edu**

National Archives

The National Archives preserves and makes available the historical records of the United States government since 1774. You can read the National Archives and Records Administration (NARA) News and find out about exhibits at the National Archives in Washington, DC. You can also find out about the genealogy holdings at the National Archives. —*LAD*

Access: **gopher://gopher.nara.gov/**

The African-American Mosaic

Access: **http://lcweb.loc.gov/exhibits/African.American/ intro.html**

See *African-Americans: The African-American Mosaic for a review.*

American South Home Page

Access: **http://sunsite.unc.edu/doug-m/pages/south/south.html**

See *United States: American South Home Page for a review.*

Humor

Douglas Adams

For everything you ever wanted to know about Douglas Adams, the infamous author of *The Hitchhikers Guide to the Galaxy*, visit this newsgroup. You might even see a post from the man himself. The discussions range from quantum physics to Douglas Adams appearing with Pink Floyd. —*LAD*

Access: **news:alt.fan.douglas-adams**

Humor & Jokes

If you want to build up your joke repertoire, this is the place for you. You can find jokes about topics ranging from PC to Christmas Cheer. You can also find comical ASCII art and smilies. —*LAD*

Access: **gopher://155.187.10.12:70/11/fun/humour**

Jokes Galore

If you ever need a break from your daily drudgery, this is the thing to read. Just make sure you sit in a place where you can laugh out loud. I've had many a strange look while reading this newsgroup too close to people who were working too hard. —*LAD*

Access: **news:rec.humor**

The Usenet Oracle

This follows the ancient tradition of oracular consultation and reply. Hercules consulted the Delphic Oracle; King Cepheus consulted the Oracle of Ammon (who told him to chain his daughter Andromeda to the rocks of Joppa: some oracles are more malevolent than others). There's a twist, however: as atonement for a reply, the Usenet Oracle often asks a question in return. Your emailed reply is reviewed by the Oracle "priesthood" and if it's worthy, becomes an

"Oracle" posting itself. Befitting of the Internet anarchy, the Oracle is actually members of the list, asking and answering questions of one another. The priesthood maintains the quality and timbre of the Oracularities, but the members are the source. —*TL*

Access: to subscribe, send email to **oracle-request@cs.indiana.edu**

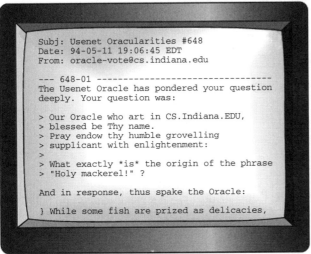

```
Subj: Usenet Oracularities #648
Date: 94-05-11 19:06:45 EDT
From: oracle-vote@cs.indiana.edu

--- 648-01 --------------------------------
The Usenet Oracle has pondered your question
deeply. Your question was:

> Our Oracle who art in CS.Indiana.EDU,
> blessed be Thy name.
> Pray endow thy humble grovelling
> supplicant with enlightenment:
>
> What exactly *is* the origin of the phrase
> "Holy mackerel!" ?

And in response, thus spake the Oracle:

} While some fish are prized as delicacies,
```

The Usenet Oracle offers its periodic Oracularities via the Internet.

USENET Rec.Humor Page

This page contains excerpts from the rec.humor USENET news-groups. It also contains top ten lists, tasteless jokes, song spoofs, goofy headlines and links to other humor-related sites. —*GB*

Access: **http://www.cs.odu.edu/~cashman/humor.html**

Three Stooges

Access: **news:alt.comedy.slapstick.3-stooges**

See **Television: Three Stooges** *for a review.*

The Toy Box

Access: **http://orange-room.cc.nd.edu/ToyBox/ToyBox.html**

*See **Fun: The Toy Box** for a review.*

INTERNET

National Information Infrastructure

Access: **gopher://iitfcat.nist.gov:95**

*See **Government, U.S.: National Information Infrastructure** for a review.*

■■■■■ Internet. Publishing ■■■■■

Alternative X

Alternative X is an electronic publishing company focused on the '90s alternative/countercultural scene. Founded by avant-pop novelist, musician and essayist Mark Amerika, Alternative X's purpose is to "feature publications created by people who are actively engaged in the world of alternative art, writing, music, philosophy, electronic media and anything/everything else that might interest the emerging generation of creative thinkers and doers." *—GB*

Access: **http://marketplace.com/0/alt.x/althome.html**

Electric Press

The Electric Press designs multimedia catalogs, brochures and newsletters for World Wide Web (WWW) display. Through its online brochure, get an overview of the company, marketing information about the Internet, and reasons why you should use the Electric Press to meet online marketing needs. Access a "tasty electronic-publishing sampler," featuring samples of online catalogs, electronic newsletters and product brochures that the Press has designed.

Other products provided include Internet storefronts for FTP, Gopher and WWW, design and conversion services, instant Internet mail, and a Personal Surfer Internet Index—an online directory customized for your organization. —*ST*

Access: **http://www.elpress.com/homepage.html**

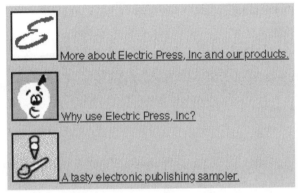

Find out all about WWW publishing services through this electronic brochure.

Kaleidospace

Access: **http://kspace.com/**

*See **Art: Kaleidospace** for a review.*

 **Internet. Resources**

See also Internet, World Wide Web.

The Best of the Internet

Find out what people consider to be the best things on the Internet. Here people post articles from other newsgroups that they think are the best of the Internet. You never know what you might find here. If you find yourself wanting to read too many newsgroups, read this one for a wide range of information. —*LAD*

Access: **news:alt.best.of.internet**

Computer Networks & Internet Guides

IRC, PPP, SLIP, RFC. And other strange Internet rituals. Just what is the Internet anyway and why should I care? How big is the Net? How do I participate in a newsgroup discussion without totally humiliating myself? I don't care what the Internet is—just tell me how I can buy stuff. Gophers are funny-looking rodents—what the heck are they doing on the Net? Is it an infestation? Where can I find government information? Stop! Enough questions, already. Get to this site, get hip, get connected, get answers. —*JW*

Access: **gopher://riceinfo.rice.edu:70/1/Subject/Networks**

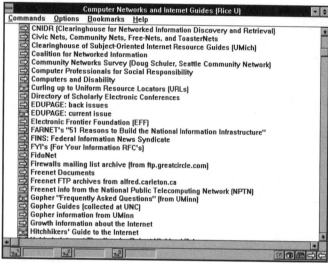

Want Net info? Here it is.

Cool Stuff in the Internet

Here's where you'll find some of the hippest links to video and multimedia on the Web. If you have a hardwired Net connection and are running X Windows on your Mac, or if you have access to an X Windows system, check out the Video Browser at MIT for a glimpse of video on demand. —*GB*

Access: **http://www.cs.ucdavis.edu/internet-stuff.html**

Some of the hippest places to visit are found on the Cool Stuff in the Internet site.

ElNet Galaxy Homepage

This is the home page for ElNet, an Internet service provider. Light on the promotional material, it is also a vital link to a number of Net resources organized by subject. You can even download MacWeb, ElNet's answer to Mosaic. —*GB*

Access: **http://galaxy.einet.net/galaxy.html**

FAQ (Frequently Asked Questions) Central

So you're interested in a particular subject or newsgroup? Or you wonder just what people discuss in the group **alt.cows.moo.moo.moo**? (Why cows have been left off of the "Information Superhighway" and devices to connect them to the Net.) Or on a more serious note, why doesn't my #$#@ clone boot? (The **comp.sys.ibm.pc.hardware.systems** FAQ.) The answer to all the questions can be summed up in the statement, "Read the FAQ!" One of the wonderful resources on the Internet is the accumulation of diverse information into the easy-to-read guides/tutorials called Frequently Asked Questions (FAQs). This Gopher menu collects all of the FAQs into two easy-to-browse menus, which separate the FAQs into computer-related subjects and "everything else." —*Chris Colomb*

Access: **gopher://gopher.cs.ttu.edu/11/Reference%20Shelf/ FAQs%20%28Frequently%20Asked%20Questions%29**

Fishnet Homepage

This home page is the site for an amazing one-man Internet side-show. Fishnet is a weekly publication that gleans some of the best and most interesting items from the Net and stirs them together into a spicy infostew. Here you can browse back issues by date or see a list of all the subjects that Fishnet has covered. —*GB*

Access: **http://www.cs.washington.edu/homes/pauld/fishnet**

Global Network Navigator

GNN is a series of publications and information services provided by O'Reilly & Associates, the computer book publishers. From the GNN home page you can access *GNN NetNews*, a weekly publication of news from the Internet, *GNN Magazine*, a quarterly with feature articles, how-to's, reviews of Net resources and an advice and commentary section, the electronic version of the *Whole Internet Catalog*, with hotlinks to all of its resource listings, an "arcade," a travel center and The Internet Center, which includes a Help Desk for new Net citizens. You have to subscribe to GNN, but the subscription is free of charge. —*GB*

Access: **http://nearnet.gnn.com/gnn/gnn.html**

GNN's home page.

Gopher Jewels

Gopher Jewels is a moderated list service of interesting finds from Gopher sites. It covers dozens of categories on everything from agriculture and forestry to fun to library sciences. The interface is attractive and easy to use. —*GB*

Access: **http://galaxy.einet.net/GJ/index.html**

The Guide to Network Resource Tools

A hypertext introduction to all the major Internet networking tools (WAIS, Gopher, NetNews, X.500, Hytelnet, telnet, etc.). Covers where to find them, how to use them and where to go for more information. —*GB*

Access: **http://www.earn.net/gnrt/notice.html**

InterLinks Internet Access

For an easy-to-use, searchable database of mostly "light" resources, try InterLinks. The database of resources from all over the Internet is divided into subject categories such as Internet Resources, Fun and Games, News and Weather and Reference Shelf. InterLinks also supplies a list of the 50 most popular files accessed as a constantly changing best-of-the-Internet list. —*ST*

Access: **http://alpha.acast.nova.edu/start.html**

International Internet Association

The International Internet Association (IIA), the largest nonprofit provider of free Internet access and services in the world, works to ensure that all aspects of society have the opportunity to participate in online technology. At the IIA's Gopher server, browse the latest free electronic books available on the Internet or access the anti-censorship bulletin board for articles, contact information and a direct telnet connection. Find out how you can get lower telephone rates to decrease your Internet connection bills. Or connect directly to the IIA through telnet. —*ST*

Access: **gopher://gopher.iia.org:70**

Internaut

The online cousin to *The Online User's Encyclopedia*, a comprehensive guide to computer networks from TCP/IP to FidoNet, BITNET, UUCP, WWIVNet and RIME. Online resources include back issues of *Internaut*, with overview articles, how-to's and letters to the editor. Also contains information about the encyclopedia and where to get it. —*GB*

Access: **http://www.zilker.net/users/internaut/index.html**

Internet Connections List

Scott Yanoff's Special Internet Connections List is a popular Web starting point because of the wide variety of Web sites and Internet services it offers. If you want to get a better idea of the wealth of information that's out there, try making this list your home page for a while. —*GB*

Access: **http://info.cern.ch/hypertext/DataSources/Yanoff.html**

Internet Mail Guide

NorthWestNet offers a 300-page guide to the Internet, covering electronic mail, file transfer, remote login, discussion groups, online library catalogues and supercomputer access. This is an excellent site for Internet learning and training materials. —*TL*

Access: **ftp://ftp.nwnet.net/**

Internet Mailing Lists

A comprehensive list of Internet mailing lists is periodically made available by anonymous FTP. It is also posted in the **news.answers** newsgroup whenever it's updated. The list includes nearly every mailing list that's generally available on the Internet, along with subscription information and descriptions of list activity. —*TL*

Access: **ftp://rtfm.mit.edu/pub/usenet/news.answers/mail/mailing-lists**

Internet Phone Books & Email

Here's a nice Gopher menu from the Computer Science department at Texas Tech University that centralizes a number of resources to aid in one of the Net's bigger headaches—trying to find someone's email address. There is also an Inter-Network Email From-To Guide, which helps overcome the difficulties of sending mail between different networks and services, a nice Internet email address verification service to confirm that an address actually exists, and the Netfind service for Internet-wide email address searches. If you're wondering if a country is connected to the Net, there's a service to search for its Internet country code. You can find the email address of your congressional representative, and there's even a searchable directory for zip, postal and area codes. —*Chris Colomb*

Access: **gopher://gopher.cs.ttu.edu/11/Phone%20Books**

Internet Resource Guide

A clearinghouse of subject-oriented resource guides available on the Internet. This Web page has links to the Gopher site at the University of Michigan Library where the guides are accessible. They are divided into sections: Humanities, Social Sciences, Sciences and Multiple Subject Coverage. You can also search the full text of the collection. A number of HTML versions of some of these guides are also available. —*GB*

Access: **http://http2.sils.umich.edu/~lou/chhome.html**

The Internet Society

The Internet Society is an international organization for the Internet, its technology and its applications. It purpose is to maintain and extend the development and availability of the Internet. At the Internet Society's Gopher server, you'll find lots of valuable general information about the Internet. Read articles, news and press releases released by the Society. A FAQ directory gives listings of Internet service providers and answers questions about how to connect and what the Internet is. A regularly updated archive of presentation and reference materials contains information on Internet size, growth, traffic and architectures. You'll also find information on Internet standards, practices and conduct. —*ST*

Access: **gopher://gopher.isoc.org:70/11/isoc**

The Internet Society is a great starting place for learning about the Internet.

Internet Talk Radio

Tune in to Internet Talk Radio, broadcasting interviews and news over the Internet's own radio network, the MBONE. Internet Talk Radio provides in-depth technical information to the Internet community, freely available in archives such as this one. This is not a complete archive site of the broadcasts, but it does include the most notable or interesting programs. One feature you'll always find here is "Geek of the Week," a weekly interview with prominent members of the technical community. Also available are excerpts from Internet Town Hall meetings, a forum on Internet issues. —*ST*

Access: **http://www.ncsa.uiuc.edu/radio/radio.html**

The Internet Tools List

A large catalog describing the various tools that can be used on the Internet for information retrieval, computer-mediated communication and other services. A number of the tool listings are hotlinked to FTP sites so the software being discussed can be easily downloaded. —*GB*

Access: **ftp://ftp.rpi.edu/pub/communications/internet-tools.html**

Unraveling the URL

Most of the Internet resources reviewed in this book are identified by URLs (Uniform Resource Locators), a standardized addressing system designed to be used with Web browsing software (such as Ventana Mosaic, included on the CD-ROM at the back of this book). URL addresses can refer to World Wide Web sites, which are accessed using the HyperText Transport Protocol (HTTP), as well as sites using other Internet protocols, including FTP, Gopher, telnet and newsgroups.

URL addresses consist of four parts: **protocol://hostname.domain:port/path**.

- The **protocol** indicates the type of site on which the resource is located.
- The **hostname.domain** is the Internet address of the site.
- The **port** is the numerical connection point where the server can be found. (The port is usually not necessary to include, since most protocols default to a specific port.)
- The **path** is the specific location of the resource. This might be a directory name, a file name, or both. (Some URLs include no path at all.)

The URL for the Ventana Online Visitor's Center home page looks like this:

http://www.vmedia.com:80/home.html

This tells us that the Visitor's Center home page is the file **home.html**, located at the World Wide Web site **www.vmedia.com**, port **80**.

Following are typical URLs for FTP, Gopher and telnet sites (note that you must have a telnet client properly installed and configured in order to initiate telnet sessions with Mosaic):

ftp://ftp.vmedia.com:21/pub/

gopher://gopher.vmedia.com:70/

telnet://kells.vmedia.com:23/

Newsgroup URLs look a little bit different: **news:newsgroup**. For example,

news:comp.infosystems.www

If you're not using Ventana Mosaic or another Web browser, simply translate the elements of a URL address into whatever format is appropriate for your client.

InterNIC

InterNIC was created as a central help resource for Internet questions. Three valuable services are located here: Information Services, Directory and Database Services and Registration Services. At Information Services, get help with getting connected to the Internet and using Internet tools. A reference desk responds to requests for basic Internet information, and Info Source provides a collection of documents designed to make finding out about the Internet easier. At Directory and Database Services, directories of "white pages" and "yellow pages" will guide you to specific people and organizations on the Internet. Registration services help with registering Internet domains. —*ST*

Access: **gopher://ds1.internic.net:70** *OR* **http://ds1.internic.net/**

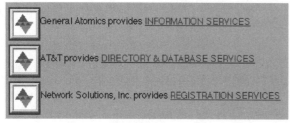

InterNIC—the Internet's help desk.

Online Texts About the Internet

Visit a library of Internet help books for newbies. The entire text of both *Big Dummy's Guide to the Internet*, by Adam Gaffin, and *Zen and the Art of the Internet*, by Brendan Kehoe, are available in this archive for free downloading. *Big Dummy's Guide* is *the* Internet resource guide, helping newcomers survive hooking into the Net and teaching them how to avoid common pitfalls (the kind that get you laughed at by Net wizards). *Zen and the Art of the Internet* teaches network basics and shows you how to use all the popular Internet tools, giving tips that Net gurus often consider too trivial to explain. —*ST*

Access: **gopher://gopher.well.sf.ca.us:70/11/matrix/ internet/inetbooks**

```
Chapter 1:  Setting up and jacking in
     1.1  Ready, set...
     1.2  Go!
     1.3  Public-access Internet providers
     1.4  If your town doesn't have direct access
     1.5  Net origins
     1.6  How it works
     1.7  When things go wrong
     1.8  FYI

Chapter 2: E-mail
     2.1. The basics
     2.2  Elm -- a better way
     2.3  Pine -- even better than Elm
     2.4  Smileys
     2.5  Sending e-mail to other networks
     2.6  Seven Unix commands you can't live without
     2.7  When things go wrong

Chapter 3:  Usenet I
     3.1  The global watering hole
     3.2  Navigating Usenet with nn
     3.3  nn commands
     3.4  Using rn
     3.5  rn commands
     3.6  Essential newsgroups
     3.7  Speaking up
     3.8  Cross-posting
```

Big Dummy's Guide to the Internet *turns any newbie into an Internet pro.*

Planet Earth Home Page

This is your one-stop destination spot for resources all over the Internet, organized into general categories. Click on an interactive map to link to different categories. As an alternative, graphical panels break down the map into manageable chunks that are easier to download. If you're just getting started on the Internet, follow links to general information, search tools and popular sites. If travel is more your thing, connect to the world through interactive maps and country home pages. Don't forget to take a look at the "Webmaster's" home page for more neat stuff, such as movies and slide shows of the earth. —*ST*

Access: **http://white.nosc.mil/info.html**

View of planet earth.

Do-It-Yourself Earth

This image of the planet earth was created with a program called Xearth. You can also create your own images of the earth, using interactive forms. To do so, connect to **http://www.mps.ohio-state.edu.** —*ST*

SUSI Search Engine

SUSI is undoubtedly the best spider in the Web. SUSI stands for "Simple Unified Search Interface," and that's exactly what it is. Using fill-in-the-blank boxes, buttons and pull-down menus, SUSI lets you search about 40 of the Web's best information indexes. Chances are, if you can't find it here, you won't find it anywhere. —*GB*

Access: **http://web.nexor.co.uk/susi/susi.html**

Testing Newsgroups & Mailing Lists

So many people send messages to newsgroups and mailing lists to make sure they work that a number of test-only newsgroups and mailing lists have been established for just this purpose. Don't test anywhere but here. For newsgroup testing, join **alt.test.** For mailing list testing, subscribe to **bit.listserv.test.** Neither of these resources makes very good reading. —*TL*

Access: **news:alt.test** *AND* **news:bit.listserv.test**

Unique & Interesting Net Resources

The New User's Guide to Unique and Interesting Resources on the Internet is available from the New York State Education and Research Network. Measuring over 145 pages, it lists some 50 databases, information resources, and more. There are a number of other good resources in this directory as well, including Jean Armour Polly's excellent *Surfing the Internet.* —*TL*

Access: **http://nysernet.org/pub/resources/html/**

USENET 101

If you want to avoid posting news that will be considered flame-bait then you should browse **news.announce.newusers.** You can read the rules for USENET posting plus read FAQs and introductions to USENET and posting. —*LAD*

Access: **news:news.announce.newusers**

What's New on comp.infosystems.announce?

The kind folks at Rochester have automated the process of keeping up on all the new Web pages as they're announced. Rather than having to spend several hours a day scanning and archiving all the new site announcements on **comp.infosystems.announce**, What's New scans USENET automatically and lists each new resource as soon as it hits the Net. Each listing is hyperlinked to the page announced for quick and easy Net surfing. —*GB*

Access: **http://www.cs.rochester.edu/users/grads/ferguson/announce/**

Chat About Chat

Access: **news:alt.irc**

See *Chat: Chat About Chat* for a review.

Chat Detox

Access: **news:alt.irc.recovery**

See *Chat: Chat Detox* for a review.

Kids On Campus Internet Tour

Access: **http://www.tc.cornell.edu:80/Kids.on.Campus/KOC94/**

See *Children: Kids On Campus Internet Tour* for a review.

List of Commercial Services on the Web

Access: **http://www.directory.net/**

See *Internet, World Wide Web: List of Commercial Services on the Web* for a review.

Nexor List of Web Robots

Access: **http://web.nexor.co.uk/mak/doc/robots/active.html**

See *Internet, World Wide Web: Nexor List of Web Robots* for a review.

3W: The Internet With Attitude

Access: **http://www.3W.com/3W/index.html**

See *Zines: 3W* for a review.

USENET FAQs

Access: **Gopher://mudhoney.micro.umn.edu:70/00/Gopher**

See Frequently Asked Questions Lists: USENET FAQs for a review.

Ventana Online

Access: **http://www.vmedia.com/**

See Computers, Resources & Publications: Ventana Online for a review.

The Virtual Tourist

Access: **http://wings.buffalo.edu/world/**

See Internet, World Wide Web: The Virtual Tourist for a review.

The Web Overview at CERN

Access: **http://info.cern.ch/hypertext/WWW/LineMode/Defaults/default.html**

See Internet, World Wide Web: The Web Overview at CERN for a review.

What's New With NCSA Mosaic

Access: **http://www.ncsa.uiuc.edu/SDG/Software/Mosaic/Docs/whats-new.html**

See Internet, World Wide Web: What's New With NCSA Mosaic for a review.

World Wide Web Chat

Access: Run IRC client, specifying desired IRC server, *OR* telnet to a telnettable server; do command **/join #www**.

*See **Internet, World Wide Web: World Wide Web Chat** for a review.*

The World Wide Web Worm

Access: **http://www.cs.colorado.edu/home/mcbryan/WWWW.html**

*See **Internet, World Wide Web: The World Wide Web Worm** for a review.*

━━━━━ Internet. Software & Tools ━━━━━

Archie

The number of computer-related files available on the Net is overwhelming. Rather than searching directories, consider letting the Archie program search for you. There are a number of Archie servers; you can telnet to most of them and log on as "archie." —*TL*

Access: **telnet://archie@archie.rutgers.edu/**
OR **telnet://archie@archie.sura.net/**
OR **telnet://archie@archie.unl.edu/**

The Internet Adapter™

The Internet Adapter (or TIA) is an Internet access program that lets you use popular TCP/IP software such as Mosaic and Eudora with a standard UNIX dial-up account. It converts a UNIX shell account into a "pseudo-SLIP" account, saving you from having to have a full SLIP/PPP account. This Web site, maintained by Cyberspace Development, creators of TIA, provides background and ordering information for this unique software. —*GB*

Access: **http://marketplace.com:80/tia/tiahome.html**

Subscribing to Mailing Lists & Electronic Publications

To subscribe to a discussion list, send the following message from your email account:

subscribe <list name> <Your Name>

<list name> is the name of the group. Send this message to the "to subscribe" address listed in the Access information. Include the message in the message section of the email, not in the subject line, because most listservers ignore the subject line. —*LAD*

The Guide to Network Resource Tools

Access: **http://www.earn.net/gnrt/notice.html**

*See **Internet, Resources: The Guide to Network Resource Tools** for a review.*

The Internet Tools List

Access: **ftp://ftp.rpi.edu/pub/communications/internet-tools.html**

*See **Internet, Resources: The Internet Tools List** for a review.*

The WebCrawler

Access: **http://www.biotech.washington.edu/WebCrawler/WebQuery.html**

*See **Internet, World Wide Web: The WebCrawler** for a review.*

Internet, World Wide Web

See also Internet, Resources.

Best of the Net

GNN Magazine's annual awards for the overall best Web pages. Looking at these "best of" lists is very helpful when designing your own pages for Web-wide consumption. —*GB*

Access: **http://src.doc.ic.ac.uk/gnn/meta/internet/feat/best.html**

Best of the Web

The Best of the Web Awards is an annual contest that gives awards to Web pages that exhibit "the quality, versatility, and power of the World Wide Web." They see their mission as two-fold: to promote the Web to new/potential users by showing its highlights; and to help information providers see what they can do with HTML/ HTTP. Hotlinks are provided to the 14 annual award-winners and all the runners up, making this single site a major access point to dozens of the best sites and sounds in cyberspace. —*GB*

Access: **http://wings.buffalo.edu/contest/**

CERN WWW Virtual Library

This library is the granddaddy of all Web hotlink pages, having its humble origins in the days when the Web was text-only. The Virtual Library's "by subject" approach to Web indexing is a helpful way to begin your Web travels. —*GB*

Access: **http://info.cern.ch/hypertext/DataSources/bySubject/ Overview.html**

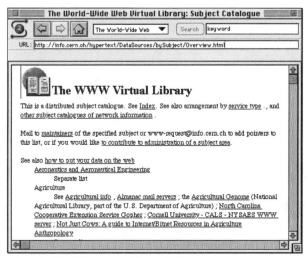

The World-Wide Web Virtual Library.

List of Commercial Services on the Web

This comprehensive list of commercial World Wide Web (WWW) sites lists several hundred institutions, organizations and companies with a Web presence. You can browse an alphabetical listing of all sites or search for keywords through an interactive interface. Check back often for regular updates of what's new on the commercial WWW scene. The commercial services list is provided as a free public service by Open Market. Make this your first stop before any WWW shopping spree. —*ST*

Access: **http://www.directory.net/**

Nexor List of Web Robots

This Web Robots page links you to most of the better "robots," programs that automatically hunt the Web and index the results of their searches. Having a Web robot is like having your own data-sniffing hound dog! —*GB*

Access: **http://web.nexor.co.uk/mak/doc/robots/active.html**

The Virtual Tourist

At the Virtual Tourist, a full-color, clickable map shows you at a glance what's out there on the World Wide Web. Clicking on the geographical region that interests you transports you to one of three types of information services: country maps of WWW sites, hyper-linked lists of WWW sites or virtual tourist guides of a region. Map symbols tell you exactly what kind of information service you are accessing. The Virtual Tourist is a resource guide that is perfect for the around-the-world WWW tourist. —*ST*

Access: **http://wings.buffalo.edu/world/**

The Web Overview at CERN

Web documents maintained by the creators of the World Wide Web. A broad overview of the Web, organized by subject, listing Web servers by country and by type of services offered. —*GB*

Access: **http://info.cern.ch/hypertext/WWW/LineMode/ Defaults/default.html**

The WebCrawler

The WebCrawler serves three functions: (1) it builds indexes for doc-uments it finds on the Web, (2) it acts as a Net-wide agent, searching for documents of particular interest to the user, and (3) it's a testbed for experimenting with Web search strategies. —*GB*

Access: **http://www.biotech.washington.edu/WebCrawler/ WebQuery.html**

What's New With NCSA Mosaic

What's New is the unofficial newspaper of the WWW. It announces new servers and Web-related tools as well as exciting new sites on the WWW or updates to existing ones. The announcements link instanta-neously to the Web pages and sites referenced. Listings are arranged chronologically and archived over the past year, so you may have to browse to find something that sparks your interest. —*ST*

Access: **http://www.ncsa.uiuc.edu/SDG/Software/Mosaic/ Docs/whats-new.html**

World Wide Web Chat

Discussion of the increasingly popular World Wide Web, and its various related topics (e.g., browsers such as Mosaic and Netscape, home pages, links, hypertext, etc.). This channel is bound to find heavier traffic in coming months due to the proliferation of WWW pages addressing various aspects of IRC—from resources to channel descriptions. Channels themselves are even spawning their own pages dedicated solely to that channel, a way of broadening the community experience beyond the limits inherent in IRC's structure (for instance, WWW pages can and do display images depicting frequent channel participants, while IRC cannot as of this writing). —*DR*

Access: Run IRC client, specifying desired IRC server, *OR* telnet to a telnettable server; do command **/join #www**

The World Wide Web Worm

The WWW Worm is a robot program that scours the WWW for available resources. It searches on a keyword you enter, scanning HTML document titles and URLs. Search results are often closely matched to what you want to find. But because of the huge database searched—essentially the entire WWW, over 100,000 multimedia resources—the robot may take a long time to return results. —*ST*

Access: **http://www.cs.colorado.edu/home/mcbryan/ WWWW.html**

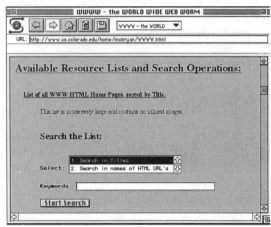

Tunnel through the WWW using this interactive *form at the WWW Worm.*

Art Links on the World Wide Web

Access: **http://amanda.physics.wisc.edu/outside.html**

See Art: Art Links on the World Wide Web for a review.

CyberNet

Access: **http://venus.mcs.com/~flowers/html/gcybernet.html**

See Cyberculture: CyberNet for a review.

SUSI Search Engine

Access: **http://web.nexor.co.uk/susi/susi.html**

See Internet, Resources: SUSI Search Engine for a review.

What's New on comp.infosystems.announce?

Access: **http://www.cs.rochester.edu/users/grads/ferguson/announce/**

See Internet, Resources: What's New on comp.infosystems.announce? for a review.

Webster's Weekly

Access: **http://www.awa.com/w2/**

See **Magazines & Publications: Webster's Weekly** *for a review.*

INTERNET GIANTS

CMU English Server

Located at Carnegie Mellon University (one of the largest, most in-fluential continents in the online world), the English Server is a valuable resource to anyone interested in cultural theory and post-modernism. You'll find everything here from serious cultural criti-cism to the goofier sides of trendy academia (check out "Panic Bauldrillard"). There's enough here to keep you jacked in for days, so if you pay for your Net connection by the hour, make sure to set a timer before you dive in. (See also **Journals & Newspapers** in the **Magazines & Publications** section.) —*GB*

Access: **http://english-server.hss.cmu.edu/**

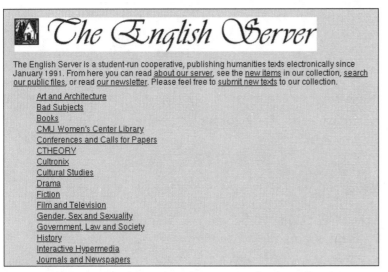

The English Server

The English Server is a student-run cooperative, publishing humanities texts electronically since January 1991. From here you can read about our server, see the new items in our collection, search our public files, or read our newsletter. Please feel free to submit new texts to our collection.

Art and Architecture
Bad Subjects
Books
CMU Women's Center Library
Conferences and Calls for Papers
CTHEORY
Cultronix
Cultural Studies
Drama
Fiction
Film and Television
Gender, Sex and Sexuality
Government, Law and Society
History
Interactive Hypermedia
Journals and Newspapers

For anyone interested in cultural theory and postmodernism, visit CMU's English Server.

Master Gopher at UMN

The Gopher at the University of Minnesota—Gopher's birthplace—can point you to all you need to know about Gopher itself, including news, FAQs, licensing information, protocols and where to get software. But there's a lot more. Get computer information in a huge archive of Apple, IBM and other miscellaneous computer-related files. Visit Fun and Games for role-playing games, MUDs, humor, recipes, movie reviews and rock lyrics. Look at News for National Weather Service forecasts, NASA news, wire services and a bunch of newspapers. Also, you can connect to other Gopher and FTP servers from this centralized site. —*ST*

Access: **gopher://gopher.tc.umn.edu/1**

SunSITE

SunSITE, located at the University of North Carolina, Chapel Hill, has something for everyone on its jam-packed FTP, Gopher and WWW servers. On the WWW, visit a strange variety of multimedia exhibits, everything from the Vatican Library to Dr. Fun. You'll also find the U.S. government hypertexts and a heliocentric view of the infoverse, where you can explore UNC-Chapel Hill, North Carolina, the U.S. and the world beyond. At the SunSITE Gopher, check out an Internet library, frequently used Internet resources and a NEWS archive (with News, Weather, Entertainment and Sports information). Visit the FTP site for UNIX, multimedia, Linux and WAIS software or for electronic publications, Internet talk radio archives and much more. —*ST*

Access: **http://sunsite.unc.edu** *AND* **gopher://sunsite.unc.edu/1** *AND* **ftp://sunsite.unc.edu**

World Wide Web Home

The birthplace of the World Wide Web, here you'll find the "web" about the Web. Everything you might need or want to know about the WWW or pointers to it can be found here. Access this site for a look at the definitive WWW project page, a list of client and server software, technical details about the WWW and places to start browsing the Web, including the Virtual Library. —*ST*

Access: **http://info.cern.ch/**

WU Archive

One of the biggest and busiest FTP sites on the Internet, the Washington University archive is *the* place to go for software. You'll find lots of free downloadable software to fit any purpose, like graphics programs, system-specific software for Amiga, DOS, Macintosh, OS/2 and lots more, and a collection of miscellaneous e-mail programs, newsreaders and other Internet tools. A multimedia archive includes audio clips, Internet talk radio and a collection of GIFs. Also access USENET archives for many computer-related newsgroups. —*ST*

Access: **ftp://wuarchive.wustl.edu**

Yahoo—A Guide to the WWW

What isn't covered in the Yahoo database? Yahoo serves as a hierarchical hotlist for the Web which you can search or add new entries to. There are over 21,000 entries on subjects like art, business, computers, education, entertainment, government, law, news and science. You can also see "what's new" (entries added in the last five days) and "what's cool." A random link propels you toward a random URL in the Web. You'll probably find what you're looking for at Yahoo. —*ST*

Access: **http://akebono.stanford.edu/yahoo/**

INTRIGUE

Conspirators Unite

Wackos and rational people alike are drawn to **alt.conspiracy.** Some of them may be right... —*TL*

Access: **news:conspiracy.alt**

Rumor Mill

If you love setting up your gullible friends, but you're running low on good material, check out **talk.rumors** for the late-breaking "unofficial" news. Your friends will be impressed at your nose for news. Just make sure you don't start believing everything you read here. —*LAD*

Access: **news:talk.rumors**

JOBS

See Career.

JOURNALISM & MEDIA

Computer-Assisted Reporting & Research

This discussion group is a forum for the use of computers in journalism. The topics range from text processing and graphics to online databases and computer communications. It was started to ease communication between journalists, journalism educators and news researchers. —*LAD*

Access: to subscribe, send email to
listserv@ulkyvm.louisville.edu

Send messages to **carr-l@ulkyvm.louisville.edu**

Medialist

A database of email addresses for major daily newspapers, magazines, TV and radio stations, etc. Many of the entries for the newspapers and magazines include email addresses for the section and column editors (Op Ed page, Letters, Arts, Story Ideas, etc.). —*GB*

Access: **ftp://ftp.std.com/customers/periodicals/Middlesex-News/medialist**

C-SPAN

Access: **gopher://c-span.org/**

See **Television: C-SPAN** *for a review.*

Digital Future

Access: **gopher://marketplace.com/11/fyi**

See **Magazines & Publications: Digital Future** *for a review.*

HotWired

Access: **http://www.wired.com/**

See **Magazines & Publications: HotWired** *for a review.*

Journals & Newspapers

Access: **http://english-server.hss.cmu.edu/Journals.html**

See **Magazines & Publications: Journals & Newspapers** *for a review.*

Mother Jones

Access: **http://www.mojones.com/motherjones.html**

See **Magazines & Publications: Mother Jones** *for a review.*

KIDS

See Children.

LANGUAGE

MARVEL Language & Linguistics

The Machine-Assisted Realization of the Virtual Electronic Library (MARVEL) Gopher has a great archive of linguistics and language information. MARVEL has links to archives of linguistics information from universities around the country, various dictionaries (including a Spanish/English dictionary), an acronym dictionary, jargon dictionaries and a thesaurus. A link finds Gophers in French and Esperanto. —*LAD*

Access: **gopher://marvel.loc.gov/11/global/lit**

Spanish Counting Books

Access: **http://davinci.vancouver.wsu.edu/buckman/ SpanishBook.html**

See *Children: Spanish Counting Books* for a review.

LAW

Information Law Alert

Information Law Alert is the authoritative online source for news on legal disputes involving intellectual property, wireless communications and telecommunications. —*GB*

Access: **gopher://marketplace.com/11/ila**

The Legal Domain Network

This Web site is a repository for legal information on the Net. Here you can gain access to law-related USENET discussion groups such

as **law**, **alt.dear.whitehouse**, **alt.freedom.of.information.act**, **alt.politics**, **comp.org.eff** (the Electronic Frontier Foundation), **misc.int-property** (intellectual property rights) and **misc.legal.**
—*GB*

Access: **http://www.kentlaw.edu/lawnet/lawnet.html**

Unraveling the URL

Most of the Internet resources reviewed in this book are identified by URLs (Uniform Resource Locators), a standardized addressing system designed to be used with Web browsing software (such as Ventana Mosaic, included on the CD-ROM at the back of this book). URL addresses can refer to World Wide Web sites, which are accessed using the HyperText Transport Protocol (HTTP), as well as sites using other Internet protocols, including FTP, Gopher, telnet and newsgroups.

URL addresses consist of four parts: **protocol://hostname.domain:port/path**.

- The **protocol** indicates the type of site on which the resource is located.
- The **hostname.domain** is the Internet address of the site.
- The **port** is the numerical connection point where the server can be found. (The port is usually not necessary to include, since most protocols default to a specific port.)
- The **path** is the specific location of the resource. This might be a directory name, a file name, or both. (Some URLs include no path at all.)

The URL for the Ventana Online Visitor's Center home page looks like this:

http://www.vmedia.com:80/home.html

This tells us that the Visitor's Center home page is the file **home.html**, located at the World Wide Web site **www.vmedia.com**, port **80**.

Following are typical URLs for FTP, Gopher and telnet sites (note that you must have a telnet client properly installed and configured in order to initiate telnet sessions with Mosaic):

ftp://ftp.vmedia.com:21/pub/

gopher://gopher.vmedia.com:70/

telnet://kells.vmedia.com:23/

Newsgroup URLs look a little bit different: **news:newsgroup**. For example,

news:comp.infosystems.www

If you're not using Ventana Mosaic or another Web browser, simply translate the elements of a URL address into whatever format is appropriate for your client.

Pepper & Corazzini, L.L.P.

Pepper and Corazzini, L.L.P., is a law firm specializing in communications law. Its practice covers radio, television, cable, satellite, MMDS, radio common carrier and cellular matters. Their law offices online include a useful series of articles on issues surrounding telecom and information law. —*GB*

Access: **http://www.iis.com/p-and-c/**

Electronic Frontier Foundation

Access: **gopher://gopher.eff.org/00/about.eff**

See **Cyberculture: Electronic Frontier Foundation** *for a review.*

LIBRARIES

Colorado Alliance of Research Libraries

Colorado Alliance of Research Libraries (CARL) may be the most extensive resource for library access and research. CARL offers access to academic and public library online catalogs, current article indexes such as UnCover and Magazine Index, databases such as the Academic American Encyclopedia and Internet Resource Guide, and a gateway to scores of other library systems. —*TL*

Access: **telnet://pac.carl.org/**

Conservation Online (CoOL)

CoOL is a project of the Preservation Department of Stanford University Libraries. It's a searchable database of conservation information. You can search by organization, subject or people. —*JW*

Access: **gopher://palimpsest.stanford.edu:70**

Online Book Initiative

The goal of the Online Book Initiative is to create a library for Net-users of freely available books and other electronic texts, including conference proceedings, reference materials, catalogs, magazines, manuals, technical documentation and anything else that's text and that's online. The Initiative also provides pointers to other e-text collections. In the archive, read a FAQ about the project or find out how to subscribe to electronic mailing lists that bring people together in the effort. Enter the repository for an alphabetical directory of online materials. There's something for everyone here, with texts from Ambrose Bierce to Virgil and everything in between. —*ST*

Access: **gopher://gopher.std.com:70/11/obi**

Wiretap Online Library

The Wiretap Online Library is an impressive collection of electronic texts. Everything's here—the classics, government reports and documents, humor, FAQ collections. Since the Online Library only exists as a Gopher site, you don't have the benefits of hypertext browsing and multimedia, but when you see what's available here, you'll probably be too overwhelmed to care. —*GB*

Access: **gopher://wiretap.spies.com/**

Alex: A Catalogue of Electronic Texts on the Internet

Access: **gopher://rsl.ox.ac.uk:70/11/lib-corn/hunter**

See *Literature, Collections: Alex: A Catalogue of Electronic Texts on the Internet* for a review.

Dartmouth Dante Project

Access: **gopher://gopher.lib.virginia.edu:70/11/alpha/dante**

See *Literature, Authors: Dartmouth Dante Project* for a review.

Electronic Texts From CCAT

Access: **gopher://ccat.sas.upenn.edu:3333**

See *Literature, Collections: Electronic Texts From CCAT for a review.*

Latin Texts

Access: **gopher://wiretap.spies.com:70/11/Library/Classic/Latin**

See *Classics: Latin Texts for a review.*

National Archives

Access: **gopher://gopher.nara.gov/**

See *History, U.S.: National Archives for a review.*

Poetry at Internet Wiretap

Access: **gopher://wiretap.spies.com:70/11/Library/Classic/Poetry**

See *Poetry: Poetry at Internet Wiretap for a review.*

Project Gutenberg

Access: **gopher://gopher.msen.com:70/11/stuff/gutenberg**

See *Literature, Collections: Project Gutenberg for a review.*

Thesaurus Linguae Graecae

Access: **gopher://tlg.cwis.uci.edu:7011**

See *Classics: Thesaurus Linguae Graecae for a review.*

Vatican Exhibit

Access: **http://sunsite.unc.edu/expo/vatican.exhibit/Vatican.exhibit.html**

*See **History, World: Vatican Exhibit** for a review.*

LITERATURE

See also Books; Classics; Libraries.

Rare Books Discussion

This discussion group focuses on matters related to rare book and manuscript librarianship, including special collections and related issues. You can find out about traveling collections and new discoveries. —*LAD*

Access: to subscribe, send email to **listserv@rutvm1.rutgers.edu**

Send messages to **exlibris@rutvm1.rutgers.edu**

Labyrinth Electronic Publishing Project

Access: **http://www.honors.indiana.edu/docs/lab/laby.html**

*See **Magazines & Publications: Labyrinth Electronic Publishing Project** for a review.*

Literature.Authors

Dartmouth Dante Project

The Dartmouth Dante Project seeks to combine computer technology with more than 600 years of commentary tradition on Dante's *Divine Comedy*. The Project gives scholars access to the full texts of important critical works, many of which are rare and difficult to obtain. Anyone can search the database of commentaries remotely through the Internet. Through this Gopher server, you can read about the Project and then connect directly to it through a telnet link. Once you have connected by telnet to Dartmouth, you will see a list of the commentaries in the database which you can select from. —*ST*

Access: **gopher://gopher.lib.virginia.edu:70/11/alpha/dante**

Douglas Adams

Access: **news:alt.fan.douglas-adams**

See **Humor: Douglas Adams** *for a review.*

Definitions of Science Fiction

Access: **gopher://gopher.lysator.liu.se:70/11/sf_lsff/Definitions**

See **Science Fiction: Definitions of Science Fiction** *for a review.*

Science Fiction Newsgroups

Access: **news:rec.arts.sf.misc**

See **Science Fiction: Science Fiction Newsgroups** *for a review.*

■■■■■ Literature.Collections ■■■■■

Aesop's Fables

Project Gutenberg has a collection of Aesop's fables. Nearly 300 of Aesop's fables are available for a moral to give. The fables range from "Hercules and the Wagoner" to "Truth and the Traveler." —*LAD*

Access: **gopher://spinaltap.micro.umn.edu:70/11/Gutenberg/aesop**

Alex: A Catalogue of Electronic Texts on the Internet

Alex serves as a library catalog for electronic texts freely available over the Internet. Here you'll find over 700 books and shorter works archived by author and title, including texts from Project Gutenberg, the Internet Wiretap, the Online Book Initiative, the English Server and many other online collections. This very complete resource maintained by Hunter Monroe covers the whole gamut of topics, including science, religion, reference, poetry, music, fiction, history, law, drama and classics. You can search the entire archive or browse; texts are grouped by author, title, subject, host, language and date. —*ST*

Access: **gopher://rsl.ox.ac.uk:70/11/lib-corn/hunter**

The adventures of Sherlock Holmes/Doyle, Arthur Conan, Sir, 1859-1930
The adventures of Sherlock Holmes/Doyle, Arthur Conan, Sir, 1859-1930
The adventures of Tom Sawyer/1903/Twain, Mark, 1835-1910/PG 74 WT
The adventures of Tom Sawyer/1876/Twain, Mark, 1835-1910
The adventures of Tom Sawyer/Twain, Mark, 1835-1910
The Aeneid
The Aeneid/1909/Virgil/Translated by Dryden, John, 1631-1700/629k/WT

Browse the shelves of a virtual library at Alex.

Children & Youth Literature List

This mailing list serves as a forum for discussing children and juvenile books. Discussions about new books as well as the classics are welcome on the list. You can also participate in discussions regarding the topics of children and juvenile books. —*LAD*

Access: to subscribe, send email to
listserv@bingvmb.cc.binghamton.edu

Send messages to **kidlitr-l@bingumb.cc.binghamton.edu**

The Complete Works of Shakespeare

Here you can find all of Shakespeare's plays and sonnets, as well as a glossary for those words that have changed meaning over time. The plays are divided into tragedies, histories and comedies. An index allows for quick reference. If you have the urge or need to brush up your Shakespeare, you've found the right place. —*LAD*

Access: **gopher://spinaltap.micro.umn.edu:70/11/Gutenberg/shake**

Electronic Books Archive

Access a completely free library of the great "classics" of literature at this archive. You can look for books by title, author or library call letters. Complete novels ready to download and read include *Dr. Jekyll and Mr. Hyde, Peter Pan* and *Moby Dick*. You'll also find the complete works of Shakespeare and the full King James Bible. Reference books like *Roget's Thesaurus* and *The CIA World Factbook* are available. Special document archives are also located here, such as the historical documents archive, which has the Constitution, Bill of Rights and the Gettysburg Address, among many more documents. —*ST*

Access: **gopher://spinaltap.micro.umn.edu:70/11/Ebooks**

Electronic Texts From CCAT

This vast archive of electronic texts features a little of everything: classical works, late antique and medieval texts, fiction, poetry, historical documents and religious texts. Here you'll find everything from Sophocles's *Oedipus* to Mary Shelley's *Frankenstein*, from Milton to Yeats, from the Magna Carta to the Koran. The full text of each work is available for downloading, and the text of selected works is also searchable by keyword. Every lover of letters can find something of interest in this online library. —*ST*

Access: **gopher://ccat.sas.upenn.edu:3333**

Miscellaneous Cyberprose

"No one should ever work. Work is the source of nearly all the misery in the world. Almost any evil you'd care to name comes from working or from living in a world designed for work. In order to stop suffering, we have to stop working." Thus begins Bob Black's treatise, "The Abolition of Work." He actually has a lot of quite serious and thought-provoking stuff to say. Check this out, along with other works such as "Ada, Enchantress of Numbers," the letters of Augusta Ada Byron and "Sarfatti's Illuminati." —*JW*

Access: **gopher://gopher.well.sf.ca.us:70/1/Publications/ Miscellaneous**

Project Gutenberg

Project Gutenberg is a massive Internet project that encourages the creation and distribution of electronic texts. This library of "great books" is available for anyone on the Internet to use free of charge. The first text the Project put online was the Declaration of Independence; project leaders hope to have 10,000 e-texts in distribution by the year 2001. Choose from a number of classic literary works, such as *Moby Dick*, *Peter Pan* and *Paradise Lost*. Or access useful reference books like *Webster's Dictionary*, the periodic table and *The Hacker's Dictionary*. —*ST*

Access: **gopher://gopher.msen.com:70/11/stuff/gutenberg**

By Title

- ? Search Electronic Books
- 1990 USA Census Information
- Aesop's Fables
- Agrippa
- Aladdin and the Wonderful Lamp
- Alice's Adventures in Wonderland
- CIA World Factbook 1991
- Clinton's Inaugural Address
- Complete Works of Shakespeare

Read the "great books" online at Project Gutenberg.

Shakespeare's Complete Plays

They're all here, every play the Bard wrote archived for your enjoyment and education. Plays are grouped in separate directories by type—comedies, tragedies, histories—and arranged chronologically within the directories. A contents file leads you to the particular play you want. You'll even find a glossary of Shakespearean terms to help elucidate the text. Say good-bye to lugging around heavy tomes for your English class or drama project; all you need now is your computer to access all of Shakespeare's works. —ST

Access: **gopher://english-server.hss.cmu.edu:70** choose the directories **Drama/Shakespeare**

Bulfinch's Mythology

Access: **gopher://gopher.vt.edu:10010/11/53**

See **Mythology: Bulfinch's Mythology** for a review.

Electronic Books

Access: **gopher://gopher.tc.umn.edu:70/11/Libraries/ Electronic%20Books**

See **Books: Electronic Books** for a review.

Electronic Cafe

Access: **http://www.cyberspace.org/u/ecafe/www/index.html**

See **Cyberculture: Electronic Cafe** for a review.

Kaleidospace

Access: **http://kspace.com/**

See **Art: Kaleidospace** for a review.

The Labyrinth

Access: **http:/www.georgetown.edu/labyrinth/labyrinth-home.html**

*See **Medieval Studies: The Labyrinth** for a review.*

Science Fiction Resource Guide

Access: **ftp://gandalf.rutgers.edu/pub/sfl/sf-resource.guide.html**

*See **Science Fiction: Science Fiction Resource Guide** for a review.*

Literature, Titles

See also Books.

Alice's Adventures in Wonderland

The Lewis Carroll classic, now converted into an e-book, is complete and ready for downloading at this Gopher server. The electronic version of the Millennium Fulcrum Edition is provided as shareware from Project Gutenberg (see review of this in the **Literature, Collections** section). Be sure to read the Introduction to the electronic text for more information on how you can contribute. Each chapter is divided into a separate file for easier downloading, and the whole text is searchable by keyword. Gather your kids around the computer and read them the electronic *Alice's Adventures in Wonderland* as their next bedtime story. —*ST*

Access: **gopher://spinaltap.micro.umn.edu/11/Ebooks/By%20Title/Alice**

Alice's Adventures in Wonderland

- Search Alice in Wonderland
- Alice Intro
- Chapter I: Down the Rabbit-Hole
- Chapter II: The Pool of Tears
- Chapter III: A Caucus-Race and a Long Tale
- Chapter IV: The Rabbit Sends in a Little Bill
- Chapter IX: The Mock Turtle's Story
- Chapter V: Advice from a Caterpillar
- Chapter VI: Pig and Pepper
- Chapter VII: A Mad Tea-Party
- Chapter VIII: The Queen's Croquet-Ground
- Chapter X: The Lobster Quadrille
- Chapter XI: Who Stole the Tarts?
- Chapter XII: Alice's Evidence

Enter Wonderland through cyberspace with this electronic version of the Lewis Carroll classic.

The Oedipus Trilogy

This directory features the complete texts of the famous dramatic trilogy by Sophocles. This Project Gutenberg text has been divided into separate files for easier downloading. It is the electronic version of the Loeb Library Edition, published by Harvard University Press and translated by F. Storr. You'll find *Antigone, Oedipus at Colonus* and *Oedipus the King*, all ready for use as scholarly references, for classroom study or for personal reading. —*ST*

Access: **gopher://spinaltap.micro.umn.edu/11/Ebooks/ By%20Title/oedipus**

Jayhawk

Access: **http://www.klab.caltech.edu/~flowers/jayhawk/**

See **Books:** **Jayhawk** *for a review.*

Umney's Last Case by Stephen King

Access: **http://www.eu.net/king/**

See Books: **Umney's Last Case** *by Stephen King* for a review.

Macintosh

Mac Everything

This FTP site at Stanford houses a wealth of Macintosh applications, utilities, graphics and sound files. —*TL*

Access: **ftp://sumex-aim.stanford.edu/**

Macintosh Chat

#macintosh is an open IRC channel to foster discussion of the Macintosh platform and topics related to it. There is even a mailing list (called "poundmac-list") devoted to discussions of the #macintosh channel, so I guess you could say it is popular with IRCers! (Note, however, that this is a closed list and approval is granted only if the user has been on #macintosh for a significant amount of time.) An official #macintosh home page on the World Wide Web states that common channel topics include the following:

- Cmon baby... Set my Intel based PC on fire!!

- Just because a binary is -fat- doesn't mean it doesn't work.

- Promote global warming! Save on heating costs! Buy a Pentium.

- News Flash: Studies find that the Pentium is the cause of Global Warming.

- I want my, I want my... PowerPC!

Take note: the IRCers that operate this channel warn new users that pirating is not tolerated on #macintosh; such an action by a user can result in him/her being kicked off (or even banned from) the channel. Even references to such acts that appear in your conversations can fall under their warning, so be careful! —*DR*

Access for #macintosh IRC channel: Run IRC client, specifying desired IRC server, *OR* telnet to a telnettable server; do command **/join #macintosh**

Access for #macintosh WWW home page:
http://disserv.stu.umn.edu/~thingles/PoundMac/

Macintosh Newsgroup

Have any questions about your Mac? This is the place to find the answers on any subject, from hardware to software. You can always find a guru listening in on this newsgroup. (Just make sure you post to the right subgroup listed below.) —*LAD*

Access: **news:comp.sys.mac.*(apps, comm, games, hardware, misc, programmer, system)**

Robert Lentz's Macintosh Resources

Bob Lentz has obviously spent a lot of time combing the globe for Mac-related resources so you don't have to. Here you'll find lists of Mac FTP sites, publication archives, product information and just about everything else that exists on the Web for the benefit of Mac owners. —*GB*

Access: **http://www.astro.nwu.edu/lentz/mac/home-mac.html**

Digital Future

Access: **gopher://marketplace.com/11/fyi**

See **Magazines & Publications: Digital Future** *for a review.*

TidBITS

Access: **http://www.dartmouth.edu/Pages/TidBITS/TidBITS.html**

See **Computers, Resources & Publications:** **TidBITS** *for a review.*

MAGAZINES & PUBLICATIONS

See also Zines.

Digital Future

Digital Future (formerly called *FYI*) is a weekly electronic newsletter covering information media. It tracks late-breaking news about the cable TV industry, CD technology, computer hardware and software, the latest developments at the FCC, online services and telecommunications. A full-blown edition is available as a paid subscription while an abridged edition is available online for free. The site also archives back issues of the abridged edition. —*GB*

Access: **gopher://marketplace.com/11/fyi**

Electronic Newsstand

The Electronic Newsstand is your friendly, street-corner newsstand on the Internet. Here you can browse at no charge the table of contents and several current articles from many different publications. The Newsstand, which is searchable by keyword, also archives previously featured material. If you like a particular publication, you can directly order single issues or subscriptions. Currently, the Newsstand features more than 175 titles, so there's bound to be something for everyone. Shoppers will also find here an electronic bookstore, a CD store with more than 80,000 titles, an electronic cars showroom, news services and a merchandise mart. —*ST*

Access: **http://www.enews.com/** *AND* **gopher://enews.com:2100/** *AND* **telnet://enews.com** (log in as **enews**)

Now on The Newsstand:

- Introduction to the Electronic Newsstand
- Magazines, Periodicals, and Journals (all titles)
- Business Publications and Resources
- Electronic Bookstore
- Music! (9 magazines and 80,000 CD titles)
- Travel/Lufthansa Takes Off...
- The Electronic Car Showroom(tm) (Featuring Lincoln-Mercury)
- News Services
- The Merchandise Mart
- WIN A TRIP TO EUROPE SWEEPSTAKES
- Search All Electronic Newsstand Articles by Keyword

There's something for everyone at the Electronic Newsstand.

HotWired

Wired is one of the most exciting magazines to appear in years. It combines a progressive, youthful design with hard-hitting journalism from the cutting edge of digital culture. Since its beginning, *Wired* has been interested in maintaining a vital presence in cyberspace. As part of this, the magazine recently unveiled its Net-based publication HotWired. The new electronic mag is not the print version online, but an entirely new venture, with breath-taking multimedia art and all new thought-provoking articles. Those interested in the future of Net-based publishing should keep an eye on HotWired's efforts. —*GB*

Access: **http://www.wired.com/**

Journals & Newspapers

A massive electronic newstand maintained by Carnegie Mellon University. (See **CMU English Server** in the **Internet Giants** section.) Here you can access electronic editions of print magazines as well as zines on a wide variety of subjects. Links are provided to mags ranging from *American Demographics*, *The New Yorker* and *Federal Commu-*

nications Law Journal to *Communications of the ACM, Electronic Journal of Virtual Culture* and *Computer-Mediated Communication Magazine.* Over 60 publications are accessible as well as an alphabetical listing of other journals available on the Internet. —*GB*

Access: **http://english-server.hss.cmu.edu/Journals.html**

Labyrinth Electronic Publishing Project

Don't miss this unique online experiment to electronically publish poetry, fiction and art produced by students and faculty at Indiana University. Here you can access chapbooks of poetry by both undergraduates and faculty, all of which can be searched electronically. There is also an interesting collection of anonymous poetry. A gallery features visual art from selected artists. After viewing the pieces on exhibit, you can comment on a work or read comments others have made. Search the entire archive for something specific or just browse through this electronic equivalent of a university literary magazine. —*ST*

Access: **http://www.honors.indiana.edu/docs/lab/laby.html**

Become an art critic at the online gallery for the Labyrinth Electronic Publishing Project. (Copyright 1994 Honors Division of Indiana University.)

Mother Jones

The Web site for *Mother Jones*, the radical expose magazine that has dedicated itself to exposing abuses of power, challenging conventional wisdom, and offering fresh solutions to reoccuring problems. This electronic newsstand has back issues and material related to the magazine and its mission. The magazine hopes to use its site "to support the strong and growing Internet activist network by acting as a nexus for information about important issues." Reader's input, other relevant Internet resources, as well as articles and input from *Mother Jones* magazine are brought together to help provide a better understanding and discussion of the issues addressed in the magazine. —*GB*

Access: **http://www.mojones.com/motherjones.html**

Newsletter & Journal List

An exhaustive listing of all the newsletters and journals that are available on the Internet can be obtained from this mailing list. When subscribing, leave the subject field blank, and place two commands in the message field:

get ejournl1 directry

get ejournl2 directry

The listing includes the address and subscription information for each periodical (most are mailing lists), and comments about content. —*TL*

Access: to subscribe, send email to **listserv@acadvm1.uottawa.ca**

PCWeek Best News Sources & Online Mags

The *PCWeek* page is a news junkie's paradise. Nowhere else on the Net can you browse the *San Francisco Examiner and Chronicle*, USENET FAQs, the NASDAQ Financial Executive, *PowerPC News* and others, all from the same site. Don't be fooled though—even *PCWeek* wants to have some fun every once in a while! You can link to Adam Curry's The Vibe music server, InterText online fiction and other recreational sites. —*GB*

Access: **ftp://www.ziff.com/~pcweek/best-news.html**

Webster's Weekly

Webster's Weekly is a weekly features magazine published exclusively on the Web. It has columns on music and movies, politics and psychology, mad rantings and humor. Published every Wednesday. —*GB*

Access: **http://www.awa.com/w2/**

A sneak peek at Webster's Weekly.

Alternative X

Access: **http://marketplace.com/0/alt.x/althome.html**

See Internet, Publishing: Alternative X for a review.

bOING bOING

Access: **http://www.zeitgeist.net/public/Boing-boing/bbw3/boing.boing.html**

See Zines: bOING bOING for a review.

Dr. Dobb's Journal

Access: **ftp://ftp.mv.com/pub/ddj/**

See Computers, Resources & Publications: Dr. Dobb's Journal for a review.

Literary E-Journals

Access: **gopher://gopher.cic.net:70/11/e-serials/general/literature**

See **Zines: Literary E-Journals** *for a review.*

Unraveling the URL

Most of the Internet resources reviewed in this book are identified by URLs (Uniform Resource Locators), a standardized addressing system designed to be used with Web browsing software (such as Ventana Mosaic, included on the CD-ROM at the back of this book). URL addresses can refer to World Wide Web sites, which are accessed using the HyperText Transport Protocol (HTTP), as well as sites using other Internet protocols, including FTP, Gopher, telnet and newsgroups.

URL addresses consist of four parts: **protocol://hostname.domain:port/path**.

- The **protocol** indicates the type of site on which the resource is located.
- The **hostname.domain** is the Internet address of the site.
- The **port** is the numerical connection point where the server can be found. (The port is usually not necessary to include, since most protocols default to a specific port.)
- The **path** is the specific location of the resource. This might be a directory name, a file name, or both. (Some URLs include no path at all.)

The URL for the Ventana Online Visitor's Center home page looks like this:

http://www.vmedia.com:80/home.html

This tells us that the Visitor's Center home page is the file **home.html**, located at the World Wide Web site **www.vmedia.com**, port **80**.

Following are typical URLs for FTP, Gopher and telnet sites (note that you must have a telnet client properly installed and configured in order to initiate telnet sessions with Mosaic):

ftp://ftp.vmedia.com:21/pub/

gopher://gopher.vmedia.com:70/

telnet://kells.vmedia.com:23/

Newsgroup URLs look a little bit different: **news:newsgroup**. For example,

news:comp.infosystems.www

If you're not using Ventana Mosaic or another Web browser, simply translate the elements of a URL address into whatever format is appropriate for your client.

Online Book Initiative

Access: **gopher://gopher.std.com:70/11/obi**

*See **Libraries: Online Book Initiative** for a review.*

MATHEMATICS

Gallery of Interactive Online Geometry

Create your own mathematical art through a variety of interactive tools. Each of the seven tools contains a sample image and an explanation of how the image was created. Then use interactive forms to change variables and create your own image. One fun tool is Orbifold Pinball, which explores the effects of negatively curved space in a pinball-style game. Or try Cyberview, an interactive three-dimensional viewer that works with most WWW browsers. —*ST*

Access: **http://www.geom.umn.edu/apps/gallery.html**

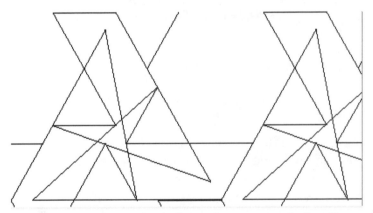

Create art like this at the Gallery of Interactive Online Geometry.

Eisenhower National Clearinghouse for Mathematics & Science Education

Access: **gopher://enc.org:70**

See Education, Resources: Eisenhower National Clearinghouse for Mathematics & Science Education for a review.

Medicine

History of Medicine

This invaluable resource contains a searchable database of nearly 60,000 medical prints and photos. Designed as an online catalog, the database provides material for study and research. A sampler of the online collection reflects its diversity, including a photograph of Lincoln visiting soldiers' graves and a recent poster for a medical film festival. If you like what you see, search the database by using text expressions or browse by retrieving ten random items. Also, take a look at many exhibitions, including "Caesarean Section: A Brief History" and "The Art of Medicine at the Twenty-first Century." —*ST*

Access: **http://www.nlm.nih.gov/hmd.dir/hmd.html**

Fred Hutchinson Cancer Research Center

Fred Hutchinson is one of the leading cancer research centers in the U.S. And the fact that it's in my home town, Seattle, makes it an instant hotlist item. But seriously, it's a great resource for the latest information on cancer research and treatment. (Bonus: Find out the current time and date in Seattle from wherever you are.) —*JW*

Access: **gopher://gopher.fhcrc.org:70**

The Virtual Hospital

The Virtual Hospital is a continuously updated medical database of multimedia information that provides patient-care support and distance learning to practicing physicians. The latest medical information is instantly available here. Several multimedia textbooks are online, all illustrated with inline images that you can click on for relevant graphics and animations. Choose a patient simulation case from a large menu to virtually treat different kinds of patients. For fun, visit the Medical Museum to see the History of the Microscope exhibit or go through the Virtual Hospital demo, which simulates how people use the virtual hospital as a research tool. —*ST*

Access: **http://indy.radiology.uiowa.edu/**

MEDIEVAL STUDIES

The Labyrinth

When you venture into this vast network of medieval studies resources, don't worry about getting lost—you can always use "Ariadne's thread" to find your way back to the home page. An online library contains electronic texts in Latin and Middle English. All texts can be searched or you can page through works, like Chaucer's *Canterbury Tales*. Subject menus link to information on topics such as national cultures, manuscripts and Latin. Another valuable service is a teaching-resources archive, with learning aids and syllabi. You can also connect to an online forum that features an ongoing discussion of medieval topics. —*ST*

Access: **http://www.georgetown.edu/labyrinth/labyrinth-home.html**

Return to Labyrinth Home Page

Follow Ariadne's thread to get around in the Labyrinth.

MICROSOFT WINDOWS

Microsoft Windows Newsletter

Subscribe to this electronic newsletter through email. It features announcements and resource pointers for Windows and for the upcoming Windows 95 release. It is maintained by Microsoft's Personal Operating Systems Division. —*LAD*

Access: to subscribe, send email to **enews@microsoft.nwnet.com**

University of Indiana Windows Resource

If you run Windows and you're on the Internet, you should know this site. Whether you're looking for something specific or just want to browse, you won't be disappointed. You can find a large selection of games, including hextris and reversi, and Winsock applications, like IRC II for Windows and a talk daemon to talk one on one. And if you're tired of the same old windows icons, you can find more to add to your collection. —*LAD*

Access: **ftp://ftp.cica.indiana.edu/pub/pc/win3/**

One of the many icons you can find at the University of Indiana Windows Resource.

Windows News

The announcement newsgroup **comp.os.ms-windows.announce** offers important news and announcements about this popular platform. Moderators keep the noise down, and the information is relevant. —*TL*

Access: **news:comp.os.ms-windows.announce**

Windows Questions Answered

If you want to get the most out of MS Windows or if you just have an annoying problem that won't go away, you should read this newsgroup. You can find tips and expand your Windows literacy, plus troubleshoot with other Windows users. —*LAD*

Access: **news:comp.os.ms-windows.*(misc, apps, networking, programmer)**

PC Newsgroup

Access: **news:comp.sys.ibm.pc.*(hardware, programmer, soundcard, games, misc)**

See Computers, Resources & Publications: PC Newsgroup for a review.

Movies

See also Multimedia.

Cardiff's Movie Database Browser

A huge database of movie information, presented in an easy-to-search format. You can look up films by title, actor or even by quotes. Can't figure out what to rent at the video store tonight? Stop in here first and have a look around. Remember a famous line but can't put your finger on who said it and in what film? Search by the quotation. A film buff's dream come true. —*GB*

Access: **http://www.cm.cf.ac.uk/Movies/**

Film Talk

You probably won't find any highly paid glamour critics in the virtual aisles of this IRC space, but film discussions *are* the order of the day here at #movies. Who knows, maybe some Netter practicing his or her critiques here will one day move on to other areas of the electronic frontier. But for now, the ability to get many points of view (POV for you film buffs), at once and in rapidfire succession, a pseudo-random collage of simultaneous opinions, is definitely unique to IRC—and probably will be for some time to come. —*DR*

Access: Run IRC client, specifying desired IRC server, *OR* telnet to a telnettable server; do command /**join #movies**

Movie Review Archive

Wondering which movie to watch tonight? Check out the Movie Review Archive. You can find reviews of current movies from USENET or read reviews of movies from 1987 to the present. You can also search for movies in case you don't remember when they came out, or you can search for other work by your favorite actor or actress. —*LAD*

Access: **gopher://spinaltap.micro.umn.edu:70/11/fun/Movies**

Movie Reviews

When you're wondering if a new film is worth seeing, check out rec.arts.movies.reviews. Most new movies are reviewed—in fact, many include more than one review in case you want more than one opinion. It's a good way to avoid that box-office bomb. —*LAD*

Access: **news:rec.arts.movies.reviews**

Movie Sounds

Want to hear clips from your favorite movies? You can hear Arnold Schwarzenegger's famous "I'll be back," and even Barney versus Star Trek. Download clips from *2001* and *2010* to make your computer talk like HAL 9000. You'll find sounds in both WAV and AU formats. —*LAD*

Access: **ftp://sunsite.unc.edu/pub/multimedia/sun-sounds/** *OR* **ftp://sunsite.unc.edu/pub/multimedia/pc-sounds/**

Unofficial Star Wars Home Page

This jam-packed archive contains all the information you could possible need on the famous science-fiction trilogy. Multimedia files include a sound library, a sound-effect archive, an image gallery and a video archive. There is also a huge catalog of collectible books, videos, music and toys for the die-hard collector. Trivia files about the actors and movies include a guide to bloopers and mis-cuts, a list of memorable quotes and a catalog of missing scenes. If you're inspired to enter the Star Wars universe yourself, access reviews, charts, guides and an explanation of hyperspace travel from West End Roleplaying Games. —*ST*

Access: **http://force.stwing.upenn.edu:8001/~jruspini/ starwars.html**

WIRETAP Film Server

As you can see from figure below, what we have here is an eclectic conglomeration of movie mania. Answers: Yumi Shirakawa, Sean Young, The Pleasure Garden. Questions: Who played "the woman who sees Mogera while bathing" in Chikyu Boeigun? (Hint: try Godzilla Cast Lists.) Who was originally cast as Vicky Vale in Batman (the Michael Keaton version)? (Hint: try Movie Trivia.) Alfred Hitchcock's directorial debut was a two-reel silent film that was never completed. What is the name of the film? (Hint: try Summary of Archivist's Screening 12/92.) —*JW*

Access: **gopher://wiretap.spies.com:70/1/Library/Media/Film**

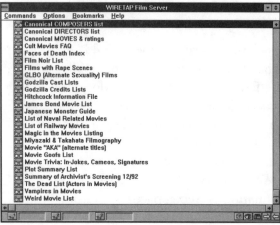

The magic and madness of movies.

Film & Television Reviews

Access: **gopher://english-server.hss.cmu.edu:70/ 11ftp%3aEnglish%20Server%3aFilm%26TV%3a**

See Television: Film & Television Reviews for a review.

Film Music Discussion List

Access: to subscribe, send email to **listserv@iubvm.ucs.indiana.edu**

Send messages to **filmus-l@iubvm.ucs.indiana.edu**

See Music: Film Music Discussion List for a review.

Kaleidospace

Access: **http://kspace.com/**

See Art: Kaleidospace for a review.

Star Trek Home Page

Access: **http://www.cosy.sbg.ac.at/rec/startrek/index.html**

See Star Trek: Star Trek Home Page for a review.

MUDs, MOOs & MUSHes

Jay's House MOO

The only WWW server to be running inside a MOO, this site houses an ongoing project to investigate text-based virtual-reality systems. Here, you can read about research projects, find out who's logged in to the MOO and meet Ron, the first hypertextified user of the MOO. Try out an experimental, hypertext object browser with a searchable interface that gives you a preview of Jay's House. An on-site library houses texts such as a guide to object naming and research papers on MOOs. Finally, enter Jay's House MOO through a telnet link; an online help system tells you how to interact in the MOO. —*ST*

Access: **http://jh.ccs.neu.edu:7043/**

MediaMOO

Originally developed as a virtual hangout and testbed for media researchers, MIT's cyberspace extension of The Media Lab has grown to a virtual community of thousands. Here, you can stop and chat with the creme de la cybercreme of media intelligentsia, play with the literally thousands of virtual toys that dot the MOOscape, and become an active participant in the creation of a new medium. Log in and look around. Ride the edge. —*SC*

Access: **telnet://purple-crayon.media.mit.edu:8888/**

MUD Institute

If you've ever wondered what the inside of a MUD looks like, the Mud Institute (TMI) is for you. When you log into TMI, you're automatically given wizard status, which gives you the ability to look at and create the files that make up a MUD. TMI is also involved in making a MUDlib to improve the speed and features of MUDs. You can also read bulletin boards to find out if any MUDs are looking for people to code areas or guilds for their MUD. This is a good place to start if you want to program on a MUD, but you don't want to play and gain levels to become a wizard. —*LAD*

Access: **telnet://tmi.lp.mud.org:5555/**

```
Welcome to...

     tttttttt mmmm   mmmm  iiii       twotwotwotwo
     t  tt  t mmmm mmmm    ii          two  two
        tt     mm mmm mm   ii          two  two
        tt     mm  m  mm   ii   ####    two  two
        tt     mm  m  mm   ii   ####    two  two
        tt     mm     mm   ii          two  two
        tt     mm     mm   ii          two  two
       tttt   mmmm   mmmm  iiii       twotwotwotwo

              Mudlib Development Site

Tmi-2 is running the TMI-2 1.1.1 mudlib on MudOS 0.9.19.4.3

Current users: Lem, Jeearr, Kupe, Grendel, Eldrich, Wyrmslayer, Kamini,
Terry, Gothic, Eyes, and Firedoom.

By what name do you wish to be known?
```

The login screen for TMI-2.

Abyss IV (DikuMUD)

Access: **telnet://129.89.68.89:4000/**

*See **Games: Abyss IV** for a review.*

Apocalypse IV MUD (DikuMUD)

Access: **telnet://157.182.168.20:4000/**

*See **Games: Apocalypse IV MUD** for a review.*

BatMUD, A World Apart

Access: **telnet://bat.cs.hut.fi:23/**

*See **Games: BatMUD, A World Apart** for a review.*

ChromeMUSH (TinyMUSH)

Access: **telnet://colossus.acusd.edu:4444/**

*See **Games: ChromeMUSH** for a review.*

Diversity University (MOO)

Access: **telnet://erau.db.erau.edu:8888/**

See Education, Institutions: Diversity University for a review.

EVIL! Mud

Access: **telnet://intac.com:23/**

See Bizarre: EVIL! Mud for a review.

Final Frontiers II

Access: **telnet://ugly.microserve.net:2499/**

See Games: Final Frontiers II for a review.

Logo of the United Federation of Planets, one of the key groups on Final Frontiers II.

Games of Death MUD (DikuMUD)

Access: **telnet://cyberspace.com:4000/**

See Games: Games of Death MUD for a review.

GarouMUSH (TinyMUSH)

Access: **telnet://kyriath.cygnuys.com:7000/**

See Games: GarouMUSH for a review.

Genocide (LPMud)

Access: **telnet://pip.shu.edu:2222/**

See Games: Genocide for a review.

Global MUSH

Access: **telnet://lancelot.cif.rochester.edu:4201/**

See Games: Global MUSH for a review.

GrimneMUD (DikuMUD)

Access: **telnet://gytje.pvv.unit.no:4000/**

See Games: GrimneMUD for a review.

InfinityMUD (LPMud)

Access: **telnet://infinity.ccs.neu.edu:3000/**

See Games: InfinityMUD for a review.

Separating the MUDs From the MUSE

A MUD is a Multi-User Dimension; a MUSE is a Multi-User Simulation Environment. They're both similar to adventure games, with one significant exception: participation isn't limited to an individual. When 20 people are all participating in a simulation at the same time, the dynamic compounds elaborately. Players connect to the host computer, adopt a character and personality of their choosing, and enter into the synthetic world, consisting of a web of connected rooms and movable props. —*TL*

MediaMOO

Access: **telnet://purple-crayon.media.mit.edu:8888/**

See *MUDs, MOOs & MUSHes: MediaMOO* for a review.

MUME "Multi Users in Middle Earth" (DikuMUD)

Access: **telnet://lbdsun4.epfl.ch:4242/**

See *Games: MUME* for a review.

NannyMUD (LPMud)

Access: **telnet://mud.lysator.liu.se:2000/**

See *Games: NannyMUD* for a review.

Nanvaent

Access: **telnet://corrour.cc.strath.ac.uk:3000/**

See *Games: Nanvaent* for a review.

NuclearWar (LPMud)

Access: **telnet://nuclearwar.astrakan.hgs.se:4080/**

See *Games: NuclearWar* for a review.

Overdrive (LPMud)

Access: **telnet://castor.acs.oakland.edu:5195/**

See *Games: Overdrive* for a review.

Paradox

Access: **telnet://adl.uncc.edu:10478/**

See *Games: Paradox* for a review.

The Revenge of the End of the Line (LPMud)

Access: **telnet://mud.stanford.edu:2010/**

See *Games: The Revenge of the End of the Line* for a review.

Spatial Wastes

Access: **telnet://chestnut.enmu.edu:2001/**

See *Games: Spatial Wastes* for a review.

The Sprawl

Access: **telnet://chiba.picosof.com:7777/** and
http://chiba.picosof.com:7777/

See *Games: The Sprawl* for a review.

Star Wars MUSH

Access: **telnet://100.3.240.54:4402/**

See *Games: Star Wars MUSH* for a review.

ToonMUSH III (TinyMUSH)

Access: **telnet://brahe.phys.unm.edu:9999/**

See *Games: ToonMUSH III* for a review.

MULTIMEDIA

Index to Multimedia Sources

If graphics are what you crave, if plain text doesn't cut it for you, or
if you just want some nifty stuff to impress that friend who's looking over your shoulder, then the Index to Multimedia Sources is the

place to go. It doesn't include a link to every multimedia resource, but it comes close. Here you can find links to media archives, multimedia software, conference announcements, media-related companies and much more. —*GB*

Access: **http://cui-www.unige.ch/OSG/MultimediaInfo/**

Rob's Multimedia Lab

At this famous site for multimedia resources, you'll find downloadable graphics, movies and sounds of all kinds. Tons and tons of GIFs are stored in the archive, sorted chronologically, alphabetically or in a range of subject categories, such as Escher, Jurassic Park, raytraces and Star Wars. Sound directories range from film and TV quotes to music to sound effects. You'll also find many MPEG movies, from MRI images to Beavis and Butt-head, including weather images and movies. Other links take you to even more sound, image and movie archives on the Internet. —*ST*

Access: **http://www.acm.uiuc.edu/rml/**

Download publicly accessible GIF files like this one from Rob's Multimedia Lab.

Music

American Music Resource

If it's music, if it's American, it's here. Did you know that John Philip Sousa coined the phrase "canned music" around the turn of the century to express his disdain for the prospect of phonograph recordings replacing live performances? The following figure shows the Topic Index for this site. There's also a Subject Index (actually by performer) and a searchable database. —*JW*

Access: **gopher://calypso.oit.unc.edu:70/1/sunsite.d/amr.d/**

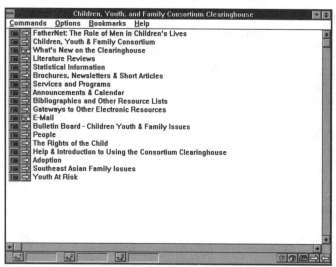

"With a song in my heart..."

Barbershop Quartet Gopher

Hum along with me now: "Down by the ooold mill streeeam..." Ah, those dulcet tones of yesteryear. But wait! Can it be true? Yes indeedy, barbershop quartets live and prosper in the age of rap, raves and heavy metal. Find out where to get barbershop arrangements, check the Calendar of Barbershop Events for up-to-date info, download music notation software or read the Acapella FAQ. If you're a contest judge (or have aspirations in that direction), go to

The Judges' Corner for articles like "Heart, Farce, and Arrangement" and "Tune It or Die." —*JW*

Access: **gopher://timc.pop.upenn.edu:70**

Classical Music Discussion List

The classical music list was created to facilitate discussions regarding classical music. All topics and periods are discussed, ranging from Gregorian Chants to Baroque. The exchange of ideas isn't quite as scholarly as a graduate level of classical music study. —*LAD*

Access: to subscribe, send email to **listserv@brownvm.brown.edu**

Send messages to **classml@brownvm.brown.edu**

Adam Curry's The Vibe

Former MTV VJ Adam Curry has had his share of problems in cyberspace. He is currently being sued by MTV for using the Internet site name mtv.com. He's now changed his address to the one below, where he maintains a number of services, one called The Vibe, which has music reviews, commentary, musician interviews, concert information, chart action and back issues of Curry's electronic gossip sheet, The Cyber-Sleaze Report. Adam Curry's Recording Studio offers musical selections that can be downloaded. There are also links to Web pages devoted to different rock artists. —*GB*

Access: **http://metaverse.com/vibe/index.html**

Film Music Discussion List

This discussion list focuses on dramatic music for films and television. Topics range from reviews of current film scores and soundtracks to discussion of film composers and the history and theory of film music. You can also find out how to get in touch with film music professionals. —*LAD*

Access: to subscribe, send email to **listserv@iubvm.ucs.indiana.edu**

Send messages to **filmus-l@iubvm.ucs.indiana.edu**

HardCORE

Excerpts from the info file for this site (HardCORE.411): "The electronic magazine of hip-hop music and culture....Brought to you as a service of the Committee of Rap Excellence....We at C.O.R.E. support underground hip-hop (none of that crossover bullshucks). That means we also support the 1st Amendment and the right to uncensored music." —JW

Access: **gopher://fir.cic.net:70/1/Zines/HardCORE**

Internet Underground Music Archive

IUMA sports great graphics and award-winning page design (Best of the Net '94) and provides an innovative service to the Net music community. The Archive gives needed exposure to little-known bands, providing bios, commentary and reviews, and audio excerpts. Legal issues around music and music on the Internet are also covered. The musical excerpts are available in MPEG format only. —GB

Access: **http://sunsite.unc.edu/ianc/index.html**

The Internet Underground Music Archive.

Noteworthy Music

Satisfy all your music tastes through this limitless CD catalog. Search the inventory by artist, album, song, music category or record label. Select a check box to immediately order the album; when you turn the page, the top will display the number of albums you've ordered and the total amount of your order. You have to set up a NetMarket account to order—you can create it at the page listed under "Access" below. Then choose the "Go to Netmarket" button to enter the market where you will find a link to Noteworthy Music. —ST

Access: **http://www.netmarket.com/**

Elvis Aaron Presley Home Page

Elvis has been sighted on the World Wide Web! At his home page, you can tour Graceland through photos and music. Or wander through the Elvis Exhibit, a collection of photos of the King. A sound archive lets you sample some tunes and spoken clips. Fun software includes Windows applications you can download, such as a program that detects Elvis's presence in the vicinity of your computer. An interactive application allows you to read what other visitors to the site have to say about the King and add your own comments. —ST

Access: **http://128.194.15.32/~ahb2188/elvishom.html**

Rare Groove

This site acts as both a magazine and radio station for hip-hop and house music. On the magazine side, articles include techno and hip-hop reviews, DJ playlists and regional reports from Boston, San Francisco, Florida and North Carolina. The radio side features a song of the week and a mix of the week, which you can listen to and immediately provide feedback on. Get various charts of top tunes, sampling some of them to see which you like. Or go to the listening booth to listen to song snippets. —ST

Access: **http://RG/RG.html**

Underworld Industries' Web's Edge

Underworld Industries' "Cultural Playground" is the home of Underworld Industries' group dedicated to linking underground music, art and the Internet. —GB

Access: **http://kzsu.stanford.edu/uwi.html**

American South Home Page

Access: **http://sunsite.unc.edu/doug-m/pages/south/south.html**

*See **United States: American South Home Page** for a review.*

Art Links on the World Wide Web

Access: **http://amanda.physics.wisc.edu/outside.html**

*See **Art: Art Links on the World Wide Web** for a review.*

Cyberpoet's Guide to Virtual Culture

Access: **http://128.230.38.86/cgvc/cgvc1.html**

*See **Cyberculture: Cyberpoet's Guide to Virtual Culture** for a review.*

Electronic Cafe

Access: **http://www.cyberspace.org/u/ecafe/www/index.html**

*See **Cyberculture: Electronic Cafe** for a review.*

Electronic Newsstand

Access: **http://www.enews.com, gopher://enews.com:2100** *AND* **telnet://enews.com** (log in as **enews**)

*See **Magazines & Publications: Electronic Newsstand** for a review.*

Kaleidospace

Access: **http://kspace.com/**

*See **Art: Kaleidospace** for a review.*

University of California at Irvine Bookstore

Access: **http://bookweb.cwis.uci.edu:8042/**

See **Books:** *University of California at Irvine Bookstore* *for a review.*

MYTHOLOGY

Bulfinch's Mythology

Brush up on your mythology by accessing these famous works by Thomas Bulfinch. The three "volumes" of mythology cover Greek and Roman myths and the legends of medieval times. Here you'll find the entire text of Bulfinch's works: *Legends of Charlemagne or Romance of the Middle Ages, The Age of Chivalry or Legends of King Arthur* and *The Age of Fables or Stories of Gods and Heroes.* A great educational resource, these works are also suitable for pleasure reading—so curl up with your computer and a little Bulfinch. —*ST*

Access: **gopher://gopher.vt.edu:10010/11/53**

Subscribing to Mailing Lists & Electronic Publications

To subscribe to a discussion list, send the following message from your email account:

subscribe <list name> <Your Name>

<list name> is the name of the group. Send this message to the "to subscribe" address listed in the Access information. Include the message in the message section of the email, not in the subject line, because most listservers ignore the subject line. —*LAD*

NATURAL HISTORY

Smithsonian Natural History Archive

This Gopher is a repository for information compiled and maintained by the Smithsonian staff. You can find information relating to biology, zoology and paleontology. There are links to other related Internet resources. You can also find out about the Smithsonian's modernization and computerization projects. (Also see Jan Weingarten's review in the **Science** section.) —*LAD*

Access: **gopher://nmnhgoph.si.edu/**

News

See also Journalism & Media.

Report Chat Channel

When news is breaking, especially a crisis, the #report channel is likely to be where the latest information will be available from IRCers around the globe. When active, #report has been called "better than the *New York Times*" by some IRC observers—probably because it provides real-time immediate feedback from real people, without mass-media filters and time lags, and because of the reputation this channel received after two 1991 crises (Gulf War and Russian coup; see related reviews in the **History, World** section). Note: If you cannot find the #report channel on IRC, try looking for the channel #discuss (remember, channels are not always forever on IRC, and may evolve over time with different names and participants), or ask someone in the channels designed for IRC-related questions (usually called #IRC_Prefect, #Twilight_Zone or #dead). —*DR*

Access: Run IRC client, specifying desired IRC server, *OR* telnet to a telnettable server; do command **/join #report**

USA Today Headline News, Sports, etc.

You can telnet from Mosaic (if you have NCSA Telnet installed) and read the day's issue of *USA Today.* You have to obtain an account before you're able to access the paper, but the account is free. —*GB*

Access: **telnet://freenet-in-a.cwru.edu**
telnet://freenet-in-b.cwru.edu
telnet://freenet-in-c.cwru.edu
login as **visitor**

Unraveling the URL

Most of the Internet resources reviewed in this book are identified by URLs (Uniform Resource Locators), a standardized addressing system designed to be used with Web browsing software (such as Ventana Mosaic, included on the CD-ROM at the back of this book). URL addresses can refer to World Wide Web sites, which are accessed using the HyperText Transport Protocol (HTTP), as well as sites using other Internet protocols, including FTP, Gopher, telnet and newsgroups.

URL addresses consist of four parts: **protocol://hostname.domain:port/path**.

- The **protocol** indicates the type of site on which the resource is located.
- The **hostname.domain** is the Internet address of the site.
- The **port** is the numerical connection point where the server can be found. (The port is usually not necessary to include, since most protocols default to a specific port.)
- The **path** is the specific location of the resource. This might be a directory name, a file name, or both. (Some URLs include no path at all.)

The URL for the Ventana Online Visitor's Center home page looks like this:

http://www.vmedia.com:80/home.html

This tells us that the Visitor's Center home page is the file **home.html**, located at the World Wide Web site **www.vmedia.com**, port **80**.

Following are typical URLs for FTP, Gopher and telnet sites (note that you must have a telnet client properly installed and configured in order to initiate telnet sessions with Mosaic):

ftp://ftp.vmedia.com:21/pub/
gopher://gopher.vmedia.com:70/
telnet://kells.vmedia.com:23/

Newsgroup URLs look a little bit different: **news:newsgroup**. For example,

news:comp.infosystems.www

If you're not using Ventana Mosaic or another Web browser, simply translate the elements of a URL address into whatever format is appropriate for your client.

Vanderbilt Television News Archive

Feeling (correctly) that television news was not being adequately preserved and chronicled, Vanderbilt University began this archive in 1968. It's still the only place that records, abstracts and indexes national television newscasts on a regular basis. But it's not just a stuffy old archive gathering dust—anyone can borrow videos from the Archive's collection. Since this is a nonprofit institution, they have to charge you something—you can get info about rates and availability from the following address: Television News Archive, Vanderbilt University, 110 21st Avenue South, Suite 704, Nashville, TN 37203. Phone: 615/322-2927; fax: 615/343-8250. —*JW*

Access: **gopher://tvnews.vanderbilt.edu:70**

World Headlines

Interested in finding out more about the world news than your local paper offers? You'll want to check out misc.headlines, where you can get your daily news fix. —*LAD*

Access: **news:misc.headlines**

C-SPAN

Access: **gopher://c-span.org/**

See Television: C-SPAN for a review.

Gulf War IRC Logs

Access: **ftp://sunsite.unc.edu/pub/academic/communications/ logs/Gulf-War/**

See History, World: Gulf War IRC Logs for a review.

PCWeek Best News Sources & Online Mags

Access: **ftp://www.ziff.com/~pcweek/best-news.html**

See Magazines & Publications: PCWeek Best News Sources & Online Mags for a review.

PowerPC News

Access: **http://power.globalnews.com/**

See *Computers, Resources & Publications: PowerPC News* for
a review.

Russian Coup IRC Log

Access: **ftp://sunsite.unc.edu/pub/academic/communications/
logs/report-ussr-gorbatchev**

See *History, World: Russian Coup IRC Log* for a review.

TidBITS

Access: **http://www.dartmouth.edu/Pages/TidBITS/
TidBITS.html**

See *Computers, Resources & Publications:* **TidBITS** for a review.

OCEANOGRAPHY

O

Safari 1994: Barkley Sound Expedition

For ten days, a team of scientists, archaeologists and kids explored
the ocean environment of Barkley Sound, British Columbia. This
site describes their experiments, discoveries and experiences. The
main highlight is an interactive map of an aquarium-like touch tank
you can click on or "touch" to get information about the animals
inside or view in motion through a hyperlinked animation. You can
also visit the 3D Icon Gallery of thumbnail photos of various marine
plants and animals. Click on one to get a larger photograph and
information about that specimen. —ST

Access: **http://oberon.educ.sfu.ca/splash.htm**

Safari Touch Tank

"Touch" fish and plant life in this touch tank at the Barkley Sound Expedition. (Used with permission of Excite Center, Simon Fraser University.)

PALEONTOLOGY

University of California Museum of Paleontology

Colorful interactive maps guide you through the huge exhibits at this famous museum. Enter the exhibits by way of one of three topics: phylogeny, geological time or evolutionary thought. As you move deeper into one topic, you will discover more cross-links to other topics. The phylogeny section is the best entrance for the first-time visitor, with exhibit halls of fossils, including dinosaur and mammal exhibits. One highlight you shouldn't miss is the Great White Shark exhibit. A fossil specimen database links to an online catalog which can be searched for more specialized research on specimens in the museum. —*ST*

Access: **http://ucmp1.berkeley.edu/welcome.html**

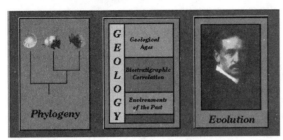

Navigate through the Museum of Paleontology using this interactive map.

Honolulu Community College

Access: **http://www.hcc.hawaii.edu/**

*See **Education, Institutions: Honolulu Community College** for a review.*

PERSONALS

Debra Listens

If you're feeling lonely and would like a conversation with a willing listener. Debra is reminiscent of the early BASIC programs that played the part of a Freudian psychoanalyst, though she's much more conversational and talented—if that's the appropriate term to use to describe a machine. —*TL*

Access: **telnet://debra.dgbt.doc.cn:3000/**

FurryMUCK (MUCK)

Warm and fuzzy, cute and cuddly, FurryMUCKers are an odd but amiable lot. Dedicated to creating a society not made of nasty stuff like cyberpunks or adventurers, FurryMUCK is a world of soft glades, burbling streams and forest glens populated with animals, not people. Don't be fooled, though—taking animal form seems to loosen people up a bit. Don't be surprised when that cute bunny wabbit nuzzling your leg wants more than a pat on the head! —*SC*

Access: **telnet://sncils.snc.edu:8888/**

Virtual Meetmarket

Now you can meet that special someone, a new best friend or just someone to talk to through this dating service on the World Wide Web. Browse personals and reply immediately through email. There is no cost to publish your own personal; just download a personal template and fill in the blanks. You can use a full page of hypertext and even link in pictures from an archive of GIF images. We've all heard about couples who met, fell in love and got married through the Internet. Using the Virtual Meetmarket, that might happen to you. —ST

Access: **http://www.wwa.com:1111/**

Male seeking Female:

- CA2323.California_Gentleman
- CA2465.Aim_to_please
- CA2931.Slow_Soft_Shy
- CO2135.Looking_For_You
- CO2746.Renaissance_Man_in_Northern_Colorado
- FL2666.From_Hindustan
- IL2692_Bored_in_Southern_Illinois

Browse intriguing personals like these at the Virtual Meetmarket.

Chatting in the Hot Tub

Access: Run IRC client, specifying desired IRC server, *OR* telnet to a telnettable server; do command **/join #hottub**

See **Chat: Chatting in the Hot Tub** *for a review.*

Netsex

Access: Run IRC client, specifying desired IRC server, *OR* telnet to a telnettable server; do command **/join #netsex**

See **Sex: Netsex** *for a review.*

Penpal Network

Access: **news:soc.penpals**

See **Fun: Penpal Network** *for a review.*

Pull a Stool Up to the #ircbar

Access: Run IRC client, specifying desired IRC server, *OR* telnet to a telnettable server; do command **/join #ircbar**

See **Chat: Pull a Stool Up to the #ircbar** *for a review.*

Truth or Dare

Access: Run IRC client, specifying desired IRC server, *OR* telnet to a telnettable server; do command **/join #netsex**

See **Sex: Truth or Dare** *for a review.*

PHILOSOPHY

Noble Savage Philosophers Mailing List

This mailing list focuses on philosophical topics and studies. The subtopics within this field are varied. Subscribers are free to express their ideas for debate and discussion. If you have questions about your favorite philosopher, or wonder who disagreed with him, then this is the mailing list for you. —*LAD*

Access: to subscribe, send email to **listserv@rpicicge.bitnet**

Send messages to **nsp-l@rpicicge.bitnet**

Philosophy & Religion Journals

Electronic Journal of Analytic Philosophy, Ioudaios, Lchaim, LogBank (Journal on Philosophical Logic), *Muslim News, New Age Magazine, Psycoloquy,* the *Religious Studies Publications Journal, Thinknet* and the *Observer*. Need I say more? This Gopher's a veritable gold mine for anyone who wants to be au courant with the latest in religion, philosophy and alternative paths. —*JW*

Access: **gopher://marvel.loc.gov/11/global/phil/journals**

Religious & Philosophical Studies

Access: **gopher://dewey.lib.ncsu.edu/11/library/disciplines/religion**

*See **Religion: Religious & Philosophical Studies** for a review.*

PHOTOGRAPHY

Black Star Photography Archive

Connect to an archive of resources for amateur and professional photographers alike. A photography database has information on film, paper and photographic chemistry. Here you can also connect to the International Center for Photography, view various photography studies or visit the Michigan State University Online Photography Gallery. Other tidbits you'll find in the archive include FAQs on film and developing, exhibition information and photography magazines. —*ST*

Access: **gopher://gopher.blackstar.com** *OR* **http://www.blackstar.com/**

View photography exhibitions at the Black Star Photography Archive.

Photography Database

The Photography Database offers information about the chemistry of photography, as well as advice and techniques on developing film. You can find out pros and cons about different materials for use in developing film. —*LAD*

Access: **gopher://gopher.panix.com:70/11/Photography**

Smithsonian Images

Visit the latest Smithsonian exhibits without having to travel to Washington, DC. You can get pictures (in both GIF and JPEG format) in various categories including art, science and nature, people and places, and air and space. A special directory features newly added pictures. —*LAD*

Access: **ftp://photo1.si.edu/images/**

Snapshots From the UMBC Computer Department

Probably in any other context, pictures like this would bore you to death. However, having the ability to snoop in on someone's office hundreds or even thousands of miles away does have its appeal. Here are up-to-the-minute snapshots of what's going on in the computer department at the University of Maryland, Baltimore. The pictures are relatively small and in GIF format, so even if you have a low-powered Mac and a SLIP connection, you can still snoop. Take a peek. —*GB*

Access: **http://www.cs.umbc.edu/video-snapshots/**

Art Links on the World Wide Web

Access: **http://amanda.physics.wisc.edu/outside.html**

*See **Art: Art Links on the World Wide Web** for a review.*

P

NASA Earth Pix

Access: **ftp://explorer.arc.nasa.gov/**

*See **Weather: NASA Earth Pix** for a review.*

POETRY

Poetry Archive at SunSITE

Here you'll find a vast searchable library with something for every poetry lover. An archive of the "classics" lets you search all of Yeats, Shakespeare's sonnets, plus the works of many other famous poets like e.e. cummings, Sylvia Plath and Thomas Hardy. If contemporary poetry is more to your taste, search the index of *Poetry* magazine for the past six years. Lovers of "modern" poetry can search an archive of rock and roll lyrics. A searchable version of *Roget's Thesaurus* is even available for aspiring wordsmiths. —*ST*

Access: **gopher://president.oit.unc.edu:70/11/sunsite.d/poetry.d**

Poetry at Internet Wiretap

This poetry library features all the "classics" of poetry. Here you'll find all your old favorites like Wordsworth's "The Daffodils," Frost's "Stopping By Woods on a Snowy Evening," Tennyson's "Charge of the Light Brigade," Poe's "The Raven," even "The Night Before Christmas." Many more poems are included in the electronic library. Be sure to put it on your hotlist because it will probably become your personal volume of poetry. —*ST*

Access: **gopher://wiretap.spies.com:70/11/Library/Classic/Poetry**

Poetry in Motion

Poems are made online, before your eyes, and criticisms are usually immediate. If you always wanted to be a creator, listener and critic all at once, here's a great experimental ground to do so. Note that a poetry contest is planned soon, at the time of this writing (may already be in progress as you read this). Although you can find poems in progress here, even completed ones, it can also be great fun to watch things degenerate into nonpoetic babble. Still, the occasional good poem is worth the effort to check out this channel—and, if they're not so good, you'll feel that much better about your own "magnum opus."

I especially loved how this channel enabled me to create a "collaborative improvized" poem with a stranger I never met before! Then others joined in with lines of their own! Truly an experience unique to IRC. You gotta try it yourself. (And another plus: the people were friendlier on this channel than on many other IRC channels.) —*DR*

Access: Run IRC client, specifying desired IRC server, *OR* telnet to a telnettable server; do command **/join #poems**

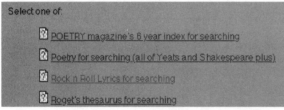

Select one of:

- POETRY magazine's 6 year index for searching
- Poetry for searching (all of Yeats and Shakespeare plus)
- Rock n Roll Lyrics for searching
- Roget's thesaurus for searching

Search all types of poetry through this Gopher interface at SunSITE.

Poetry Newsgroup

If you're a poet, an aspiring poet or a poetry appreciator, **rec.arts.poems** is for you. You can post your original poems and get feedback from others, or just read the poetry others post. —*LAD*

Access: **news:rec.arts.poems**

Alex: A Catalogue of Electronic Texts on the Internet

Access: **gopher://rsl.ox.ac.uk:70/11/lib-corn/hunter**

*See **Literature, Collections: Alex: A Catalogue of Electronic Texts on the Internet** for a review.*

P

Electronic Texts From CCAT

Access: **gopher://ccat.sas.upenn.edu:3333**

*See **Literature, Collections: Electronic Texts From CCAT** for a review.*

Labyrinth Electronic Publishing Project

Access: **http://www.honors.indiana.edu/docs/lab/laby.html**

*See **Magazines & Publications: Labyrinth Electronic Publishing Project** for a review.*

Stream of Consciousness

Access: **http://kzsu.stanford.edu/uwi/soc.html**

*See **Zines: Stream of Consciousness** for a review.*

POLITICS

Political Talkfest

If you love to talk politics but your friends walk away when you start, here you'll find nonstop politics. You can post your views. Chances are that someone out there will respond. The worst thing that can happen is that no one will reply, but all your friends will stay happy. —*LAD*

Access: **news:talk.politics.misc**

The center of American politics—the White House.

Mother Jones

Access: **http://www.mojones.com/motherjones.html**

See Magazines & Publications: **Mother Jones** *for a review.*

PROGRAMMING

See Computers, Programming.

PSYCHOLOGY

Psyche Discussion Forum

This group encourages discussions about issues arising from the interdisciplinary study of consciousness. It also serves as a forum to discuss the PSYCHE electronic journal, which publishes consciousness-related articles and reports. —*LAD*

Access: to subscribe, send email to **listserv@iris.rfmh.org**

Send messages to **psyche-d@iris.rfmh.org**

Rivendell Resources

"Everyone dies. The choice and the challenge is how we choose to live." That's from Elizabeth Glaser, who recently died of AIDS, but dedicated herself to the AIDS fight right to the end. Life and death—we can't have one without the other. But you can get all kinds of support for this transition that we humans often have trouble accepting and dealing with. GriefNet offers a wide range of services: there's a Bereavement and Loss Resources Directory that can connect you with support groups, agencies and other organizations; the Professional Resources Directory gives you a list of professionals who work in the areas of death, dying and bereavement; and take a look at the Annotated Bibliography if you want to find out about available books, articles, movies and other media resources on these topics. And that's just for starters. —*JW*

Access: **gopher://garnet.msen.com:70/1/causes/rivendell**

PUBLISHING

See also Books; Magazines & Publications.

Project Gutenberg

Project Gutenberg was established to encourage the creation and distribution of electronic text. The charter is ambitious: they hope to have a trillion etexts in distribution by the end of 2001. (Also see Jan Weingarten's Project Gutenberg review in the **Literature, Collections** section) —*TL*

Access: **ftp://tmrcnext.cso.uiuc.edu/**

```
Project Gutenberg Index
Title/Author

The Complete Works of William Shakespeare
Beethoven, 5th Symphony in c-minor
A Tale of Two Cities, by Charles Dickens
Flatland, by Edwin A. Abbott
The First 100,000 Prime Numbers
The Communist Manifesto,Karl Marx
Aladdin and the Magic Lamp, Traditional
Inaugural Address, US Pres Bill Clinton
Tom Sawyer Detective, Mark Twain
Tarzan, Jewels of Opar,  Burroughs
Son of Tarzan, Edgar Rice Burroughs
NAFTA, Treaty, Annexes, Tariffs
Price/Cost Indexes from 1875 to 1989
The World Factbook, US CIA, 1993 Edition
A Connecticut Yankee, Mark Twain
Beasts of Tarzan, Edgar Rice Burroughs
Frankenstein/Mary Wollstonecraft Shelley
From the Earth to the Moon, Jules Verne
Return of Tarzan, Edgar Rice Burroughs
The Online World/de Presno  [Shareware]
Terminal Compromise/NetNovel, Win Schartau
```

*A partial listing of the thousands of diverse documents
available via FTP from Project Gutenberg.*

QUOTATIONS

Definitions of Science Fiction

Access: **gopher://gopher.lysator.liu.se:70/11/sf_lsff/Definitions**

See Science Fiction: Definitions of Science Fiction for a review.

RADIO

Canadian Radio

An experimental database containing sound and text files from the
Canadian Broadcasting Corporation. Popular programs such as
Quirks and Quarks, Basic Black and Sunday Morning can be heard
online. Obviously these sound files are huge and you probably need

to have a direct Internet connection to make downloading them cost effective. Ordering information is available to buy the programs on cassette tape. —*GB*

Access: **http://debra.dgbt.doc.ca/cbc/cbc.html**

Ham Radio Server

No ham radio operator on the Internet should ever need to use a callbook again. The callsign server lets you search by callsign, last name, city or zip code. You can also use filters to limit the amount of entries found by your search. Just type **help** once you log in for a list of commands. —*LAD*

Access: **telnet://callsign.cs.buffalo.edu:2000/**

A shortwave radio.

Internet Talk Radio

Access: **http://www.ncsa.uiuc.edu/radio/radio.html**

*See **Internet, Resources: Internet Talk Radio** for a review.*

REAL ESTATE

Homebuyer's Fair

This free service not only lists houses for sale but also gives a lot of useful information about the process of buying a house. Information booths provide pamphlets on housing costs, closing and organizations that help low-income homebuyers. At the Mortgage Booth, send an electronic postcard to mortgage lenders or use the electronic calculator to find out how big a mortgage loan you can qualify for. The New Homes Guide lets you view houses for sale in the Washington, DC, area. A clickable map transports you to the area you want to live in, where you can browse through listings of available properties. —*ST*

Access: **http://www.homefair.com/homepage.html**

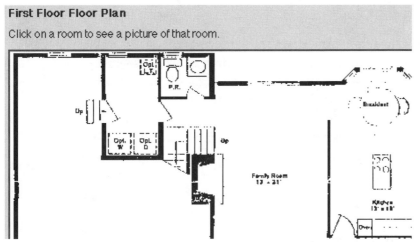

This portion of an interactive floorplan is part of the prototype real-estate display at the Homebuyer's Fair.

REFERENCE

*See also Dictionaries; Education, Resources;
Encyclopedias.*

CIA World Factbook

The CIA World Factbook contains statistical information about the countries of the world. If you're researching a country, this will probably offer more statistical information than an encyclopedia. You can even find out the exchange rates for the local currency if you plan on traveling abroad. —*LAD*

Access: **gopher://sunny.stat-usa.gov:70/11/NTDB/Wofact** *OR* **gopher://sunny.stat-usa.gov:70/11/STAT-USA/NTDB/Wofact**

Knowledge One

Knowledge One offers timely, accurate information on any subject using the convenience and speed of the Internet. The researchers have access to millions of information sources and can provide answers to almost any question, usually within an hour. Knowledge One serves students, researchers, business people and parents with a range of needs, from simple facts to in-depth research. Fill out an online quote form to ask instantly whatever you need to know. As a free trial of the service, join an update service that allows you to stay on top of an important topic, with information updates weekly, daily or hourly. —*ST*

Access: **http://KnowOne-WWW.Sonoma.edu/**

Roget's Thesaurus

Some people may use a thesaurus to find just the right word to turn that meandering missive into an exemplary epistle. But I use the thesaurus for entertainment. When my brain just can't take it anymore, I browse through Roget's online thesaurus and click on whatever catches my fancy. To get the figure shown here, I chose

"Existence"; then, in keeping with my existentialist mood, I clicked on "Unsubstantiality." Yeah, that's the ticket. I especially like that Shelley quote at the end—"an ocean of dreams without a sound." Is that cool or what? —*JW*

Access: **gopher://gopher.uoregon.edu:70/1/Reference/Roget**

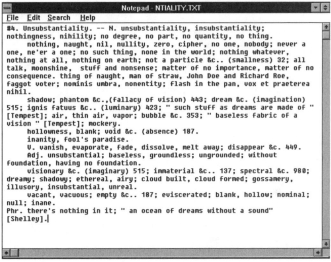

Use Roget's Thesaurus to get your brain moving.

The Virtual Reference Desk

The Virtual Reference Desk features links to dictionaries and other reference material accessible from the Internet. In addition to dictionaries, you can search thesauri, presidential speeches, women's studies resources, email addresses and an acronym dictionary. When you run across technical jargon while exploring the Internet, this is the place to come to find out what it means. —*LAD*

Access: **gopher://peg.cwis.uci.edu:7000/11/gopher.welcome/
peg/uci**

Alex: A Catalogue of Electronic Texts on the Internet

Access: **gopher://rsl.ox.ac.uk:70/11/lib-corn/hunter**

*See **Literature, Collections: Alex: A Catalogue of Electronic Texts on the Internet** for a review.*

R

Babel Computer Terms

Access: **ftp://ftp.temple.edu/pub/info/help-net**

See *Computers, Resources & Publications: Babel Computer Terms* for a review.

Britannica Online

Access: **http://www.eb.com/**

See *Encyclopedias: Britannica Online for a review.*

CERFnet Research

Access: **ftp://ftp.cerf.net/**

See *Education, Resources: CERFnet Research for a review.*

Colorado Alliance of Research Libraries

Access: **telnet://pac.carl.org/**

See *Libraries: Colorado Alliance of Research Libraries for a review.*

Computer-Assisted Reporting & Research

Access: to subscribe, send email to **listserv@ulkyvm.louisville.edu**

Send messages to **carr-l@ulkyvm.louisville.edu**

See *Journalism & Media: Computer-Assisted Reporting & Research for a review.*

Department of Commerce Database

Access: **gopher://gopher.stat-usa.gov/**

See *Business & Finance: Department of Commerce Database for a review.*

Dictionary Library

Access: **http://math-www.uni-paderborn.de/HTML/
Dictionaries.html**

*See **Dictionaries: Dictionary Library** for a review.*

Hacker's Dictionary

Access: **gopher://gopher.cs.ttu.edu/11/Reference%20Shelf/
Hacker%27s%20Dictionary**

*See **Dictionaries: Hacker's Dictionary** for a review.*

National Archives

Access: **gopher://gopher.nara.gov/**

*See **History, U.S.: National Archives** for a review.*

Project Gutenberg

Access: **gopher://gopher.msen.com:70/11/stuff/gutenberg**

*See **Literature, Collections: Project Gutenberg** for a review.*

Access: **ftp://tmrcnext.cso.uiuc.edu/**

*See **Publishing: Project Gutenberg** for a review.*

Thesaurus Linguae Graecae

Access: **gopher://tlg.cwis.uci.edu:7011**

*See **Classics: Thesaurus Linguae Graecae** for a review.*

Wiretap Online Library

Access: **gopher://wiretap.spies.com/**

*See **Libraries: Wiretap Online Library** for a review.*

RELIGION

The Bible Gateway

Now the Bible is instantly available over the WWW in this useful reference format. An interactive program produces HTML versions of Bible chapters as you request them. Using a form, you type the

Unraveling the URL

Most of the Internet resources reviewed in this book are identified by URLs (Uniform Resource Locators), a standardized addressing system designed to be used with Web browsing software (such as Ventana Mosaic, included on the CD-ROM at the back of this book). URL addresses can refer to World Wide Web sites, which are accessed using the HyperText Transport Protocol (HTTP), as well as sites using other Internet protocols, including FTP, Gopher, telnet and newsgroups.

URL addresses consist of four parts: **protocol://hostname.domain:port/path**.

- The **protocol** indicates the type of site on which the resource is located.
- The **hostname.domain** is the Internet address of the site.
- The **port** is the numerical connection point where the server can be found. (The port is usually not necessary to include, since most protocols default to a specific port.)
- The **path** is the specific location of the resource. This might be a directory name, a file name, or both. (Some URLs include no path at all.)

The URL for the Ventana Online Visitor's Center home page looks like this:

http://www.vmedia.com:80/home.html

This tells us that the Visitor's Center home page is the file **home.html**, located at the World Wide Web site **www.vmedia.com**, port **80**.

Following are typical URLs for FTP, Gopher and telnet sites (note that you must have a telnet client properly installed and configured in order to initiate telnet sessions with Mosaic):

ftp://ftp.vmedia.com:21/pub/

gopher://gopher.vmedia.com:70/

telnet://kells.vmedia.com:23/

Newsgroup URLs look a little bit different: **news:newsgroup**. For example,

news:comp.infosystems.www

If you're not using Ventana Mosaic or another Web browser, simply translate the elements of a URL address into whatever format is appropriate for your client.

passage name you want to see; within a few seconds, the passage is returned to you. Choose the version of the Bible you prefer or access chapters from all versions. A concordance function lets you search for keywords. In addition to this English gateway, a German version is available, and the program's creator is working on other language versions to make this a truly international service. —*ST*

Access: **http://unicks.calvin.edu/cgi-bin/bible/**

Catholic Archives

Interested in Catholicism? You can browse files at this site including Roman Catholic documents, Franciscan documents, Opus Dei documents and an archive of the Free Catholic Mailing List/Newsgroup. You can also find links to other sites with Catholic documents and pictures that can be downloaded. —*LAD*

Access: **gopher://auvm.american.edu:70/11/Cath0**

A picture of St. Francis of Assisi from the Catholic Archives.

R

Electronic Jewish Library

Holocaust and Holocaust Denial archives, book reviews, the Judaica eJournal, Institute of Jewish Studies, Kol Yisrael shortwave broadcasts. And pay attention, all you aspiring (or already spired) writers—they're looking for you, and the figure below gives you info on submitting stuff to the library. If you're Jewish, interested in Judaism, or write about any kind of Judaism-related stuff, check it out. —*JW*

Access: **gopher://jerusalem1.datasrv.co.il/11/Elect**

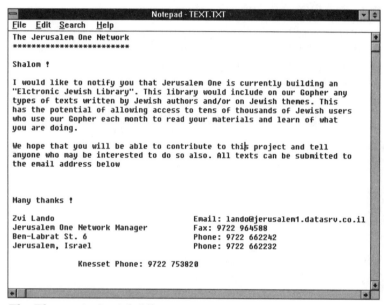

```
                    Notepad - TEXT.TXT
 File   Edit   Search   Help
 The Jerusalem One Network
 **************************

 Shalom !

 I would like to notify you that Jerusalem One is currently building an
 "Elctronic Jewish Library". This library would include on our Gopher any
 types of texts written by Jewish authors and/or on Jewish themes. This
 has the potential of allowing access to tens of thousands of Jewish users
 who use our Gopher each month to read your materials and learn of what
 you are doing.

 We hope that you will be able to contribute to this project and tell
 anyone who may be interested to do so also. All texts can be submitted to
 the email address below


 Many thanks !

 Zvi Lando                        Email: lando@jerusalem1.datasrv.co.il
 Jerusalem One Network Manager    Fax: 9722 964588
 Ben-Labrat St. 6                 Phone: 9722 662242
 Jerusalem, Israel                Phone: 9722 662232

          Knesset Phone: 9722 753820
```

The Electronic Jewish Library.

History of Islam

This nonsectarian forum lets you learn about the history of Islam. It does not host debates on the philosophy of Islam. It is used to distribute announcements and calls for papers related to Islamic history and often features discussion of short papers and queries. —*LAD*

Access: to subscribe, send email to
listserv@ulkyvm.louisville.edu

Send messages to **islam-l@ulkyvm.louisville.edu**

Nostradamus

We've all heard of Nostradamus and his prophecies, but not many have actually read the prophecies themselves. Now you can read them in both French and English. You can also read a letter Nostradamus wrote to his son and a short biography. —*LAD*

Access: **gopher://skynet.usask.ca:70/1nostradamus/ nostradamus.70**

Religion Newsgroup

If you have an interest in religion, you can often find intelligent discussions, as well as lively debates, on talk.religion.misc. —*LAD*

Access: **news:talk.religion.misc**

Religious & Philosophical Studies

Deep thinkers and travelers on the spiritual path, disembark here for a while. Search the Book of Mormon, the Koran or the King James Bible. —*JW*

Access: **gopher://dewey.lib.ncsu.edu/11/library/disciplines/ religion**

Religious Studies

At this site you can search the sacred writings of your religion or find out how other religions view certain topics and how they compare to your own. Currently, you can search the Bible, the Quran, Jainist texts and others, or browse the SunSITE Religious Studies archive. —*LAD*

Access: **gopher://sunsite.unc.edu:70/11/sunsite.d/religion.d**

Shamash: The Jewish Networking Project

If you're familiar with The New York Israel Project, look no further for your connection to the world of Judaism. Shamash is its new name. Take a look at the figure below for a glimpse of the available treasures. This project was put together by a bunch of Jewish computer activists, who connected with the New York State Research and Educational Network (NYSERNet). It's evolved into a comprehensive resource of community bulletin boards, educational information, extensive resource lists and much, much more. —*JW*

Access: **gopher://israel.nysernet.org**

Alex: A Catalogue of Electronic Texts on the Internet

Access: **gopher://rsl.ox.ac.uk:70/11/lib-corn/hunter**

See Literature, Collections: Alex: A Catalogue of Electronic Texts on the Internet for a review.

Dead Sea Scrolls Exhibit

Access:**http://sunsite.unc.edu/expo/deadsea.scrolls.exhibit/intro.html**

See History, World: Dead Sea Scrolls Exhibit for a review.

Electronic Texts From CCAT

Access: **gopher://ccat.sas.upenn.edu:3333**

See Literature, Collections: Electronic Texts From CCAT for a review.

Philosophy & Religion Journals

Access: **gopher://marvel.loc.gov/11/global/phil/journals**

See Philosophy: Philosophy & Religion Journals for a review.

Vatican Exhibit

Access: **http://sunsite.unc.edu/expo/vatican.exhibit/Vatican.exhibit.html**

See History, World: Vatican Exhibit for a review.

RUSSIA

Moscow Kremlin Online Excursion

The excursion is set up as if you were actually taking a walking tour of the Kremlin, with talks about the history and layout along the way. You have a choice of walking through Red Square or Cathedral Square. In the squares, look around at the surrounding buildings and choose which to visit. Every stop on the tour is accompanied by full-color photos. —*ST*

Access: **http://www.kiae.su/www/wtr/kremlin/begin.html**

Russian Chat

#russian is an IRC channel where Russians and non-Russians from around the world (or, if you prefer, Net) meet to chat, exchange news and, according to the #russian WWW home page, "kick each other's butt." Speaking of home pages, the #russian page is one of the most complete in listing details about frequent visitors to the channel. Another passage from this page (presumably written by a Russian): "Unfortunately for some of us [and fortunately for others], ... citizens of the former USSR are scattered around the world and some of them who knew each other before need visas and other bureaucratic s**t to meet each other in person. Thus, #russian is the only way for such people to converse with their relatives and friends who may live in hundreds of kilometers from them." Yet another ringing endorsement of IRC's power and usefulness.

#russian channel visitors (channelers, if you prefer ;-) include regulars from about a dozen countries including the U.S., Ukraine, Latvia and, of course, Russia. Most of these IRCers are either students or programmers (which is often true for other channels too, since they often have more time and access bandwidth to the Net). Random chat is common on this channel, but serious discussion also takes place, especially between 22:00 and 24:00 EST—and, of course, during the occasional Russian coup or other crisis. Talk often ends on some other channel, since it's often difficult to talk seriously in a sea of 20 to 30 virtual voices.

R

Although many #russian channel users speak English, one shouldn't be offended if asked to speak Russian, since many #russian regulars get tired of non-native languages and prefer to take rest on #russian speaking Russian. Finally, note that #russian is a relatively anarchistic channel; regulars say that you can say anything you want; but anybody who doesn't like what you say can possibly kick you out. So, as on all channels having nationalistic themes, be careful out there! (Also see **Russian Coup IRC Log** in the **History, World** section.) —*DR*

Access: Run IRC client, specifying desired IRC server, *OR* telnet to a telnettable server; do command **/join #russian**

Friends & Partners

Access: **http://solar.rtd.utk.edu/friends/home.html**

See **World Cultures: Friends & Partners** *for a review.*

Russian Coup IRC Log

Access: **ftp://sunsite.unc.edu/pub/academic/communications/ logs/report-ussr-gorbatchev**

See **History, World: Russian Coup IRC Log** *for a review.*

Subscribing to Mailing Lists & Electronic Publications

To subscribe to a discussion list, send the following message from your email account:

subscribe <list name> <Your Name>

<list name> is the name of the group. Send this message to the "to subscribe" address listed in the Access information. Include the message in the message section of the email, not in the subject line, because most listservers ignore the subject line. —*LAD*

Science

The Exploratorium

This online science museum is always fun to visit, with interactive exhibits on light and color, sound and music, patterns of motion and other natural phenomena. Explore principles of science, through hearing the Doppler effect, viewing the "Bronx Cheer Bulb" or experiencing the "fading dot," for example. A multimedia library displays still images of the museum exhibits, artist-in-residence pieces and other interesting photographs, such as bubbles and prisms. Teachers and parents can order museum publications, such as "cookbooks" that teach how to construct the museum exhibits at home. Don't forget to stop by the Exploratorium store for gifts and learning tools. (Also see Jan Weingarten's Gopher review in the **Fun** section.) —*ST*

Access: **http://www.exploratorium.edu/**

The JASON Project

Travel along with a scientific expedition on a journey to the rain forest, caverns, Mayan ruins and coral reef of Belize. The project is designed to teach science by enabling students to participate remotely in an "electronic field trip." Here you can read "Letters from the Rain Forest," descriptions of thoughts, experiences and reflections on each day's activities made as the expedition took place. The letters include photos taken each day. After reading, participate by leaving comments on the public bulletin board or connecting to JASON ONLINE, a BBS designed to introduce teachers to education through telecommunication. —*ST*

Access: **http://seawifs.gsfc.nasa.gov/JASON.html**

Photographs like this one heighten the rain-forest experience at the JASON Project.

NCSA Digital Gallery CD-ROM

Sample visualizations, movies and software demos submitted by researchers all over the world. You can watch animations in the Science Theater or access image samples. On display are a variety of scientific MPEG movies and GIF files, including images of Hurricane Bob, animations of fluid dynamics, eclipse and supernova images and volume visualizations. You can even view an MRI image of a person's brain or a 3D image of a dog's heart in the medical sciences section. Click on an item in a menu for information about the image or animation—what it is and how it was created. —*ST*

Access: **http://www.ncsa.uiuc.edu/SDG/DigitalGallery/ DG_readme.html**

Smithsonian Institution Natural History Gopher

Is vertebrate zoology your thing? No? What about biodiversity, biological conservation, global volcanism or botany? Information from the National Zoo in Washington, DC? If I'm still striking out with you, you might still want to check out this Gopher. If there's anything at all in the field of natural history that rings your bell, you'll find it here. —JW

Access: **gopher://nmnhgoph.si.edu**

Unraveling the URL

Most of the Internet resources reviewed in this book are identified by URLs (Uniform Resource Locators), a standardized addressing system designed to be used with Web browsing software (such as Ventana Mosaic, included on the CD-ROM at the back of this book). URL addresses can refer to World Wide Web sites, which are accessed using the HyperText Transport Protocol (HTTP), as well as sites using other Internet protocols, including FTP, Gopher, telnet and newsgroups.

URL addresses consist of four parts: **protocol://hostname.domain:port/path**.

- The **protocol** indicates the type of site on which the resource is located.
- The **hostname.domain** is the Internet address of the site.
- The **port** is the numerical connection point where the server can be found. (The port is usually not necessary to include, since most protocols default to a specific port.)
- The **path** is the specific location of the resource. This might be a directory name, a file name, or both. (Some URLs include no path at all.)

The URL for the Ventana Online Visitor's Center home page looks like this:

http://www.vmedia.com:80/home.html

This tells us that the Visitor's Center home page is the file **home.html**, located at the World Wide Web site **www.vmedia.com**, port **80**.

Following are typical URLs for FTP, Gopher and telnet sites (note that you must have a telnet client properly installed and configured in order to initiate telnet sessions with Mosaic):

ftp://ftp.vmedia.com:21/pub/

gopher://gopher.vmedia.com:70/

telnet://kells.vmedia.com:23/

Newsgroup URLs look a little bit different: **news:newsgroup**. For example,

news:comp.infosystems.www

If you're not using Ventana Mosaic or another Web browser, simply translate the elements of a URL address into whatever format is appropriate for your client.

Biosphere & Ecology Discussion List

Access: to subscribe, send email to **listserv@ubvm.cc.buffalo.edu**

Send messages to **biosph-l@ubvm.cc.buffalo.edu**

See Environment: Biosphere & Ecology Discussion List for a review.

CERFnet Research

Access: **ftp://ftp.cerf.net/**

See Education: Resources: CERFnet Research for a review.

Earth Science Information Network

Access: **gopher://gopher.ciesin.org/**

See Environment: Earth Science Information Network for a review.

Eisenhower National Clearinghouse for Mathematics & Science Education

Access: **gopher://enc.org:70**

See Education, Resources: Eisenhower National Clearinghouse for Mathematics & Science Education for a review.

The Electronic Zoo

Access: **gopher://netvet.wustl.edu:70/11n%3a/e-zoo**

See Zoology: The Electronic Zoo for a review.

EnviroGopher

Access: **gopher://envirolink.org/**

See Environment: EnviroGopher for a review.

Geologic Information Servers

Access: **gopher://info.er.usgs.gov:70/1/** choose directory
Geologic Information/Geologic Information Servers

See Geology: Geologic Information Servers for a review.

Fred Hutchinson Cancer Research Center

Access: **gopher://gopher.fhcrc.org:70**

See Medicine: Fred Hutchinson Cancer Research Center for a review.

Safari 1994: Barkley Sound Expedition

Access: **http://oberon.educ.sfu.ca/splash.htm**

See Oceanography: Safari 1994: Barkley Sound Expedition for a review.

Smithsonian Images

Access: **ftp://photo1.si.edu/images/**

See Photography: Smithsonian Images for a review.

University of California Museum of Paleontology

Access: **http://ucmp1.berkeley.edu/welcome.html**

See Paleontology: University of California Museum of Paleontology for a review.

Virtual Frog Dissection Kit

Access: **http://george.lbl.gov/ITG.hm.pg.docs/dissect/info.html**

See Biology: Virtual Frog Dissection Kit for a review.

S

SCIENCE FICTION

Definitions of Science Fiction

Isaac Asimov defines science fiction this way: "Modern science fiction is the only form of literature that consistently considers the nature of the changes that face us, the possible consequences, and the possible solutions." Read for yourself his and many other science fiction authors' definitions of the genre in this collection of quotes in the Lysator Science Fiction Archive. Other famous SF writers represented include Robert Heinlein, Frank Herbert, Brian Aldiss, Ray Bradbury, L. Sprague DeCamp and many more. This document makes great browsing for any science fiction fan. —*ST*

Access: **gopher://gopher.lysator.liu.se:70/11/sf_lsff/Definitions**

The Doomsday Brunette by John M. Zakour

This is "the first Internet-browsable, downloadable, interactive, science-fiction, humorous, satirical, mystery, electronic book," or so the introduction says. You can only read the first three chapters of the book in this demonstration. Hyperlinked words within the futuristic text lead you to definitions of unknown terms, either from a realistic point of view or the main character's point of view, depending on which you pick. You also choose where the story goes at the end of every page. After going through the WWW demonstration, you'll probably want to download the entire book just to see what happens next—or rather, what you can make happen. —*ST*

Access: **http://zeb.nysaes.cornell.edu/CGI/ddb/demo.cgi**

Lysator Science Fiction & Fantasy Archive

Connect to a hypertext interface to a massive ASCII-text archive of science fiction and fantasy resources on the Internet. An experimental searching mechanism allows you to pin down specific topics, or browse through general subject areas. You'll find authors' biographies and bibliographies, book reviews, film commentaries and a list of electronically available fiction. Special series stored here include some real gems: "belated reviews" of classic works; *Dragon Zine*, a shared-world project; publisher's newsletters from Del Rey and Tor; and *Quanta*, a magazine of science fiction and fantasy. You can even visit an art gallery created by science fiction and fantasy fans. —*ST*

Access: **http://www.lysator.liu.se/sf_archive/sf_main.html**

Science Fiction Newsgroups

If you're interested in sci-fi trivia and discussing the "greats" of the genre, this is the newsgroup for you. The discussions focus mostly on books and authors. Occasionally, the topic shifts to classic science fiction TV shows and movies. —*LAD*

Access: **news:rec.arts.sf.misc**

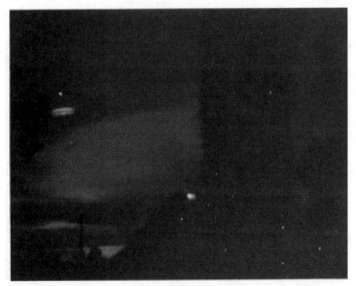

Much of science fiction is taken from what is believed to be reality, such as the Gulf Breeze UFO Sightings.

Science Fiction Resource Guide

Probably the largest collection of science fiction literature in cyberspace. Contains articles, essays, interviews, bibliographies, FAQs, sci-fi journals and information on awards and conventions. Hotlinked to all the other major sci-fi Net nodes. —*GB*

Access: **ftp://gandalf.rutgers.edu/pub/sfl/sf-resource.guide.html**

Douglas Adams

Access: **news:alt.fan.douglas-adams**

See **Humor: Douglas Adams** *for a review.*

Deus Ex Machina: *Mystery Science Theater 3000*

Access: **http://128.194.15.32/~dml601a/mst3k/mst3k.html**

See **Television: Deus Ex Machina: Mystery Science Theater 3000** *for a review.*

Future Fantasy Bookstore

Access: **http://www.commerce.digital.com/palo-alto/FutureFantasy/home.html**

See **Books: Future Fantasy Bookstore** *for a review.*

Jayhawk

Access: **http://www.klab.caltech.edu/~flowers/jayhawk/**

See **Books: Jayhawk** *for a review.*

Sex

See also Erotica.

Condom Country

From the privacy of your computer screen, you can order from the largest assortment of condoms and other sex-related items for sale on the Internet. If that isn't private enough—if someone walks by, for instance—push a "privacy" button to instantly make the screen go blank. This catalog features the best-selling condoms in the U.S., Europe and Japan; click an order button to drop the item you want into your shopping bag. You'll also find related free features at the site, such as articles on how to use a condom, an archive of condom jokes, and government information on AIDS and STDs. —*ST*

Access: **http://www.ag.com/Condom/Country/**

The Condom Country Homepage

Howdy, pardners and welcome to **Condom Country**, home to the largest assortment of condoms and other below-the-belt-buck'l items on the Web. We sure hope you feel right at home here.

Meet all your "below-the-buckle" needs at Condom Country.
(Copyright 1994 The Access Group.)

Netsex

Do I really need to describe this channel, folks?:-) Perhaps I need a new emoticon or two to make the proper impression here! Of course, on #netsex, creative use of symbols can certainly be a plus. Then again, some people don't like all that mushy stuff like

@)->>->— virtual roses; if so, you can always try that on #romance or #singles instead. —*DR*

Access: Run IRC client, specifying desired IRC server, *OR* telnet to a telnettable server; do command **/join #netsex**

Truth or Dare

"An Adult Game of Truth or Dare" is the channel's own description of this IRC version of the T-or-D game, popularized (or was it invented?) by the ongoing wake of Madonna-mania. A refresher on the rules: when someone calls on you, you're asked, "Truth or dare?" Answer "truth" and you will be given a question that you are expected to answer truthfully. Answer "dare" and you will be given a task that you will be expected to complete. After your answer or completed dare, it is your turn to pick someone and ask them, "Truth or dare?" This channel seems the perfect place for this game, with many users probably feeling less inhibited in their confessions and other verbal offerings than they would face-to-face (let alone face-to-Madonna in a black-and-white sultry setting). Fun for those who don't think risqué is a four-letter word. —*DR*

Access: Run IRC client, specifying desired IRC server, *OR* telnet to a telnettable server; do command **/join #netsex**

Chatting in the Hot Tub

Access: Run IRC client, specifying desired IRC server, *OR* telnet to a telnettable server; do command **/join #hottub**

See **Chat: Chatting in the Hot Tub** *for a review.*

SHOPPING

Downtown Anywhere

Enter a virtual city where you can "sell anything worth selling and buy anything worth buying." If you're a business owner, find out how you can purchase "real estate" in Downtown Anywhere. If you're just shopping, go to Main Street, the commercial center of the virtual city. There you can buy books, software, video games, videos, music and more. There's even a Downtown Anywhere souvenir shop. Downtown Anywhere offers many public services as well, including a library, newsstand, educational resources, a financial district and a sports arena, all with links to useful Internet resources. —*ST*

Access: **http://www.awa.com/**

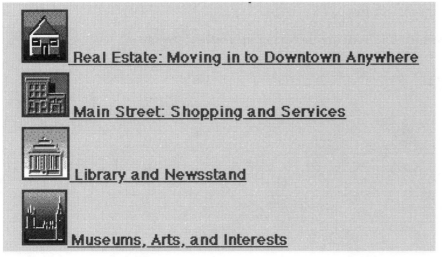

Buy real estate, go shopping or visit libraries and museums in Downtown Anywhere.

FringeWare

FringeWare is a company and Net-based community dedicated to creating an alternative marketplace for goods and services offered by Net citizens. They publish a catalog of hard-to-find software, hardware and cybercultural curios, and two magazines: *FringeWare Review* and *Unshaved Truths*. They also maintain an Internet-wide mailing list and discussion groups on cyberculture and alternative economics. —*GB*

Access: **http://io.com/commercial/fringeware/home.html**

The Global City

The Global City is a virtual community in itself, with a marketplace and newspaper available to users. Users can access the Global City Dispatch, an electronic newspaper of telecommunications, networking, Internet and World Wide Web news. You can also wander through the Global City marketplace. Visit a variety of stores to purchase books, Internet services, consulting services and computers. Storefronts lead into graphical catalogs where you can order products interactively, get company profiles, send comments, view a product line and find out what's new. To use the Global City, you must register (it's free). —*ST*

Access: **http://kaleidoscope.bga.com/km/KM_top.html**

Enter a virtual city of news and shops at the Global City.

The Internet Mall

A budding commercial Net enterprise with several dozen "stores" selling media items, personal items, computer wares, books and various services. —*GB*

Access: **http://www.kei.com/internet-mall.html**

Internet Shopping Network

Now you can "shop till you drop" at the virtual mall! On the leading edge of Net commercialization, the Internet Shopping Network offers a way to electronically shop for just about anything your heart desires. To get started, send them your credit card number and they send you an ISN password. After that, you find what you want, grab the virtual goods and the real-world equivalents are delivered to your door. I couldn't find the commemorative *Star Trek: The Next Generation* Borg plates, but I'm sure they're here somewhere. —*GB*

Access: **http://shop.internet.net/**

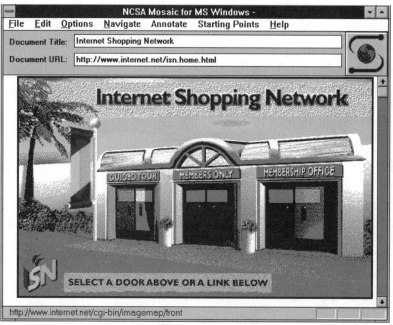

You don't need a parking spot to shop the Internet Shopping Network.

MarketPlace.com

Another burgeoning commercial site on the Internet. MarketPlace.com wants to offer the Internet community a convenient and useful online shopping environment. So far they have about eight "storefronts" occupied. —*GB*

Access: **http://marketplace.com/**

Nine Lives Consignment Clothing

The only consignment store on the Internet, here you can shop a large inventory of pre-owned, name-brand clothing. Use an interactive form to browse the entire inventory or "hire" a personal shopping assistant; an interactive form lets you create your own clothing profile and then have your computer do your shopping. You'll also find here a tour of the real store in photographs and information on how to sell clothing on consignment. The store is open only special hours—Monday through Friday, 11:00–2:00 Pacific time—so be sure to get there before it closes. —*ST*

Access: **http://chezhal.slip.netcom.com/index.html**

Unraveling the URL

Most of the Internet resources reviewed in this book are identified by URLs (Uniform Resource Locators), a standardized addressing system designed to be used with Web browsing software (such as Ventana Mosaic, included on the CD-ROM at the back of this book). URL addresses can refer to World Wide Web sites, which are accessed using the HyperText Transport Protocol (HTTP), as well as sites using other Internet protocols, including FTP, Gopher, telnet and newsgroups.

URL addresses consist of four parts: **protocol://hostname.domain:port/path**.

- The **protocol** indicates the type of site on which the resource is located.
- The **hostname.domain** is the Internet address of the site.
- The **port** is the numerical connection point where the server can be found. (The port is usually not necessary to include, since most protocols default to a specific port.)
- The **path** is the specific location of the resource. This might be a directory name, a file name, or both. (Some URLs include no path at all.)

The URL for the Ventana Online Visitor's Center home page looks like this:

http://www.vmedia.com:80/home.html

This tells us that the Visitor's Center home page is the file **home.html**, located at the World Wide Web site **www.vmedia.com**, port **80**.

Following are typical URLs for FTP, Gopher and telnet sites (note that you must have a telnet client properly installed and configured in order to initiate telnet sessions with Mosaic):

ftp://ftp.vmedia.com:21/pub/

gopher://gopher.vmedia.com:70/

telnet://kells.vmedia.com:23/

Newsgroup URLs look a little bit different: **news:newsgroup**. For example,

news:comp.infosystems.www

If you're not using Ventana Mosaic or another Web browser, simply translate the elements of a URL address into whatever format is appropriate for your client.

Vermont Teddy Bear Company

This catalog introduces you to a wonderful selection of teddy bears, perfect for any gift-giving occasion. Here you'll find special-occasion bears, such as for Mother's Day, birthdays, weddings or graduations. Also see bears suited to many different occupations, hobbies and sports. You can even order special limited-edition and other unique bears. A huge, full-color photo accompanies each bear's description. Read about how to send a Teddy Bear-gram as a gift to anyone anywhere. Then call the number provided to speak to a bear counselor and order your favorite bear. —*ST*

Access: **http://www.service.digital.com/tdb/vtdbear.html**

Find adorable bears like these at the Vermont Teddy Bear Company.

Condom Country

Access: **http://www.ag.com/Condom/Country/**

*See **Sex: Condom Country** for a review.*

Consumer News & Reviews

Access: **gopher://gopher.uiuc.edu/11/News/consumers**

See *Consumer Services: Consumer News & Reviews* for a review.

The Exploratorium

Access: **http://www.exploratorium.edu/**

See *Science: The Exploratorium* for a review.

Access: **gopher://gopher.exploratorium.edu**

See *Fun: The Exploratorium* for a review.

Future Fantasy Bookstore

Access: **http://www.commerce.digital.com/palo-alto/
FutureFantasy/home.html**

See *Books: Future Fantasy Bookstore* for a review.

Hot Hot Hot

Access: **http://www.presence.com:1235/H3/**

See *Food & Drink: Hot Hot Hot* for a review.

Internet Business Directory

Access: **http://ibd.ar.com/**

See *Business & Finance: Internet Business Directory* for a review.

List of Commercial Services on the Web

Access: **http://www.directory.net/**

See *Internet, World Wide Web: List of Commercial Services on the
Web* for a review.

Noteworthy Music

Access: **http://www.netmarket.com/**

See **Music: Noteworthy Music** *for a review.*

Sword & Crown

Access: **http://www.mcs.com/~sword/html/top.html**

See **Games: Sword & Crown** *for a review.*

Ventana Online

Access: **http://www.vmedia.com/**

See **Computers, Resources & Publications: Ventana Online** *for a review.*

Social Issues

An (Almost) Complete Privacy Toolkit

This comprehensive review by Robert Luhn originally appeared in the *Whole Earth Review* magazine. Do you want to be left alone? Do you want to know how to dig up any kind of dirt on anyone? Whether your motives are pure or dastardly, you'll find something of interest here. From books like *Steal This Urine Test: Fighting the Drug Hysteria in America* and *How to Get Anything on Anybody* to newsletters and reports like *Privacy Times* and *Genetic Monitoring and Screening in the Workplace*. Plus, ya get yer basic rundown of advocacy groups and resources such as the ACLU, Computer Professionals for Social Responsibility, and the Privacy Rights Clearinghouse Hotline. (Totally opinionated aside: Ignore these issues at your peril. One way or another, this stuff is going to shape our personal and professional lives in ever greater proportions.) —*JW*

Access: **gopher://gopher.well.sf.ca.us:70/0/WER/privacy.toolkit**

Anonymous Mail

The anon.penet.fi anonymous server lets you post to newsgroups and send email anonymously and without charge. When you send your first message to the server, it automatically allocates an ID for you. You may then use this ID in all your subsequent anonymous posts or mailings, and any mail sent to your anonymous address gets redirected to your real address. Johan Helsingius runs the anon.penet.fi server from Finland with the following disclaimer: "...remember this is a service that some people (in groups such as alt.sexual.abuse.recovery) *need*." This is a voluntary service, administered by a lone person in a faraway land. Keep that in mind if no one answers when you send your sign-up message. To find out more, send email to anon.penet.fi with the word "help" in the message field. —*TL*

Access: to subscribe, send email to **help@anon.penet.fi**

Children, Youth & Family Consortium Clearinghouse

We still don't get it—family is the only issue. Whatever's happening in our society, good or bad, is happening because of people who used to be children and were raised in some sort of family. We can't start talking about a lack of ethics in government without looking at our entire culture. Explore the gamut of family-related issues here—the figure below shows the main menu for this important site. —*JW*

Access: **gopher://tinman.mes.umn.edu:80**

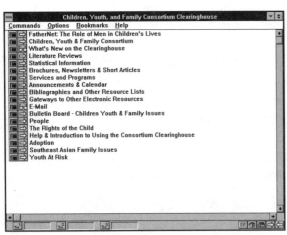

Main menu for the Children, Youth & Family Consortium Clearinghouse.

Cornucopia of Disability Information

We're working on it, but there's a lot more ground to cover when it comes to accepting people with disabilities. This Gopher has employment and educational resources, the latest legal and practical information on discrimination, information on independent living, and links to lots of related sites. —*JW*

Access: **gopher://val-dor.cc.buffalo.edu:70**

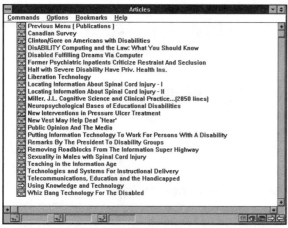

Get to these articles by choosing Publications/Articles from the Cornucopia of Disability Information Gopher.

Subscribing to Mailing Lists & Electronic Publications

To subscribe to a discussion list, send the following message from your email account:

subscribe \<list name> \<Your Name>

\<list name> is the name of the group. Send this message to the "to subscribe" address listed in the Access information. Include the message in the message section of the email, not in the subject line, because most listservers ignore the subject line. —*LAD*

S

Computer Professionals for Social Responsibility

Access: **gopher://locust.cic.net:70/11/CPSR**

See Technology: Computer Professionals for Social Responsibility for a review.

SOFTWARE

See Computers, Software; Macintosh; Microsoft Windows.

SPACE

NASA Explorations

Who knows how many satellites NASA has venturing through space? Actually, that information is in the public domain. Not only will you find the answer to the question there, but you'll also find a "jukebox" of 69 CD-ROMs of interstellar graphics taken by the *Magellen*, *Viking* and *Voyager* satellites. Many were snapped far from earth, some are in color, and all are breathtaking when you realize each one is the real thing. Investigate the CD-ROM directory. *—TL*

Access: **ftp://explorer.arc.nasa.gov/**

Though it looks like a painting, this is a Voyager *satellite photograph.*

Smithsonian Images

Access: **ftp://photo1.si.edu/images/**

See *Photography: Smithsonian Images* for a review.

Welcome to the Planets

Access: **http://stardust.jpl.nasa.gov/planets/**

See *Astronomy: Welcome to the Planets* for a review.

SPORTS

Aquanaut

Whether you're an avid diver or live near the ocean, this site is for you. You can find information about dive agencies and clubs, diving gear, Nitrox and an image library. This site also features a wreck database to find out more about shipwrecks you might want to explore. —*LAD*

Access: **gopher://gopher.opal.com:70/11/aquanaut**

The Nando X Baseball Server

The Nando X Baseball Server contains baseball news, commentary, box scores, history, graphics and even videos. —*GB*

Access: **http://www.nando.net/baseball/bbserv.html**

Welcome to the Baseball Server

Welcome to the Nando X Baseball Server.

S

Sports Schedules

Find out when your favorite team is playing next and who they're playing. You can find out when, where and which teams are playing in the National Basketball Association, the National Hockey League, Major League Baseball and the National Football League. You can also find out team schedules. Just telnet to the listed port and type in the abbreviation of your team or division. —*LAD*

Access: **telnet://culine.colorado.edu:port/** where port is
> **859** for the NBA
> **860** for the NHL
> **862** for MLB
> **863** for the NFL

SurfNet

Open a window to the world's beaches on your computer. Access the latest surfcasts and swell predictions, plus all sorts of other reports, like marine forecasts, wave heights and water temperatures. Satellite views of the West Coast show you where the surf is highest. A body boarding archive features photos and a dictionary of surf-speak. You'll also find a gallery of surfing photos and poetry, or check out the "wave of the day." Visit the beach without leaving your computer through a live video feed of the ocean from Carlsbad, California. —*ST*

Access: **http://sailfish.peregrine.com/surf/surf.html**

The surf is always up at SurfNet.

World Wide Web of Sports

Come to this site for all the sports information you could ever need. Get in-depth coverage of football, basketball, baseball and hockey with schedules, drafts and video highlights of recent games. You'll also find soccer news, such as international game results, and cycling information, with Tour de France reports. Link to other popular sports, like ultimate frisbee, volleyball, rugby, golf, running, rowing, figure and speed skating, and tennis. Or go to international games like the Olympics and the Goodwill Games. You can even create a personalized sports page using an interactive form to access only the sports information you're most interested in. —*ST*

Access: **http://tns-www.lcs.mit.edu/cgi-bin/sports/**

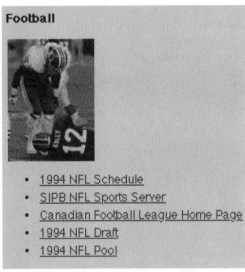

The World Wide Web of Sports links to an endless supply of sports scores and news.

The Global Cycling Network

Access: **gopher://cycling.org/**

See **Cycling: The Global Cycling Network** *for a review.*

USA Today Headline News, Sports, etc.

Access: **telnet://freenet-in-a.cwru.edu**
telnet://freenet-in-b.cwru.edu
telnet://freenet-in-c.cwru.edu
log in as **visitor**

See News: USA Today Headline News, Sports, etc. for a review.

Unraveling the URL

Most of the Internet resources reviewed in this book are identified by URLs (Uniform Resource Locators), a standardized addressing system designed to be used with Web browsing software (such as Ventana Mosaic, included on the CD-ROM at the back of this book). URL addresses can refer to World Wide Web sites, which are accessed using the HyperText Transport Protocol (HTTP), as well as sites using other Internet protocols, including FTP, Gopher, telnet and newsgroups.

URL addresses consist of four parts: **protocol://hostname.domain:port/path**.

- The **protocol** indicates the type of site on which the resource is located.
- The **hostname.domain** is the Internet address of the site.
- The **port** is the numerical connection point where the server can be found. (The port is usually not necessary to include, since most protocols default to a specific port.)
- The **path** is the specific location of the resource. This might be a directory name, a file name, or both. (Some URLs include no path at all.)

The URL for the Ventana Online Visitor's Center home page looks like this:

http://www.vmedia.com:80/home.html

This tells us that the Visitor's Center home page is the file **home.html**, located at the World Wide Web site **www.vmedia.com**, port **80**.

Following are typical URLs for FTP, Gopher and telnet sites (note that you must have a telnet client properly installed and configured in order to initiate telnet sessions with Mosaic):

ftp://ftp.vmedia.com:21/pub/
gopher://gopher.vmedia.com:70/
telnet://kells.vmedia.com:23/

Newsgroup URLs look a little bit different: **news:newsgroup**. For example,

news:comp.infosystems.www

If you're not using Ventana Mosaic or another Web browser, simply translate the elements of a URL address into whatever format is appropriate for your client.

STAR TREK

Star Trek Home Page

Access a ton of archived information on both the original *Star Trek* and *The Next Generation*, including MPEG clips, still images and sounds. Complete episode guides for all televison series and movies (even the animated series) are linked in. You'll also turn up gems like *SF-Lovers Digest*, a quick reference guide and humorous synopses. Learn facts on vessels, charted worlds, guest characters and known races in the Star Trek universe. You can also read original parodies, Star Trek jokes and top-ten lists, as well as a collection of original stories on the "third generation." —*ST*

Access: **http://www.cosy.sbg.ac.at/rec/startrek/index.html**

Star Trek Email Game

Access: to subscribe, send email to **listserv@gitvm1.gatech.edu**

Send messages to **stargame@gitvm1.gatech.edu**

*See **Games: Star Trek Email Game** for a review.*

STATISTICS

CIA World Factbook

Access: **gopher://sunny.stat-usa.gov:70/11/NTDB/Wofact**

*See **Reference: CIA World Factbook** for a review.*

Department of Commerce Database

Access: **gopher://gopher.stat-usa.gov/**

*See **Business & Finance: Department of Commerce Database** for a review.*

U.S. Census Bureau Home Page

Access: **http://www.census.gov/**

See Government, U.S.: U.S. Census Bureau Home Page for a review.

TECHNOLOGY

Computer Professionals for Social Responsibility

Computer Professionals for Social Responsibility promotes the responsible use of information technology. It directs public attention to critical issues concerning the power and application of computers, and how computers affect society. At its Gopher archive, learn all about the organization, with access to membership forms, email lists of members and so forth. You'll also find relevant documents, including federal and state bills affecting information technology, information on computer crime and security, articles covering intellectual property and privacy issues, and the National Information Infrastructure policy. A search feature allows you to quickly locate the newest additions to the archive. *—ST*

Access: **gopher://locust.cic.net:70/11/CPSR**

Digital Future

Access: **gopher://marketplace.com/11/fyi**

*See Magazines & Publications: **Digital Future** for a review.*

EFFector Online

Access: **gopher://gopher.eff.org/00/about.eff**

See Cyberculture: EFFector Online for a review.

Electronic Frontier Foundation

Access: **gopher://gopher.eff.org/00/about.eff**

*See **Cyberculture: Electronic Frontier Foundation** for a review.*

TELEPHONY

Telephony Newsgroup

Telephony—communication via wires, including telephone and TV cable lines—is probably the most fluid and consequential technology of our time, and the **comp.dcom.telecom** moderated newsgroup is a vital source of relevant information. —*TL*

Access: **news:comp.dcom.telecom**

TELEVISION

C-SPAN

At this site, you can find out all about the C-SPAN networks on cable. You can browse the programming schedules and read FAQs and press releases regarding C-SPAN. You can also look through information about C-SPAN publications and how to get program transcripts. —*LAD*

Access: **gopher://c-span.org/**

The Complete TV Guide

The ultimate online television resource will link you to your favorite shows on the Internet. An interactive feature lets you post your favorite TV links while removing everybody else's dull links, resulting in the hottest list of TV resources. A top-of-the-ratings page highlights creative, innovative and entertaining TV sites you might have missed. The comprehensive TV guide features "cards" for every TV show on the Internet, which typically link to episode guides, newsgroups, FAQs, mailing-list archives, WWW pages and sound or film clip archives. This great resource makes channel surfing easy. —*ST*

Access: **http://www.galcit.caltech.edu:80/~ta/tv/**

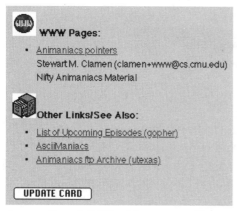

Access "cards" like this one on all your favorite television shows at the Complete TV Guide.

Deus Ex Machina: *Mystery Science Theater 3000*

Deux Ex Machina is a meta-home page linking all of the Web-accessible documents about the popular TV show *Mystery Science Theater 3000*. Animations, MST3K newsletters, pictures, sounds, show schedules, etc., are all available through this gateway. You'll be astonished by how many sites around the Internet have MST3K-related material. —*GB*

Access: **http://128.194.15.32/~dml601a/mst3k/mst3k.html**

A picture from the popular TV show Mystery Science Theater 3000.

Film & Television Reviews

If you've ever wondered what people on the Internet think about your favorite TV show or movie, this is the place to go. This site includes links to information about current hits and cult classics. You can find the song of "Brave and Bold Sir Robin" or read about *90210. —LAD*

Access: **gopher://english-server.hss.cmu.edu:70/ 11ftp%3aEnglish%20Server%3aFilm%26TV%3a** *OR* **gopher://english-server.hss.cmu.edu/** then follow the directory **Film and Television**

Three Stooges

Interested in Stooge trivia? Or just looking for the name of that one episode? Here Stooge fans discuss episodes and trivia and fight over their favorite Stooge. You can also find out where to pick up your favorite hard-to-find videos. *—LAD*

Access: **news:alt.comedy.slapstick.3-stooges**

Public Broadcasting System

Access: **gopher://gopher.pbs.org:70**

See Education, Resources: Public Broadcasting System for a review.

Star Trek Home Page

Access: **http://www.cosy.sbg.ac.at/rec/startrek/index.html**

See Star Trek: Star Trek Home Page for a review.

Vanderbilt Television News Archive

Access: **gopher://tvnews.vanderbilt.edu:70**

See News: Vanderbilt Television News Archive for a review.

Warner Brothers Central

Access: **news:alt.animation.warner-bros**

*See **Animation: Warner Brothers Central** for a review.*

TRAVEL

Arctic Adventours, Inc.

Have you dreamed of sailing to the Arctic? Or are you just craving adventure? Then visit Arctic Adventours, where you can read about adventure tour packages and even book reservations. Many different expeditions are available, such as whale safaris, mountaineering, fishing and cave paintings; all trips are described in detail and enhanced by photos. The online site provides the latest information available about destinations, prices and availability. After reading through the expedition descriptions, use an interactive form to request more information or book your trip. —ST

Access: **http://www.oslonett.no/html/adv/AA/AA.html**

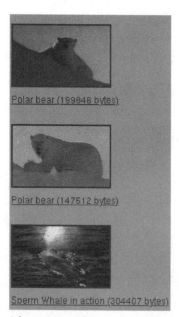

Polar bear (199846 bytes)

Polar bear (147512 bytes)

Sperm Whale in action (304407 bytes)

After seeing these photos, you won't be able to resist booking a trip to the Arctic.

Big Island of Hawaii

Visit Hawaii the multimedia way! An interactive map makes traveling around the island easy. For example, clicking on the Hawaii Volcanoes National Park takes you to the Visitor's Center, where you can get a crash course in geology or walk Devastation Trail. If you're most interested in scenery, access a repository of all the images at the site. If thoughts and impressions of Hawaii are what intrigue you, link into a directory of sound files recorded by the author. Or thumb through the tour guide, reading about Hawaii's land, people, sports and recreation, among many other subjects, all illustrated with color photos. —*ST*

Access: **http://bookweb.cwis.uci.edu:8042/Books/Moon/ moon.html**

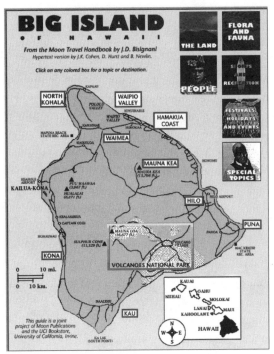

Virtually visit paradise through this interactive map of the Big Island of Hawaii.

London Information Guide

An in-depth guide to everything in London, this site is a must for exploration. Travel to London by air, land and rail using full-color maps. Or come in from orbit—a satellite photograph you can click on to zoom in closer to the city. For the tourist, there is a vast, full-color, interactive map that links to detailed information about historical sites. To get around, you'll probably have to take the subway. An innovative Tube Journey Planner Index helps you find the best route between two places on the London Underground using an interactive form. —ST

Access: **http://www.cs.ucl.ac.uk/misc/uk/london.html**

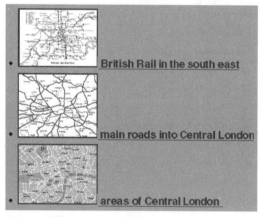

Many different maps help you get around town at the London Information Guide.

Moon Travel Handbooks

At this site you can find information about ordering the popular Moon Handbooks, as well as read the latest edition of the *Travel Matters* newsletter. (See Jan Weingarten's review below.) You can also find information about health when traveling abroad. —LAD

Access: **gopher://gopher.moon.com:7000/11/**

A Tourist Expedition to Antarctica

Sail to Antarctica through a combination of journal entries and full-color photos. Tour the cruise ship by viewing deck plans. Then proceed through the journal entries, either through a chronological index or index of geographical locations. A highlights section skips directly to the best parts of the trip, including landings at points of interest and surprising events while cruising. Or listen in on lectures given on board by eminent explorers and biologists. This rich site is a winner of the Best of the Web award for best educational resource. —*ST*

Access: **http://http2.sils.umich.edu/Antarctica/Story.html**

You feel like you've been transported to Antarctica through photographs like this one. (Copyright 1994 University of Michigan.)

Travel Information

A one-stop shop to some of the travel information found on the Net. Airline info, FAQs about tourism, specific information on countries and cities around the world, travel guides and newsletters. —*GB*

Access: **http://galaxy.einet.net/GJ/travel.html**

Travel Matters Newsletter

There is too a free lunch. Well, maybe not exactly, but if such an animal exists, your free subscription to Moon Publications' *Travel Matters* newsletter will no doubt fill you in on the details. Each quarterly issue focuses on a particular geographical area. The Winter 1995 issue zooms in on Mexico. You'll find an article on the importance of masks in Mexican professional wrestling, a traveler's tale of riding a Green Tortoise bus through Mexico, and information about immunizations. In every issue, you get book reviews, travel tips, and other goodies. Get your free subscription by calling 800/345-5473 or sending email to **travel@moon.com**. (Of course, you can always peruse the current issue online even if you don't have a subscription.) —JW

Access: **gopher://gopher.moon.com:7000/1h/travel.matters**

Travels With Samantha

This Best of the Web award-winner is an online travelogue about author Philip Greenspun's summer touring North America. As the trip progresses, the work becomes a retrospective of American people and places, illustrated along the way with maps and photos. The site features over 250 full-color photos taken during the trip, which can be viewed in their entirety through a "slide show." Who is Samantha? Samantha is the author's Mac PowerBook computer, used to record his journal. You can even send her email through an interactive form. —ST

Access: **http://www-swiss.ai.mit.edu/samantha/travels-with-samantha.html**

See America through photographs like these at Travels With Samantha.
(Reprinted with permission.)

U.S. State Department Travel Advisories

You can either search for the country you're traveling to, or see which countries currently have advisories. You can also find Consular Information Sheets provided by the State Department, which give you information about the country, what you need to enter it, the location of the American Embassy, medical and crime information, and much more. You shouldn't leave the country without knowing this information. —*LAD*

Access: **gopher://gopher.stolaf.edu/11/Internet%20Resources/ US-State-Department-Travel-Advisories**

Alternative access: **gopher://gopher.stolaf.edu/** and go into the **Internet Resources** folder, then the **US-State-Department- Travel-Advisories** folder.

Global Network Navigator

Access: **http://nearnet.gnn.com/gnn/gnn.html**

See **Internet, Resources: Global Network Navigator** *for a review.*

Guide to Australia

Access: **http://life.anu.edu.au/education/australia.html**

See **World Cultures: Guide to Australia** *for a review.*

The Jerusalem Mosaic

Access: **http://shum.cc.huji.ac.il/jeru/jerusalem.html**

See **World Cultures: The Jerusalem Mosaic** *for a review.*

Moscow Kremlin Online Excursion

Access: **http://www.kiae.su/www/wtr/kremlin/begin.html**

See **Russia: Moscow Kremlin Online Excursion** *for a review.*

The Official Touring Guide of New Brunswick

Access: http://www.cuslm.ca/tourist/welcome.html

See Canada: The Official Touring Guide of New Brunswick for a review.

Singapore Online Guide

Access: http://king.ncb.gov.sg/sog/sog.html

See World Cultures: Singapore Online Guide for a review.

Slovakia Document Store

Access: http://www.eunet.sk/slovakia/slovakia.html

See World Cultures: Slovakia Document Store for a review.

UNITED STATES

American South Home Page

This regional home page opens with some "mood music"—the "Dueling Banjos" sequence from *Deliverance*—as Elvis greets you. Here you'll find a variety of information on the South and southern culture. The highlight of this site is the Southern Historical Collection, where you should definitely pay a visit to the Doc Watson Multimedia Exhibit. There you can wander through an exhibit of photographs while listening to samples of Doc's music. Current satellite weather images of the Southeast region are also available here, and an interactive map connects directly to Internet resources and home pages by state. —*ST*

Access: **http://sunsite.unc.edu/doug_m/pages/south/south.html**

Unraveling the URL

Most of the Internet resources reviewed in this book are identified by URLs (Uniform Resource Locators), a standardized addressing system designed to be used with Web browsing software (such as Ventana Mosaic, included on the CD-ROM at the back of this book). URL addresses can refer to World Wide Web sites, which are accessed using the HyperText Transport Protocol (HTTP), as well as sites using other Internet protocols, including FTP, Gopher, telnet and newsgroups.

URL addresses consist of four parts: **protocol://hostname.domain:port/path**.

- The **protocol** indicates the type of site on which the resource is located.
- The **hostname.domain** is the Internet address of the site.
- The **port** is the numerical connection point where the server can be found. (The port is usually not necessary to include, since most protocols default to a specific port.)
- The **path** is the specific location of the resource. This might be a directory name, a file name, or both. (Some URLs include no path at all.)

The URL for the Ventana Online Visitor's Center home page looks like this:

http://www.vmedia.com:80/home.html

This tells us that the Visitor's Center home page is the file **home.html**, located at the World Wide Web site **www.vmedia.com**, port **80**.

Following are typical URLs for FTP, Gopher and telnet sites (note that you must have a telnet client properly installed and configured in order to initiate telnet sessions with Mosaic):

ftp://ftp.vmedia.com:21/pub/

gopher://gopher.vmedia.com:70/

telnet://kells.vmedia.com:23/

Newsgroup URLs look a little bit different: **news:newsgroup**. For example,

news:comp.infosystems.www

If you're not using Ventana Mosaic or another Web browser, simply translate the elements of a URL address into whatever format is appropriate for your client.

The Presidio

The full name of this site is The Presidio—Converting a Military Base to a Public Park. Snooze time? Not at all. At least not for me. I used to live a couple of blocks from the Presidio in San Francisco, wandered through it all the time, and I was not alone in grousing that the Army had a lock on some of the best land and views in the City (and a wonderful old pet cemetery). Now the U.S. Army is in the process of handing the Presidio over to the National Park Ser-

U

vice. At 2.5 percent of the area of San Francisco, it'll be the largest urban park ever converted from military use. Fascinating to read about the process, proposals from different groups vying for space, and everything it took to make this come together. —*JW*

Access: **gopher://gopher.well.sf.ca.us:70/1/Community/presidio**

Seattle USA

Okay, maybe you couldn't care less about Seattle. The point is, this is the kind of community-oriented site that will help shape the future of info access. It's a blend of community service and commercialism, and IMHO (in my humble opinion) has the potential to provide the best of both. I can get the current ferry schedules and find out which ferry is disabled (one of them always is). I can check out the local theater scene, learn about my local elected officials, and connect to the King County library system. And when I get hungry, I can order a box lunch from Larry's Market (superfantastic deli— almost enough to justify a trip to Seattle). Before you leave, don't forget your regular dose of Slugs. —*JW*

Access: **gopher://gopher.seattle.wa.us:70**

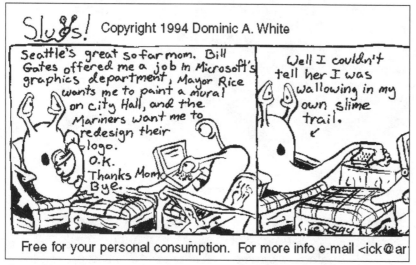

One of Seattle's many claims to fame. (Reprinted with permission.)

The African-American Mosaic

Access: **http://lcweb.loc.gov/exhibits/African.American/
intro.html**

*See **African-Americans: The African-American Mosaic** for a review.*

American Memory

Access: **http://rs6.loc.gov/amhome.html**

*See **History, U.S.: American Memory** for a review.*

Big Island of Hawaii

Access: **http://bookweb.cwis.uci.edu:8042/Books/Moon/
moon.html**

*See **Travel: Big Island of Hawaii** for a review.*

Children, Youth & Family Consortium Clearinghouse

Access: **gopher://tinman.mes.umn.edu:80**

*See **Social Issues: Children, Youth & Family Consortium Clearinghouse** for a review.*

Civil War History

Access: to subscribe, send email to **listserv@uicvm.uic.edu**

Send messages to **h-civwar@uicvm.uic.edu**

*See **History, U.S.: Civil War History** for a review.*

Friends & Partners

Access: **http://solar.rtd.utk.edu/friends/home.html**

*See **World Cultures: Friends & Partners** for a review.*

Historical Documents & Speeches

Access: **goher://dewey.ub.ncsu.edu:70/1/library/stacks/ historical-documents-us**

See History, World: Historical Documents & Speeches for a review.

Information From the White House

Access: **gopher://gopher.tamu.edu/11/.dir/president.dir**

See Government, U.S.: Information From the White House for a review.

National Archives

Access: **gopher://gopher.nara.gov/**

See History, U.S.: National Archives for a review.

Travels With Samantha

Access: **http://www-swiss.ai.mit.edu/samantha/travels-with-samantha.html**

See Travel: Travels With Samantha for a review.

U.S. Census Bureau Home Page

Access: **http://www.census.gov**

See Government, U.S.: U.S. Census Bureau Home Page for a review.

U.S. Government Hypertexts

Access: **http://sunsite.unc.edu/govdocs.html**

See Government, U.S.: U.S. Government Hypertexts for a review.

VIDEO

Art Links on the World Wide Web

Access: **http://amanda.physics.wisc.edu/outside.html**

See Art: Art Links on the World Wide Web for a review.

VIRTUAL REALITY

NCSA Virtual Reality Lab

The NCSA Virtual Reality Laboratory is a research facility exploring new methods of visualizing and interfacing with scientific data and simulations. The lab is located in the Beckman Institute for Advanced Science and Technology on the University of Illinois campus. The goal of the lab is to study and use improved methods of viewing and interacting with information. The VR Lab's Web site contains papers related to their research and project reports, with graphics and links to FTP sites, and USENET newsgroups devoted to virtual reality and other advanced imaging technologies. —*GB*

Access: **http://www.ncsa.uiuc.edu/VR/VR/VRHomePage.html**

UK VR-SIG

This site provides access to the UK Virtual Reality Special Interest Group (UK VR-SIG) and is a major link point to VR archives and discussion groups throughout the Internet. If you're interested in virtual reality, this is the place to go to connect with the VR community online. Get information on upcoming events, new research and development, and the latest software; view demos; and much more. —*GB*

Access: **http://pipkin.lut.ac.uk/WWWdocs/LUTCHI/people/ sean/vr-sig/vr-si.html**

Weather

Atmospheric Research Weather Images

Remember Hurricane Kevin way back in October of '91? If not, re-
fresh your memory by perusing the electronic weather map GIFs
under "Archives of Interesting Weather Happenings." This site's
main purpose in life is to allow the Unidata program to strut its
stuff. It provides weather data for teaching and research to universities and professors, and the pictures here are just samples. But even
for us non-U types, this site's definitely worth a gander. —*JW*

Access: **gopher://unidata.ucar.edu:70/1/Images**

NASA Earth Pix

Various earth-from-space images (GIF format) of the North American continent are available from NASA (the National Aeronautics
and Space Administration). Look in the /pub/space and pub/CD-
ROM directories. —*TL*

Access: **ftp://explorer.arc.nasa.gov/**

Northwestern Washington State, including
downtown Seattle and Puget Sound.

National Weather Service Reports

Ever wonder if you should take your umbrella on your next business trip or vacation? Now you can check out the weather and extended forecasts for the U.S., Canada and Puerto Rico. You can also find out about tropical storm forecasts if you're heading toward the ocean. —*LAD*

Access: **gopher://spinaltap.micro.umn.edu:70/11/Weather**

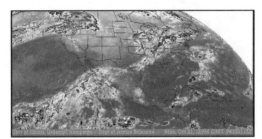

A satellite image of the U.S. from the National Weather Service Reports Gopher.

Satellite Pictures & Forecasts

For the latest satellite images and forecasts, FTP to early **bird.think.com** and look in the directory **/pub/weather/maps/**. Most of the images there are in GIF format.

Access: **ftp://early-bird.think.com/pub/weather/maps/**

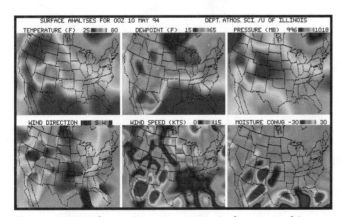

*Temperature, dewpoint, pressure, winds—everything you need to know about the weather every day at **early-bird.think.com**. (These images are posted in color.)*

Sources of Meterological Data

The "Sources of Meteorological Data" FAQ lists hundreds of meteorological sources. Look for the file **weather/data/part1** in the directory **/pub/usenet/news.answers**. The FAQ is also posted every two weeks in the **sci.geo.meteorology, news.answers** and **sci.answers** newsgroups. These sources are constantly changing and new sources appear as unique weather conditions warrant. —*TL*

Access: **ftp://rtfm.mit.edu/**

Weather Underground

A telnet (menu-driven, textual) resource that's especially rich and easy to use is the Weather Underground at the University of Michigan. Forecasts and climatic data are available for all U.S. cities with three-letter airport codes, and for all U.S. states. This site can be busy, and only 100 connections are accepted at a time. Try again if your first attempt fails. —*TL*

Access: **telnet://downwind.sprl.umich.edu:3000/**

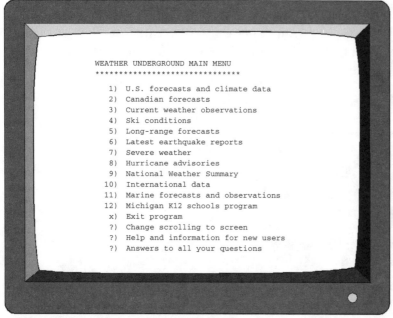

```
WEATHER UNDERGROUND MAIN MENU
********************************

    1)  U.S. forecasts and climate data
    2)  Canadian forecasts
    3)  Current weather observations
    4)  Ski conditions
    5)  Long-range forecasts
    6)  Latest earthquake reports
    7)  Severe weather
    8)  Hurricane advisories
    9)  National Weather Summary
   10)  International data
   11)  Marine forecasts and observations
   12)  Michigan K12 schools program
    x)  Exit program
    ?)  Change scrolling to screen
    ?)  Help and information for new users
    ?)  Answers to all your questions
```

The Weather Underground main menu.

Guide to Australia

Access: **http://life.anu.edu.au/education/australia.html**

*See **World Cultures: Guide to Australia** for a review.*

Women

Women's Wire

Women's Wire is a service provider focusing on the information and networking needs of women. Its Gopher server includes information about health, jobs and politics for women. You can also browse essays and speeches dealing with women's issues. —*LAD*

Access: **gopher://gopher.wwire.net/**

World Cultures

Guide to Australia

Numerous subjects are covered in this hypertext encyclopedia about Australia, but don't miss some of the highlights. Learn the history of the national flag and other Australian flags, including the Aboriginal flag, with accompanying illustrations. Interactive and static maps of the continent provide geographical information. Download travel information, such as airline timetables and U.S. State Department information. Telnet to the Bureau of Meteorology for the latest weather forecast. Even get earthquake reports or learn about vegetation monitoring from satellite. Other subjects covered include news, community, environment and government, creating a handy, all-in-one guide. —*ST*

Access: **http://life.anu.edu.au/education/australia.html**

Cultures Newsgroup

Looking for more information about one of the many cultures in our world? A multitude of information can be found in the **soc.culture.*** newsgroups. You can join in on discussions ranging from Afghanistan to Yugoslavia, and everywhere in between. —*LAD*

Access: **news:soc.culture.***

Friends & Partners

This site provides a "meeting place" for the U.S. and Russia. To learn more about this experimental project, stop in the Global Lecture Hall for a slide presentation accompanied by a recorded talk. An interactive map links to information collected from all over the Internet. Other gems to explore include listening to selections from the Slavyanka Men's Slavic Chorus CD or studying Russian with audio examples. End your visit by spending some leisurely time in the interactive coffee house to talk with other visitors. —*ST*

Access: **http://solar.rtd.utk.edu/friends/home.html**

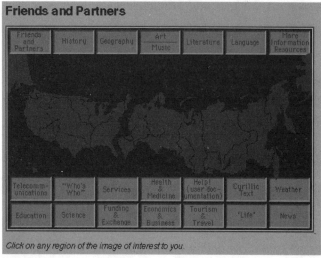

The United States and Russia are linked through this interactive map.

The Jerusalem Mosaic

Enter one of the world's most venerated cities through one of four "gates," each featuring a different way to explore Jerusalem. The "Faces of Jerusalem" gate opens into a collection of photos of the ethnic and cultural mix of people who call Jerusalem home. Access a collection of maps made through the ages at the "Maps of Jerusalem" gate. Go through the "Views of Jerusalem" gate to see the city from all angles. The "Paintings of Jerusalem" gate leads to 20 paintings, each illustrating a different artistic outlook on the city. —*ST*

Access: **http://shum.cc.huji.ac.il/jeru/jerusalem.html**

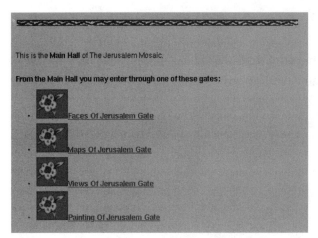

The gates of Jerusalem offer four virtual entranceways to the city.

Singapore Online Guide

Take a customized tour of Singapore using the Interactive Tour Agent, an innovative feature found at this site. Fill out a form detailing when you want to visit, how long you will stay and what you are most interested in seeing. Send the form off and within seconds you get back a personalized tour guide of Singapore, with a schedule that you can follow in the time frame of your visit. The guide tells you what to see and do, and gives useful information on subjects ranging from feasting to formalities. When you're finished, don't forget to fill out the feedback form; you might receive a free gift! —*ST*

Access: **http://king.ncb.gov.sg/sog/sog.html**

Slovakia Document Store

This site opens with the statement, "There's something to be said about being number two." This attitude makes the Slovakia home page a fun place to explore with very few pretensions. Don't miss the picture tour around Slovakia called "The Eye of the Beholder." An interactive map links to photographs (including satellite images) and brief histories of different places in Slovakia. To tour the capital, use the Bratislava Navigator, which provides maps, listings of theaters, galleries and museums, and a picture tour of the city. —*ST*

Access: **http://www.eunet.sk/slovakia/slovakia.html**

Brit Chat

Access for #England IRC channel: Run IRC client, specifying desired IRC server, *OR* telnet to a telnettable server; do command **/join #England**

Access for #England WWW home page: **http://www.fer.uni-lj.si/ ~iztok/england.html**

*See **England: Brit Chat** for a review*

Global Chat

There are a number of very popular chat channels devoted to various nationalities. In addition to **Brit Chat** (reviewed in the **England** section) and **Russian Chat** (listed in the **Russia** section), some of the most active are #viet, #korea, #hk (hong kong, I presume), #taiwan, #aussie or #australia, #sweden, #germany, #francais and #francaise, and #europe (for that unified feeling). Naturally I cannot list them all, and some may not use English as the primary language, but if you get out a (recent!) globe, it'll be the next best thing to a real world tour. —*DR*

Russian Chat

Access: Run IRC client, specifying desired IRC server, *OR* telnet to a telnettable server; do command **/join #russian**

See **Russia: Russian Chat** *for a review.*

Smithsonian Images

Access: **ftp://photo1.si.edu/images/**

See **Photography: Smithsonian Images** *for a review.*

Unraveling the URL

Most of the Internet resources reviewed in this book are identified by URLs (Uniform Resource Locators), a standardized addressing system designed to be used with Web browsing software (such as Ventana Mosaic, included on the CD-ROM at the back of this book). URL addresses can refer to World Wide Web sites, which are accessed using the HyperText Transport Protocol (HTTP), as well as sites using other Internet protocols, including FTP, Gopher, telnet and newsgroups.

URL addresses consist of four parts: **protocol://hostname.domain:port/path**.

- The **protocol** indicates the type of site on which the resource is located.
- The **hostname.domain** is the Internet address of the site.
- The **port** is the numerical connection point where the server can be found. (The port is usually not necessary to include, since most protocols default to a specific port.)
- The **path** is the specific location of the resource. This might be a directory name, a file name, or both. (Some URLs include no path at all.)

The URL for the Ventana Online Visitor's Center home page looks like this:

http://www.vmedia.com:80/home.html

This tells us that the Visitor's Center home page is the file **home.html**, located at the World Wide Web site **www.vmedia.com**, port **80**.

Following are typical URLs for FTP, Gopher and telnet sites (note that you must have a telnet client properly installed and configured in order to initiate telnet sessions with Mosaic):

ftp://ftp.vmedia.com:21/pub/

gopher://gopher.vmedia.com:70/

telnet://kells.vmedia.com:23/

Newsgroup URLs look a little bit different: **news:newsgroup**. For example,

news:comp.infosystems.www

If you're not using Ventana Mosaic or another Web browser, simply translate the elements of a URL address into whatever format is appropriate for your client.

ZINES

See also Magazines & Publications.

Bad Subjects

Bad Subjects is an Internet magazine of nonacademic articles and responses to those articles. You can read the first 16 issues or search the articles by topic. You can also find out how to submit articles to be published in subsequent issues. —*LAD*

Access: **gopher://english-server.hss.cmu.edu/** then follow the Bad Subjects link

bOING bOING

bOING bOING has brazenly dubbed itself The World's Greatest Neurozine. In its quarterly print form it covers the wild and wacky fringes of pop and cyberculture. The new *bOING bOING* Online features an art gallery (mainly of comic art), articles from past issues and online exclusives. Excerpts from *bOING bOING*'s first book, *The Happy Mutant Handbook* (Putnam/Berkeley, 1995), will soon be appearing online. —*GB*

Access: **http://www.zeitgeist.net/public/Boing-boing/bbw3/ boing.boing.html**

Stroll through bOING bOING*'s art gallery.*

Hypermedia Zine List

Zines (small, do-it-yourself publications on any topic of interest) have moved onto the Net. But, like their tiny-circulation print cousins, electronic zines (or e-zines) can be incredibly hard to find. Luckily, there's a one-stop shop for electronic zine access: the Hypermedia Zine List. The list also includes links to USENET newsgroups about zines, other zine archives and even a list of zines that are readable on the Web. —GB

Access: **http://www.acns.nwu.edu/ezines/**

International Teletimes

This general-interest zine presents informed opinion and observation drawn from the experience of living in a particular place, raising a global awareness and general knowledge of different lifestyles. Each issue of the zine covers a specific theme; some recent themes have been favorite authors, travel, TV and film, history and the environment. All back issues are archived by subject so that you can connect to what most interests you. You can also follow regular columns on cuisine and wine, as well as creative-writing selections. —ST

Access: **http://www.wimsey.com/teletimes.root/ teletimes_home_page.html**

Read about people and places all over the Internet in International Teletimes. (Copyright 1994 International Teletimes.)

Z

Intertext

Intertext is an electronically distributed magazine of fiction read by thousands of people on six continents. You'll find in the magazine a large selection of original fiction, as well as regular columns from the editor and assistant editor. At the World Wide Web site, you can read the current issue or access back issues from a volume library. You can also choose specific stories from a list arranged by author. Use an interactive form at the site to subscribe for notices of new and upcoming issues. Don't miss this best-established of all the Internet fiction e-zines. —*ST*

Access: **http://ftp.etext.org/Zines/InterText/intertext.html**

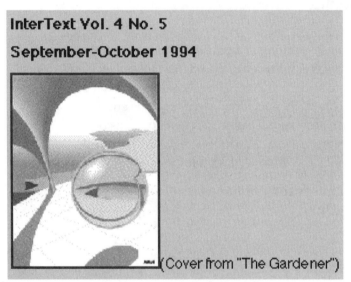

InterText Vol. 4 No. 5

September-October 1994

(Cover from "The Gardener")

Read the best original fiction on the World Wide Web at Intertext. (Artwork copyright 1994 Jeff Quan.)

Literary E-Journals

This Gopher archive indexes several literary electronic magazines, published and distributed solely through the Internet. Offerings here include *Locus*, the newspaper of the science-fiction field; *Powderkeg*, a literary magazine formatted to retain the "look" of printed magazines; and *Random Access Humor* and *Schidt*, humor zines. You'll also find a variety of poetry, creative writing and essay offerings in zines with titles like *Electronic Antiquity, Blooball* and *Toxic Custard Workshop Files.* Explore the peculiar world of electronic zine publishing through this archive. —*ST*

Access: **gopher://gopher.cic.net:70/11/e-serials/general/literature**

Stream of Consciousness

Each issue of this Web-based experimental poetry zine consists of several visual poems stored as GIF or JPEG files. The reader clicks on the inline image of the poem that interests them and it's launched as an external image. Although this publication is new (only three issues so far), and the work represented is hit and miss, the idea behind has potential. If you're interested in visual poetry and experimental writing, you might want to check this site out and get involved in its evolution. —*GB*

Access: **http://kzsu.stanford.edu/uwi/soc.html**

3W: The Internet With Attitude

This WWW magazine publishes useful articles on networking, the Internet, service providers, software, the WWW, electronic publishing, multimedia and Internet resources. Regular features include information for beginning Internet users and WWW coverage. One unique feature is Internet A–Z, an alphabet of Internet resources covering every subject in-depth. Although available by subscription only, you can sample articles at this site. Also be sure to follow the "value-added" link for free goodies such as a list of e-zines, letters from the Internet and other Internet-related articles. —*ST*

Access: **http://www.3W.com/3W/index.html**

Zines Newsgroup

The ultimate reference to zines both electronic and conventional is the newsgroup alt.zines. Here you'll find everything from subscription offers for traditional (mailed paper) zines, Internet mailing-list zines, zines in Windows Help format, zines in PostScript format

Z

and zines in Macintosh TeachText format. You'll also find the zine-scene invertebrate life-forms here (which are often the best): the text-only zines, which are often posted directly to the newsgroup. —*TL*

Access: **news:alt.zines**

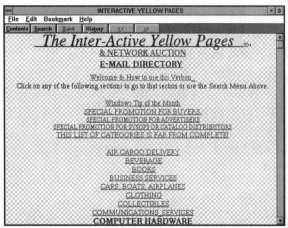

The Inter-Active Yellow Pages, a Windows Help-format zine containing listings for resources popular in the computing community.

Cyberpoet's Guide to Virtual Culture

Access: **http://128.230.38.86/cgvc/cgvc1.html**

See **Cyberculture: Cyberpoet's Guide to Virtual Culture** *for a review.*

ZOOLOGY

The Electronic Zoo

The Electronic Zoo is a comprehensive list of Internet resources about animals. You can find links or resources based on the tool you use to access the information. The Electronic Zoo also features search capabilities. —*LAD*

Access: **gopher://netvet.wustl.edu:70/11n%3a/e-zoo**

Smithsonian Natural History Archive

Access: **gopher://nmnhgoph.si.edu/**

See **Natural History: Smithsonian Natural History Archive** for *a review.*

Appendix: Mosaic & the World Wide Web

"Surfing the Net" has become a cliché for describing many kinds of Internet activities. The World Wide Web (WWW) takes the analogy a step further. Using what are called *hypertext links*, you can jump from topic to topic, finding information, files, pictures, sounds and even movies, all with a single click of your mouse.

Internet Roadside Attractions readers can take advantage of the Web and its revolutionary features. Ventana Mosaic, included on the CD-ROM bundled in the back of the book, is one of the best software tools for exploring the power of the World Wide Web. Both the Windows and Mac versions of Ventana Mosaic are available on the companion CD-ROM. A little later in this appendix, you'll get some hands-on experience using Mosaic, but first a little more background on the World Wide Web itself.

What Is the World Wide Web?

Created in 1989 by CERN, the European Center for Particle Physics in Switzerland, the World Wide Web is an online hypertext system spanning most of the Internet. The concept of *hypertext* (nonlinear textual presentation) was first promoted by computing theorist Ted Nelson in the early 1960s. Nelson's vision called for a global information structure that users could browse at will, freely investigating cross-referenced material. Typically, in a hypertext document the reader clicks a highlighted word or phrase (a *hotlink*) to access associated information that may be contained in the same file or in another file thousands of miles away.

The World Wide Web is a system of documents (called pages), linked together by a hypertext format. For instance, if you were reading a Web page on Rocky and Bullwinkle, and you noticed that a paragraph referred to the occasional appearance of Dudley Doright in the series, the words *Dudley Doright* might appear in a different color (usually blue) and underlined.

Clicking anywhere on *Dudley Doright* would take you to a related page that might give you the history or a personal profile of Dudley, and maybe a few pictures or a QuickTime movie of the hero.

These links also work to automate the FTP process. If you wanted to download a movie of Dudley in action from the Web, you would be able to do it easily. Instead of logging into **ftp.hanna.barbera.com** and navigating to the **pub/mounties/canadian/heroic** directory, you would just click on a picture of Dudley or the words describing that particular movie file. The file is then automatically FTPed, or transferred, to your system.

If that were all (and it's not), WWW would be a wonderful thing. But the list of Amazing Stupendous Things That WWW Does goes on. You can use the Web to search for information via Gopher or WAIS. Most of the pages have embedded pictures that you can view while you read the page, and some even include QuickTime movies or sound.

The combination of text, still images, sound and motion pictures (or video) is commonly referred to as *multimedia*. This type of presentation has become popular in education and corporate training environments, as it presents information in an interesting and entertaining format. Educators and trainers know the power of multimedia to speed learning and increase retention levels.

The combination of hypertext and multimedia, presented in a browsing context, is what is commonly defined as *hypermedia*. When we click on embedded graphics, video and sound objects in a compound-document Web page, we are fulfilling Ted Nelson's predictions for the future of global information systems. The current popularity of the World Wide Web attests to the lasting power of Nelson's concepts.

The Web Analogy

The reason the WWW is a web, and not a cocoon, or knothole, or some other place an insect resides, is because the hypertext links form strands that connect the pages of the Web one to another. There may be hundreds of references to one document, and many other references from that page onward. The quickest route to a Web site is not necessarily a straight line, but the least number of links needed.

What Is Mosaic?

NCSA Mosaic, developed by the National Center for Supercomputing Applications at the University of Illinois, Urbana-Champaign, is a software "front end," or interface, used to access the World Wide Web. It was designed specifically to simplify navigation through the thousands (soon to be millions) of pages that constitute the Web. The software is free from NCSA, and can be downloaded via FTP at **ftp.ncsa.uiuc.edu**. The companion CD-ROM at the back of this book includes both Mac and Windows implementations of Ventana Mosaic, a version of Mosaic enhanced for commercial use. The latest version of the Ventana Mosaic software is always available from Ventana Online (**http://www.vmedia.com/**).

Browsing the Web With Mosaic

Mosaic will install from the companion CD-ROM with the other Internet applications. To start using it, just double-click the Mosaic icon when your Internet connection has been established. The first time you use Mosaic (and every time thereafter, until you set up a new home page), the introductory page will appear, as shown in Figure A-1.

Figure A-1: Ventana Mosaic's introductory page.

At this point, you really haven't connected to a location yet; the page shown in Figure A-1 actually resides on your hard drive rather than on the Web. Go to the File menu, select Open URL and enter the following into the text field:

**http://www.ncsa.uiuc.edu/SDG/Software/Mosaic/
NCSAMosaicHome.html**

Make sure you get the uppercase and lowercase right, and don't insert any spaces. Click the OK button. After a few seconds, the NCSA Mosaic home page should appear (see Figure A-2). Every Web server site has a *home page*, or main document. From this page you can jump to other resources by simply selecting the embedded hypertext links on the current page, indicated by colored, underlined text. If the home page doesn't appear, or you get a message saying that no connection could be made, make sure you are properly hooked up to the Internet either by modem or direct connection, and that the connection is active.

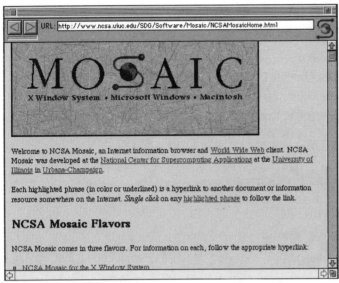

Figure A-2: The NCSA Mosaic home page.

So that you don't have to type in that long URL again, select Add current to hotlist from the Navigate menu. The next time you want to access the Mosaic home page, all you will have to do is select Hotlist from the Navigate menu (or just hit Command-H or Ctrl-H), choose NCSA Mosaic Home Page from the list itself, and click the Go To button. The hotlist is one of Mosaic's most powerful features, and you can add any URL to it that you'd like.

Navigating in the Document Window

"Pages" in Mosaic can be any length. You can scroll through a page by clicking on the up or down arrow on the scroll bar at the right of the page window. If you resize your window, the text will automatically reflow. To customize the size of the window, drag the bottom right square around until the window is the new size.

To move quickly up and down through a document, use the navigational keys on your keyboard: Home, End, Page Up and Page Down. Home will take you to the top of the page, End will take you to the bottom. Page Up will move you to the information above what you can currently see, while Page Down moves you down.

All About Links

Links are the core of the WWW. A link is a word or phrase (sometimes a picture) that connects you to another page. Mosaic allows you to traverse these links simply by clicking on these words or phrases. Links appear as underlined text (pictures usually have informative captions describing the link). Links that you haven't clicked on yet appear as blue; links that you have taken already appear as green.

Mosaic remembers the links you have chosen, so you can follow previously explored links like a trail of bread crumbs to pages you'd like to revisit.

A Quick Tour Through the Web

This section contains a sample trip of exploration through the World Wide Web that you can follow along with. The top of each new Web page (and lower sections where applicable) is shown so that you can be sure you're in the right place.

We'll start at the home page shown above. One of the best places to begin exploring is at the Starting Points for Internet Exploration link, shown in Figure A-3.

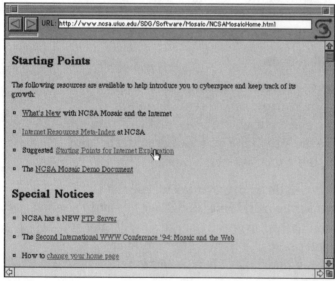

Figure A-3: The Starting Points for Internet Exploration link.

Click on the link. The bar or animated icon at the top of the
window will indicate that the program is retrieving information.
Shortly thereafter (the time it takes depends on your type of
connection), the Starting Points for Internet Exploration page will
appear, as shown in Figure A-4.

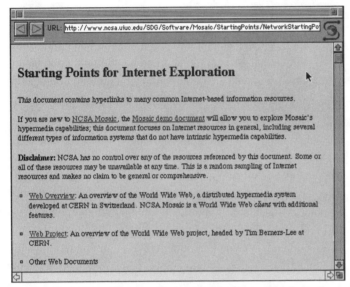

Figure A-4: The Starting Points for Internet Exploration page.

Scroll down this page just a little until you see the Information By
Subject link, shown in Figure A-5, and then click on that link.

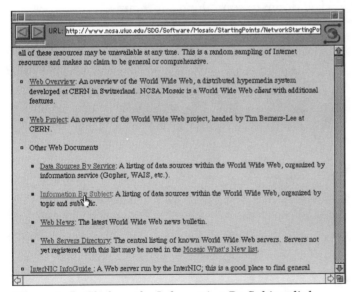

Figure A-5: Click on the Information By Subject link.

Once again, the bar or icon at the top will indicate that Mosaic is looking for the next page. When it appears, it should look like the page shown in Figure A-6.

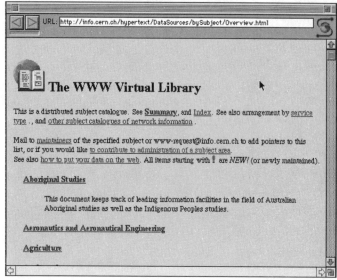

Figure A-6: The subject index of The WWW Virtual Library.

Once the page appears, take some time to scroll through the different subjects that are available. New categories are added all the time, so venture to this page as often as you can, looking for new entries. New entries are indicated by an exclamation point (!). In this particular case, let's scroll down to something fun: Games, shown in Figure A-7.

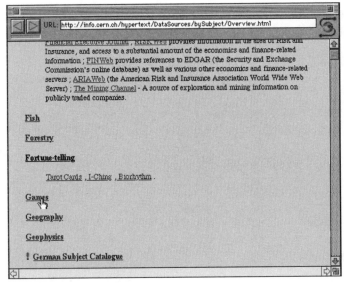

Figure A-7: The Games link.

Click on the link, and after a few seconds the Games and Recreation page will appear, as shown in Figure A-8.

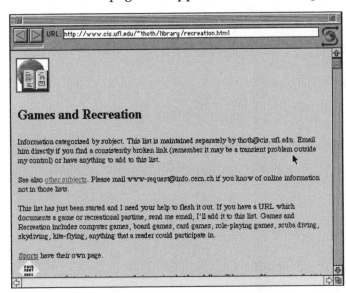

Figure A-8: The Games and Recreation page.

There are all sorts of categories and games, from computer games that can be played on the Internet to pages for card games, magic clubs and board games. Let's take a look at the Table Games section, specifically the link for the Foosball archive, shown in Figure A-9.

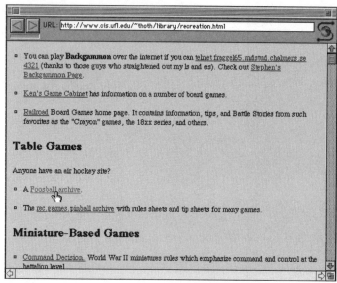

Figure A-9: The Foosball archive link.

Click on the Foosball archive link and the Foosball page will appear. This page contains a long list of files and subdirectories, as shown in Figure A-10.

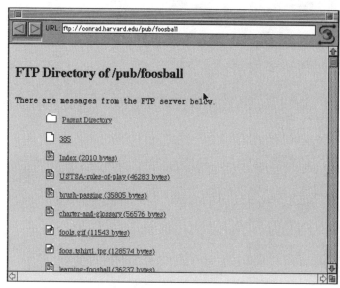

Figure A-10: The Foosball archive.

This page looks a bit different from the previous ones. That's because it is actually the directory listing from an FTP site. If you click on one of the files, it will be sent automatically to your computer using the FTP protocol that's built right into Mosaic.

But let's say you don't want to download one of these files. In fact, let's say you've just decided you're really not the slightest bit interested in foosball and would like to take a look at some of the other game options instead. To go back up a level, simply click the left arrow button near the top left corner of the window. You will be returned to the Games and Recreation page.

You can keep backtracking through all the pages you've seen using this button and click on new links at any point. Similarly, the right arrow button will move you *forward* through the pages you've already visited.

There's another way to move back and forth through pages. Select History from the Navigate menu and you will be presented with a list of all the documents you've viewed. You can select any one of them and click the Go To button to return to that page. You can use that same menu to go back to any page you've visited during your current session. To get back to where you started, simply select Home from the Navigate menu.

For now let's go back one level to The World Wide Web Virtual Library: Games and Recreation. This time, let's take a look at one of the more colorful and interesting pages. Scroll down to Miscellaneous hobbies and click on the Juggling Information Service link, shown in Figure A-11.

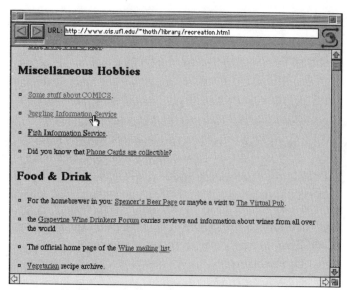

Figure A-11: The Juggling Information Service link.

The Juggling Information Service page will appear next, as shown in Figure A-12. As you scroll through the list of different options, you'll see that all sorts of things are available, like movies (in Quick-Time or MPEG format), pictures, text files and even merchandise.

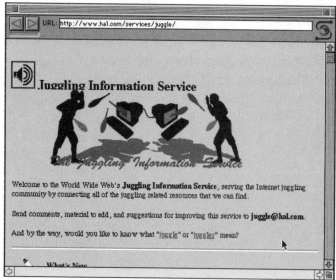

Figure A-12: The Juggling Information Service page.

Retrieving Files

If you do want to download a file, it couldn't be simpler. To demonstrate the process, let's click on the Juggling Movie Theater link on the Juggling page. The Juggling Movie Theater page is shown in Figure A-13.

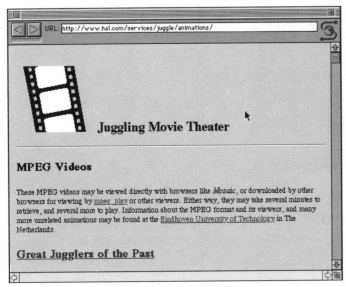

Figure A-13: The Juggling Movie Theater page.

Scroll down to the Performances in the Modern Era link and click on it. The Performances in the Modern Era page will appear, as shown in Figure A-14.

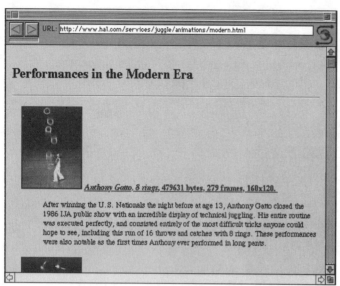

URL: http://www.hal.com/services/juggle/animations/modern.html

Performances in the Modern Era

Anthony Gatto, 8 rings, 479631 bytes, 279 frames, 160x120.

After winning the U.S. Nationals the night before at age 13, Anthony Gatto closed the 1986 IJA public show with an incredible display of technical juggling. His entire routine was executed perfectly, and consisted entirely of the most difficult tricks anyone could hope to see, including this run of 16 throws and catches with 8 rings. These performances were also notable as the first times Anthony ever performed in long pants.

Figure A-14: The Performances in the Modern Era page.

To download any of the MPEG movies, just click on the picture next to the description. (**Note:** If you have a modem connection, one of these downloads could take several minutes.)

Unfortunately, the ease of retrieving files using Mosaic doesn't make up for the general difficulty of actually finding specific files. There is no search function within Mosaic to find a file, nor is there a guarantee that you will be allowed to download files (a few are password protected).

Going Directly to Another Page

If you know the URL of any WWW page, you can go there directly. For instance, to go directly to the Juggling page you can enter the URL for that page as follows:

1. In the File menu, select Open URL.

2. Enter **http://www.hal.com/services/juggle/** into the text field and click the OK button (or press Return).

Throughout the Internet, you'll see all sorts of WWW pages noted by various groups and individuals. Because these URLs are so long, the best thing to do is to highlight the URL and copy it, and then paste it into a document (I use the Stickies provided with System 7.5; Windows users could use the Clipboard). This way you can't misspell or type incorrectly.

Setting Up a New Home Page

Let's say you *always* use the subject index to explore the WWW. There's no need for you to have to click through two other pages to get there each time you use Mosaic. To remedy this situation, you can use the subject catalogue page as your home page. It's easy to make this change.

1. Go to the page you want to use as your new home page.

2. Select the URL that appears near the top of the window by clicking the left mouse button and dragging across it until it is completely highlighted.

3. Select Copy from the Edit menu or simply hit Command-C or Ctrl-C.

4. Select Preferences from the Edit menu.

5. Place your cursor in the Home Page field, click your left mouse button once, then hit Command-V or Ctrl-V to paste the URL you copied. Click the OK button.

That's it. The next time you run Mosaic, you'll go directly to the subject catalogue page. If you ever want to use a different home page, or enter its URL in the Preferences dialog box.

Graphics & Modem Connections

If you're connected to the Internet via a SLIP or PPP modem connection, some of the pictures that are part of many WWW pages can take quite a while to reach your screen. In fact, some of them may not be worth the wait! It's easy to configure Mosaic so that it does not automatically download images. Select Preferences from the Edit menu, uncheck the Load Images Automatically check box, and click the OK button.

Accessing FTP Sites With Mosaic

Earlier we saw that Mosaic uses the FTP protocol to retrieve files with a single mouse click from whatever Web page you may be browsing. But you can also use Mosaic to download files directly from any of the literally thousands of servers that provide files to Internet users via the FTP protocol, even servers that may not have Web home pages. Typically you access FTP sites using a stand-alone FTP client program. But since Mosaic has FTP built right in, you may never need to use a stand-alone FTP program unless you want to upload files.

In the steps that follow we'll use Mosaic to get a file from the FTP server maintained by Ventana Online.

1. When your Internet connection has been established, launch Mosaic by double-clicking its icon.

2. Select Open URL from the File menu.

3. Enter **ftp://ftp.vmedia.com/** in the URL field.

4. Hit the OK button to activate your URL selection. The directory listing for the Ventana Online FTP server will appear in the main Mosaic window after a few seconds.

5. Clicking on the name of a directory takes you to that directory, where other files will be listed. Clicking on a file name downloads that file. For now, click on the file **welcome.msg**. Since this is a text file, it will be displayed in the Mosaic window. If you select a file for downloading that is not a text file, the Transfer file to dialog box will appear, where you may specify a new name and location for the file. Click OK to proceed with the download.

Accessing Gopher Sites With Mosaic

What if you don't know exactly what you're looking for on the Net and want to refine your search carefully as you explore? What if you want to delve deeply into a particular area of interest? Typical Web sites may not help you, for often the links to other information are as arbitrary, whimsical and wild as the imagination of the page's author. Gopher servers, on the other hand, serve up information in tidy hierarchical menus and submenus, sticking to a subject and presenting it in top-down outline format. With HTML documents you leap rapidly from peak to peak; using Gopher, you follow logically related information trails. There is a time and place for both methods, and fortunately Mosaic supports them both.

Gopher servers are usually accessed with specialized Gopher client programs, but Mosaic makes extra software unnecessary. Mosaic can log onto a Gopher server and then present you with the information so that it looks very much like any Web page. Menu items are blue like other Web links, and clicking on them brings up the appropriate submenus. Let's give it a try using the WELL Gopher as an example. The WELL (Whole Earth 'Lectronic Link) is a large information service known for the variety of its online forums and the lively interactions of its users, but it also maintains a very interesting Gopher site. To begin exploring it,

1. With your Internet connection established, launch Mosaic by double-clicking its icon.

Note: For the purposes of this exercise, it doesn't matter what Web page is currently displayed.

2. Select Open URL from the File menu. The Open URL dialog box will appear.

3. Type **gopher://gopher.well.com/** in the URL field and click OK. In a few seconds the top level menu of the WELL Gopher appears.

Notice that when you connect to a Gopher server, virtually all the text in the Mosaic window is comprised of hotlinks.

4. Click the top menu item, About this gopherspace. A new submenu appears.

5. Click the top item, What is this place? (The basic story). This time a text file appears.

6. After reading the file, use Mosaic's Back button to return to the top-level WELL Gopher menu. From there you can begin to explore many different areas. Feel free to browse. The WELL Gopher is especially known for its information on media, communications and cyberpunk literature.

Although every Gopher site looks about the same in terms of structure, the content varies greatly. There are Gopher sites that specialize in just about any academic field you can think of, from art to astrophysics. In addition there are some Gopher sites that are just plain fun.

Building Your Own Web Pages

Now that you've traveled the Web and seen how simple it is, you may want to start creating your own Web pages. All Web pages are written in a language called HTML (HyperText Markup Language), a subset of SGML (Standard Generalized Markup Language, a system designed for typesetting and document page description). HTML is simply ASCII text with embedded codes representing instructions for the proper display of that text. The most basic HTML commands instruct the Web browser client program regarding the display of the information (what size and style of type, etc.).

More importantly, HTML commands can include display information and links to other data types (video, graphics and audio) and even other servers. This is the real power of the Web—its ability to let you access an amazingly wide variety of information types, across the entire Internet, with a click of the mouse.

A good starting point for HTML authoring is creating a local home page for yourself—a file on your hard drive that's loaded when you start Mosaic and that contains some of your favorite links. After you feel comfortable with your authoring skills, you may want to set up your own server, or at least your own home page area on one. If you have access to a server site, it's a relatively simple matter. Some SLIP/PPP service providers even let you set up Web pages on their system as part of a shell account.

I have found that the best way to start learning the HTML techniques for creating Web pages is to study the content and structure of the pages you visit. You can look at the source code for the page you're on simply by selecting View Source from Mosaic's Edit menu. The dialog box that pops up even lets you save the source under a different file name on your own system. You can then use it as a template for your new HTML file. You can edit it in the Mac Note Pad, the Windows Notepad, or any other text editor. There are even some special editors designed specifically for automating the process of applying HTML tags to text. HTML Assistant, for instance, is available on many anonymous FTP sites. Mosaic even lets you preview or test any HTML documents you create. To view a local HTML file in Mosaic, select Open Local from the File menu.

HTML files on most Web servers have the extension HTML. Since DOS, however, does not support file-name extensions of more than three characters, Windows HTML files end with the extension HTM. If you do not use the HTML or HTM extension, Mosaic and other browsers will not recognize your files as valid HTML pages.

There are several excellent HTML reference areas online, as shown in Table A-1. These pages will give you a handle on the basics of HTML authoring.

Site	URL
CERN HTML Reference	http://info.cern.ch:80/hypertext/ WWW/MarkUp/MarkUp.html
Peter Flynn's How to Write HTML	http://kcgl1.eng.ohio-state.edu:80 www/doc/htmldoc.html
Dr. Ian Graham's Guide to HTML	http://www.utirc.utoronto.ca/ HTMLdocs/NewHTML/html

Table A-1: Popular HTML references.

If you want to start with more general information regarding the World Wide Web (straight from the horse's mouth), the best resource is the CERN Web server (**http://info.cern.ch/**). CERN engineers developed the Web, and this is a great clearinghouse for software information.

Index

T

Colophon

Internet Roadside Attractions was produced on a Macintosh Quadra 650 using PageMaker 5.0. The cover art was produced using Adobe Illustrator and QuarkXPress. Page proofs were output to a Hewlett-Packard LaserJet 4M Plus and final film output was produced using a Linotronic 330.

Text is set in Adobe Palatino and Franklin Gothic Condensed, and heads are Image Club's Badloc Compressed.

Notes

Notes

Notes

Notes

Notes

Notes

Insightful Guides

Voodoo Windows

$19.95
312 pages, illustrated

Work Windows wizardry with productivity-enhancing tips. Organized by subject, this book offers a wealth of Windows techniques, shortcuts and never-before-published tricks that will streamline your daily tasks and save time. A great reference for beginners and experienced users alike.

The Windows Shareware 500

$39.95
456 pages, illustrated

The best Windows shareware available, from thousands of contenders. Includes utilities, sounds, fonts, icons, games, clip art, multimedia and more. **BONUS**: Four companion disks: including three that feature top-rated programs, and an America Online membership disk. Includes 10 hours free online time (for new members only)!

The Visual Guide to Visual Basic for Windows, Second Edition

$29.95
1280 pages, illustrated

An A-to-Z examination of every command and technique in Microsoft's landmark GUI language, including functions, illustrations and suggested uses for each. Fully updated for Version 3.0, it offers users at all levels insight on customizing Windows and creating useful applications that look professional and perform efficiently. With more than 600 illustrations, it is truly the classic reference for Microsoft's bestselling language.

Internet Resources

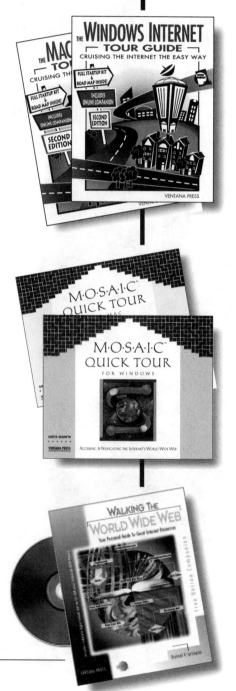

The Internet Tour Guides, Second Editions

Mac Edition: $29.95, 432 pages, illustrated
Windows Edition: $29.95, 416 pages, illustrated

Users can now navigate the Internet the easy way: by pointing and clicking, dragging and dropping. In easy-to-read, entertaining prose, the *Internet Tour Guides* lead you through installing and using the software enclosed in the book to send and receive e-mail, transfer files, search the Internet's vast resources and more! BONUS: Free trial access and two free electronic updates.

Mosaic Quick Tours

Mac Edition: $12.00, 208 pages, illustrated
Windows Edition: $12.00, 216 pages, illustrated

The *Mosaic Quick Tour*s introduce the how-to's of hypertext travel in a simple, picturesque guide. Mosaic™, called the "killer app" of the Internet, lets you view linked text, audio and video resources thousands of miles apart. Learn to use Mosaic for all your information hunting and gathering—including Gopher searches, newsgroup reading and file transfers via FTP.

Walking The World Wide Web

$29.95
350 pages, illustrated

Enough of lengthy listings! This tour features more than 300 memorable Web sites, with in-depth descriptions of what's special about each. Includes international sites, exotic exhibits, entertainment, business and more. The companion CD-ROM contains Ventana Mosaic™ and a hyperlinked version of the book, providing live links when you log onto the Internet.

Books marked with this logo include a free Internet *Online Companion*™, featuring archives of free utilities plus a reader archive and links to other Internet resources.

Internet Virtual Worlds Quick Tour

$14.00
150 pages, illustrated

Learn to locate and master real-time interactive communication forums and games by participating in the virtual worlds of MUD (Multi-User Dimension) and MOO (Mud Object-Oriented). *Internet Virtual Worlds Quick Tour* introduces users to the basic functions by defining different categories (individual, interactive and both) and detailing standard protocols. Also revealed is the insider's lexicon of this mysterious cyberworld. Available March 1995.

Internet E-Mail Quick Tour

$14.00
150 pages, illustrated

E-mail is becoming the vehicle of choice for communication within the business and computer-using communities. The *Internet E-Mail Quick Tour* makes using e-mail easy, saving you time and money when sending and receiving electronic mail. Learn to subscribe to commercial online services or use e-mail through a service provider connected directly to the Internet. Advice ranges from e-mail history to how to avoid problems on the global information superhighway. Available February 1995.

Internet Chat Quick Tour

$14.00
150 pages, illustrated

Global conversations in real-time are an integral part of the Internet. The worldwide chat network is where users find online help and forums on the latest scientific research. The *Internet Chat Quick Tour* describes the best software sites for users to chat on a variety of subjects, as well as showing users where to take out verbal aggression. Available March 1995.

To order any Ventana Press title, complete this order form and mail or fax it to us, with payment, for quick shipment.

TITLE	ISBN	Quantity		Price		Total
Voodoo Mac, 2nd Edition	1-56604-177-5	_____	x	$24.95	=	$ _____
The System 7.5 Book, 3rd Edition	1-56604-129-5	_____	x	$24.95	=	$ _____
Looking Good in Print, 3rd Edition	1-56604-047-7	_____	x	$24.95	=	$ _____
Voodoo Windows	1-56604-005-1	_____	x	$19.95	=	$ _____
The Windows Shareware 500	1-56604-045-0	_____	x	$39.95	=	$ _____
The Visual Guide to Visual Basic for Windows, 2nd Edition	1-56604-063-9	_____	x	$29.95	=	$ _____
The Mac Internet Tour Guide, 2nd Edition	1-56604-173-2	_____	x	$29.95	=	$ _____
The Windows Internet Tour Guide, 2nd Edition	1-56604-174-0	_____	x	$29.95	=	$ _____
Walking the World Wide Web	1-56604-208-9	_____	x	$29.95	=	$ _____
Mosaic Quick Tour for Mac	1-56604-195-3	_____	x	$12.00	=	$ _____
Mosaic Quick Tour for Windows	1-56604-194-5	_____	x	$12.00	=	$ _____
Internet Virtual Worlds Quick Tour	1-56604-222-4	_____	x	$14.00	=	$ _____
Internet E-Mail Quick Tour	1-56604-220-8	_____	x	$14.00	=	$ _____
Internet Chat Quick Tour	1-56604-223-2	_____	x	$14.00	=	$ _____
Internet Roadside Attractions	1-56604-193-7	_____	x	$29.95	=	$ _____
				Subtotal	=	$ _____
				Shipping	=	$ _____
				TOTAL	=	$ _____

SHIPPING:

For all standard orders, please ADD $4.50/first book, $1.35/each additional.
For "two-day air," ADD $8.25/first book, $2.25/each additional.
For orders to Canada, ADD $6.50/book.
For orders sent C.O.D., ADD $4.50 to your shipping rate.
North Carolina residents must ADD 6% sales tax.
International orders require additional shipping charges.

Name _____ Company _____

Address (No PO Box) _____

City_____ State_____ Zip _____

Daytime Telephone _____

____ Payment enclosed ____VISA ____ MC Acc't # _____ Exp. Date_____

Signature _____

Mail to: Ventana Press, PO Box 2468, Chapel Hill, NC 27515 ☎ 800/743-5369 Fax 919/942-1140

Check your local bookstore or software retailer for these and other bestselling titles, or call toll free: 800/743-5369

Ventana Communications Group, Inc.
P.O. Box 2468
Chapel Hill, NC 27515
Phone: 919/942-0220
FAX: 919/942-1140

End-User Software Sublicense Agreement

PLEASE READ THIS CAREFULLY BEFORE OPENING THE DISK OR CD-ROM ENVELOPE. BY OPENING THE ENVELOPE YOU AGREE TO BE BOUND BY ALL OF THE TERMS IN THIS AGREEMENT. IF YOU DO NOT AGREE TO ALL OF THESE TERMS DO NOT OPEN THE ENVELOPE OR USE THE SOFTWARE, BUT PROMPTLY RETURN THE UNOPENED ENVELOPE TO VENTANA.

1. License The enclosed computer software, Ventana Mosaic™ ("Software") is not being sold or purchased, but is being licensed to you by Ventana Communications Group, Inc. ("Ventana"), under a nonexclusive, nontransferable and paid-up license for use only under the following terms, and Ventana, and Spyglass, Inc. ("Spyglass"), licensor of Ventana Mosaic, reserve any right not expressly granted to you herein. Under the terms of this license you own the media on which the Software is recorded, but Spyglass retains all rights of ownership to the Software and all copies of the Software. This license shall be governed by the laws of the state of North Carolina.

2. Under this license you may:

    a.) Make one (1) copy of the Software solely for backup or archival purposes.

    b.) Make use of the Software on one computer at a time, by one user at a time. If such computer is accessible by multiple users or other computers, you must obtain additional licenses for each additional user.

    c.) Transfer your rights under this license for the Software, provided that you give Ventana prior notice of such transfer and that any transferee shall read and accept all of the terms and conditions of this license.

3. Proprietary Rights. This Software is protected by copyright pursuant to federal and state law as well as international law. The Software also contains trade secrets proprietary to Spyglass. Licensee acknowledges the foregoing and agrees to reproduce Ventana's and Spyglass's copyright notices and any other proprietary notices when the Software is copied.

4. Restrictions. Subject to the provisions of federal law, you expressly agree you will not:

    a.) Make or distribute copies of the Software in any form, directly or indirectly, without prior written agreement with Ventana.

    b.) Reverse engineer, disassemble, decompile or otherwise reduce the Software to a human perceptible form or otherwise attempt to re-create the source code.

    c.) Modify, adapt, sublicense, sell, lend, rent or lease the Software.

    d.) Create any derivative work, or incorporate the Software in any other work.

    e.) Remove or in any other way obscure any copyright notices or other proprietary rights of Ventana or Spyglass.

    f.) Use the Software on more than one computer.

    g.) Export the Software without full compliance with the rules and regulations of the Bureau of Export Administration.

    h.) Use more than one copy of the Software even if more than one copy of the Software is included as part of a multiple-component package.

If any provision of the license shall be inapplicable by law to any U.S. Government end-user, each such end-user acknowledges that use, duplication or disclosure by the Government is subject to restrictions as set forth in subparagraph (c)(1)(ii) of The Rights in Technical Data and Computer Software clause at DFARS 252.227-7013.

5. Severability and Termination. If any part of this license is found unenforceable by a court, it shall be limited only to the extent necessary to make it enforceable, without otherwise affecting the license. This license shall remain in effect until terminated. The license will be terminated immediately and without notice by your failure to comply with any provisions of this License Agreement. Upon termination, you shall be entitled to retain the media but must destroy the Software and all copies thereof. You may terminate this license at your own discretion by destroying the Software and all copies or returning the same to Ventana.

6. Warranty, Disclaimer and Limitation of Liability. Ventana warrants that the Software will perform in accordance with the technical specifications set forth in the documentation. A copy of the documentation can be obtained from Ventana prior to accepting this license for the Software by contacting Ventana at the address and phone number set forth above. Ventana further warrants that the disk on which the Software has been encoded is free from original workmanship defect at the time of such encoding. Ventana's sole obligation in the event of a claim under the foregoing warranties will be to provide a replacement copy of the Software upon receipt of the Software postage prepaid and upon confirmation of such defect.

VENTANA DISCLAIMS ANY WARRANTY OF MERCHANTABILITY OR FITNESS FOR PARTICULAR PURPOSE. The Software is licensed in "as is" condition, and except as set forth herein, Ventana makes no warranty of any kind, express or implied. Some states restrict the right to exclude certain warranties, therefore your rights that you may have may vary from state to state.

In no event will Ventana be held liable for monetary damages for any amount in excess of the amount paid for the license grant pursuant to this Agreement. Ventana shall have no liability beyond the obligations set forth above, and shall in no event be liable for additional monetary damages whether incidental, consequential or otherwise, arising out of the use of the Software, irrespective of whether Ventana shall have been informed of the possibility of such damages. Because some states do not allow the exclusion or limitation of liability for consequential or incidental damages, such limitation may not apply to you.

Mosaic is a trademark of the University of Illinois.

Installing the CD-ROM

The CD-ROM included with your copy of *Internet Roadside Attractions* contains a complete hypertext version of the entire book and a copy of Ventana Mosaic, which you can use to read the hypertext version and access all the online sites. Windows users: to install the CD-ROM, load the CD and with Windows running, double-click on the File Manager. Click on the icon corresponding to your CD-ROM drive. The contents of the CD-ROM will appear. Double-click setup.exe. A program group called Roadside Attractions is created. Double-click the Roadside Attractions icon. To launch Ventana Mosaic, click the Ventana Mosaic bar and follow the instructions to launch.

Mac users: Load the CD-ROM, then click the icon for the CD-ROM drive. A program window appears. Click the Roadside Attractions icon. To launch Ventana Mosaic, click the Ventana Mosaic bar.

The Ventana Mosaic home page will automatically appear and will allow you to browse the entire hypertext of the book locally so that you can plan your Web-walking excursions before spending a penny of online time. Then after you fire up your Internet connection, you can link directly to any of the sites reviewed in the book.

To bypass the main Roadside Attractions interface screen and skip directly to browsing with Ventana Mosaic, Mac users can simply double-click on the Ventana Mosaic icon rather than the Roadside Attractions icon in the CD-ROM program window. Windows users can create a new Ventana Mosaic program item in the Ventana Mosaic program group using the vmosaic.exe file on the CD-ROM. Then double-click on the new program item rather than the Roadside Attractions item.

To access the CD-ROM home page at any time, select Open URL on Ventana Mosaic's File menu and enter one of the following URLs.

Macintosh users: **file:///Ventana/index.htm**

Windows users: **file:///D | /index.htm** where D is the letter of your CD-ROM drive.

Accessing the Online Companion

By purchasing this book you have access to an online companion, a unique feature offered only by Ventana Press. To use the *Internet Roadside Attractions Online Companion*, you first must connect to the Internet and then must register with Ventana. After you are online, you can register from the home page on your CD-ROM version of the book by simply double-clicking the link that says "Register." An interactive form appears requesting some personal information. The form asks you for a *code key*. Your unique code key is printed on a card located behind the CD-ROM at the back of the book. You only need to enter the code key once; after that, it is added to your "key ring" at Ventana, allowing you access to the online companion whenever you want. Entering the code key grants you access only to that particular online companion and only for one year from the date you enter the code key.

The registration form also asks you to enter an account name and password. You can use whatever name and password you want, but you'll need to remember them for future use. Every time you want to use the online companion, you'll need to enter your account name and password. If you have obtained access to other online companions and are now registering for a new one, click on the "Register" link and select the option for users who have already established accounts. You'll be able to use the same account and password for the online companion you're adding, after you enter your code key for that product.

During the registration process, you will have the option of entering credit card account information. This optional service makes it easy and convenient to purchase Ventana Press products from the Ventana Online catalog and to add more time to your online companion access. An optional questionnaire requesting demographic information and data on your service provider, usage patterns, and so on is also included as part of the registration procedure. You are not required to fill out the questionnaire; doing so will help us to serve you more effectively.

You can connect to the *Internet Roadside Attractions Online Companion* by following a link from the home page on the CD-ROM version of the book. Or connect directly by typing in the following URL:

http://www.vmedia.com/ira.html

(Readers without CD-ROM capabilities can also register with Ventana and use the online companion by connecting to this URL.)

The online companion has many great and useful features. Check there often for updates to the listings in the book, including new or changed URLs, additions to the listings already featured and brand-new listings for you to explore. Look at the "What's New" page to see what changes have been made since you last visited. You can also search the entire hypertext for a keyword or send email to the authors using an interactive form.